AD Non Fiction
231.72 M

McKnight, S...
to the radica...
9001097983

KINGDOM
Conspiracy

KINGDOM
Conspiracy

RETURNING *to the* RADICAL MISSION
of the LOCAL CHURCH

SCOT McKNIGHT

BrazosPress
a division of Baker Publishing Group
Grand Rapids, Michigan

Published by Brazos Press
a division of Baker Publishing Group
P.O. Box 6287, Grand Rapids, MI 49516-6287
www.brazospress.com

Printed in the United States of America

Library of Congress Cataloging-in-Publication Data is on file at the Library of Congress, Washington, DC.

ISBN 978-1-58743-360-3

Published in association with the literary agency of Daniel Literary Group, Nashville, TN 37215.

14 15 16 17 18 19 20   7 6 5 4 3 2 1

For Fitch

Therefore, as we have opportunity, let us do good to all people, especially to those who belong to the family of believers.

Galatians 6:10

We do not need definite beliefs because their objects are necessarily true. We need them because they enable us to stand on steady spots from which the truth may be glimpsed.

Christian Wiman, My Bright Abyss

In eternity this world will be Troy, I believe, and all that has passed here will be the epic of the universe, the ballad they sing in the streets.

Marilynne Robinson, Gilead

Christianity is mostly a matter of politics—politics as defined by the gospel. The call to be part of the gospel is a joyful call to be adopted by an alien people, to join a countercultural phenomenon, a new polis called the church.

Whether they think of themselves as liberal or conservative, as ethically or politically left or right, American Christians have fallen into the bad habit of acting as if the church really does not matter as we go about trying to live like Christians.

Stanley Hauerwas and Will Willimon, Resident Aliens

It is essential, in my view, to abandon altogether talk of "redeeming the culture," "advancing the kingdom," "building the kingdom," "transforming the world," "reclaiming the culture," "reforming the culture," and "changing the world." Christians need to leave such language behind them because it carries too much weight. It implies conquest, take-over, or dominion, which in my view is precisely what God does not call us to pursue.

James Davison Hunter, *To Change the World*

These days I do not often meet Christians so passionate about evangelism that they question the need for doing justice. I am much more likely to meet Christians so passionate about justice that they question the need for evangelism. . . . In short, working for justice is cool. Proclaiming the gospel is not.

Andy Crouch, *Playing God*

"Thy kingdom come"—this is not the prayer of the pious soul of the individual who wants to flee the world, nor is it the prayer of the utopian and fanatic, the stubborn world reformer. Rather, this is the prayer only of the church-community of children of the Earth . . . who persevere together in the midst of the world, in its depths, in the daily life and subjugation of the world.

Dietrich Bonhoeffer, *Berlin: 1932–1933*

Writers are really people who write books not because they are poor, but because they are dissatisfied with the books which they could buy but do not like.

Walter Benjamin, *Illuminations*

Grant, O merciful God, that your Church, being gathered together in unity by your Holy Spirit, may show forth your power among all people, to the glory of your Name; through Jesus Christ our Lord, who lives and reigns with you and the Holy Spirit, one God, for ever and ever. Amen.†

The Book of Common Prayer

Contents

1

SKINNY JEANS KINGDOM

Recently I was speaking at a pastors' conference when a pastor friend of mine cornered me in a back hallway and asked this question: "Scot, what *in the world* does 'kingdom' mean? The skinny-jeans guys on my staff are now all talking 'kingdom this' and 'kingdom that,' and I have no idea what they are talking about. To me, it sounds like nothing but social justice. But," he then quipped, "what do I know? They call me Mr. Pleated Pants!" Skinny Jeans versus Pleated Pants indeed. But this rise in kingdom talk can't be reduced to age differences; we are talking here about a break from how things were and are to a new way of being Christian. Kingdom theology is on the rise.

Skinny Jeans Kingdom People

Tim Suttle, a Skinny Jeans kind of pastor and leader of the alternative country rock band Satellite Soul, tells his story of moving from the spiritual gospel to the kingdom gospel.[1] What awakened Suttle from the simplicity and inadequacy of the spiritual gospel was the piercing discomfort of wondering if he was making any difference in the world because, as he believes, "we should be seeing the world changing all around us." Why? Because "the good news can change the world." This difference-making and world-changing mission he sees at work in Jesus is time and time again called "kingdom" work in his book *An Evangelical Social Gospel?* As he puts it later in the book, "To profess true salvation . . . we must judge the authenticity of our conversion according to its social manifestations, not simply its inner, personal ones." Suttle illustrates the kind of break I'm talking about. But this break from how things were and are carries within it a potent undercurrent.

For one entire semester, owing to the recommendation of my friend J. R. Briggs, I listened to Derek Webb's haunting, edgy, politically critical song "A King and a Kingdom." The most haunting lines of his song come from the chorus: "My first allegiance," he declares, "is not to a flag, a country, or a man . . . [but] to a king and a kingdom."

Every time I listened to Webb's voice I wondered what he meant by "kingdom." The king was Jesus, the kingdom was . . . well, what is the kingdom in this song? And what about the church? Webb's song belongs to the Skinny Jeans crowd my pastor friend spoke of, and they all like the word "kingdom," and they all seem to know what it means, and as a whole they're a bit sketchy about the local church or the church as an institution. Which is what Derek Webb admitted in a recent interview when asked about an album called *She Must and Shall Go Free.*

> I wrote it after having spent 10 years prior to that in [the band] Caedmon's Call and playing in a lot of churches and in church culture—living in the church kind of world. At the end of my 10 years in that band, I found myself with a lot of questions about the Church and about the Church's role, my role in the Church, and the Church's role in culture. Do I have to go to church? Is that a part of Christianity? What role does the Church play, uniquely, in culture? So, my first record was trying to answer some of those questions.[2]

As he wrote "A King and a Kingdom" he was committed to the kingdom but not so sure about the church. But on his most recent album, *I Was Wrong, I'm Sorry & I Love You*, Webb apologizes for his posture toward the church, the bride of Christ. As Matt Connor, an expert on Webb's songs, puts it, "Webb, it seems, had to leave the church to love it. He's come back a better man for the journey. *I Was Wrong, I'm Sorry & I Love You* is a triumphant return [to the church]."[3]

Another pastor told me that on any weekend he wants he can solicit large buckets of money and lots of volunteers if he needs them for "kingdom work" and social activism, for compassion for the poor, for AIDS, and for building water wells in Africa. But, he said to me, "If I ask for money for evangelism, I'm lucky if anyone gives a dime!"

When I was at dinner with a group of pastors, one said this: "I talked with a young man in our church who had been on seven mission trips. Each 'mission' trip," the pastor said with some emphasis, "had *nothing* to do with telling people about Jesus or establishing a church or teaching the Bible, but with service projects like building medical facilities." I asked the pastor, "Did the young man use the word 'kingdom' for what he was doing?" The pastor responded, "Over and over." His last words haunted me that evening: "These young adults, God bless 'em, think 'kingdom' has nothing to do with 'church.'"

A missionary wrote this to me recently: "Religious work in Africa is very interesting. Almost no missionaries are doing Bible teaching, evangelism, discipleship, or church planting. We're all doing orphanages or trade schools or working with the deaf or HIV/AIDS education, etc. I'm puzzled as to why that is our reality." He didn't say it, but I suspect that those missionaries who are "doing" those good deeds think they are doing "kingdom work."

One of the most influential proponents of this Skinny Jeans view of the kingdom is Jim Wallis, and after he recently engaged in a public conversation about the gospel with Albert Mohler Jr., president of Southern Baptist Theological Seminary, he offered his own summary of the evening. Mohler, Wallis said, reduces the gospel to atonement and personal redemption; Wallis expands the gospel to its full parameters. Wallis calls his gospel the "gospel of the kingdom." What does that mean? Here are his words:

> Thus, for me, "social justice" is integral to the meaning of the gospel—a holistic message that includes both personal salvation and social transformation. This is the gospel of the kingdom, not an atonement-only gospel. In the latter, it almost seems that Jesus wasted his first three years with all those teachings, parables, and healings. He might have just gone straight to the cross to make atonement for our sins.[4]

3

For Wallis, the kingdom is about social justice and social transformation flowing from personal redemption. Kingdom work, then, is about what is done for the common good—the theme of his 2013 book, *On God's Side*, an expression that comes from Abraham Lincoln. The subtitle shows the orientation of his gospel of the kingdom: *What Religion Forgets and Politics Hasn't Learned about Serving the Common Good*. We could extend this discussion for chapters and chapters, enlisting other voices, like Charles Marsh, who sees "God's beloved community" in the expansive ways that many today speak of as the kingdom;[5] or Walter Wink, who sees the kingdom as a world marked by justice and equity and peace and nonviolence and the end of domination and systemic injustices (the powers);[6] or even, and importantly, Tyler Wigg-Stevenson, who warns the Skinny Jeans activists that we do not build the kingdom (God does) and that the world is not ours to save[7]—but enough has been said to get the general drift.

It's time now to offer a summary definition of "kingdom" in the Skinny Jeans approach. What do these folks mean by "kingdom"?[8] After three decades of teaching about kingdom in the Bible and three decades of listening to the growing use of the word, I have come to this conclusion about this prevailing, and seemingly uncorrectable, Skinny Jeans usage:

Kingdom means
good deeds
done by good people (Christian or not)
in the public sector
for the common good.

Boiled down to its central elements, kingdom mission in the Skinny Jeans approach is working for social justice and peace, and the foundation for most of these efforts, besides the writings of folks like Bill McKibben or Wendell Berry, is a selection of life-giving and important texts from the Bible. One thinks of the marvelous concern for the poor in Deuteronomy; of the prophetic critique of exploitation, which is always a moral concern and never a theoretical economic theory and system;[9] of the relentlessly piercing words and practices of Jesus; and of the overall impact of a vision of justice and peace in the future kingdom. In Western liberal democracies—where rights are assumed and protected or, when they are not, someone is at work to grant them—we are in constant need of reminding ourselves of the simplest narrative at work in the Bible: an oppressed and enslaved people, the children of Israel, were liberated through Passover from their oppressors (Egypt) and led by the hand of God through a desert and through water into the land where they were given instructions by God on how to live as a nation. Put baldly, this is a political narrative—a narrative of God granting an entire nation political freedom. Should that liberation narrative not shape how we work for the "common good"? Of course it should.

Some quick observations about this four-line definition of the word "kingdom": First, this gauzy definition of one of the Bible's strongest words is not what "kingdom" *ever* means in the Bible; the Bible never calls working for the common good "kingdom work." Second, this word's meaning matters because its meaning shapes what happens when we do kingdom "work" or kingdom "mission." I'll add a third: when people do kingdom "work" in accordance with this understanding of kingdom, they fail to do kingdom "mission." Sorry, but I have to add a fourth: there is a profound irony in how this crowd uses the term "kingdom." Statisticians are all telling us that Millennials are leaving the church, and it is usually observed that they are leaving the church because it has become too political. Agree? If you agree, listen to this: Millennials, who are shaping the Skinny Jeans vision of kingdom, have turned the kingdom message of Jesus into a politically shaped message. Perhaps we should ask if they are leaving churches not so much because the message is too political but because the politics are too conservative.

Hard, harsh words. So let me tell a story and ask a question, a question that will take the rest of this book to answer. But in the process—just in case you are a Skinny Jeans proponent and are now irritated with me—I will also contend that the Pleated Pants folks are no more accurate in their understanding of "kingdom."

Skinny Jeans and Jane Addams

I'm from Freeport, Illinois, and yes, the rumor is true: our high school's nickname was, is, and always will be the Pretzels. But forget this inane nickname, because I want to talk about one of our (unathletic) heroes. I remember as a child that when someone mentioned Jane Addams, we all gave a collective but silent round of applause for one of our own, even if she did go off to "big city" Rockford for her college education and then disappear into the even bigger city—Chicago—for her life's calling.[10] What mattered to us was that Jane grew up in Cedarville, just a five-mile bike ride north of Freeport. Jane was the first American woman to be awarded the Nobel Peace Prize, which she received in 1931 for her determined and relentless advocacy of peace and justice for all people. Jane established a "settlement" home on the West Side of Chicago called the Hull House. Louise Knight, her biographer, sums up Jane's progressivist life in these words: "She worked to end child labor, support unions and workers' rights, protect free speech and civil rights, respect all cultures, achieve women's suffrage and women's freedom, and promote conditions that nurtured human potential and therefore, she believed, the spread of peace."

Jane's driving ambition was "to put the ideal of universal, democratic fellowship into action." That is, Jane Addams was able to perceive the implications of democracy and radically apply them to all dimensions of life—family, work, race, gender, labor, economics, education, international relations, and free speech. She had unconditional regard for all people, and she believed that the federal government had the power to make radical democracy happen. As with all advocates for social justice, Addams devoted her life to the oppressed, the ignored, the marginalized, and the silent. One of the more penetrating of her own insights was that *benevolence implied hierarchy*. Put more directly, benevolence was the action of wealthy white and privileged people toward those of lower social orders; as such, benevolence perpetuated the opposite of democracy. So Addams had to slay her participation in benevolence, and she instead strived for a more radical sense of equality.

What does this have to do with kingdom? To answer this, I want to probe Addams's faith. She grew up in the home of a very independent-minded Quaker-like Presbyterian father who never could sign off on a church creed since he believed in freedom of conscience, the lack of coercion, and a life of self-determination. Jane inherited that firm resolution from her father and only joined a church after college when she realized it fit her sense of social

justice and social Christianity as expressed in the social gospel. She repudiated Christian theologies of salvation, the importance of repentance from
sin in order to be reconciled with God, the atoning work of Christ, and a
traditional sense of heaven. For her the "real meaning of Christ's message
was to trust one's own moral judgment, to listen to one's conscience," which
she called the peace of Christ. She was a devoted follower of Leo Tolstoy's
sense of nonresistance. What comes home to the reader of Jane Addams's
life is that she *socialized* the moral vision of Jesus into a *sociopolitical platform designed to lead us to justice, peace, and equality.* For her the vision
of Jesus was designed to reshape the world. An evangelical observer of Addams had this to say of her: "She seems to be a Christian without religion."
And Jean Bethke Elshtain's important study of Addams has this to say of
her faith: "There was religion at Hull-House, she would later tell critics. . . .
The good news of the Incarnation and Resurrection had been siphoned off,
and Addams had refilled the wineskin with a social message, an account of
Christianity's origins that offered the poor what she thought they needed: a
serviceable story that promised comfort for the time being, strength for the
journey, and hope of social transformation in the here-and-now."[11]

What happens in Jane Addams happens constantly in those who turn to
the political or cultural process in the world as their way of doing kingdom
work. Christ becomes a symbol of a way of life, which for Addams was
democracy; the ethic of Jesus is reduced to secular analogies, and in so
doing everything central to Jesus—the cross, the resurrection, atonement,
new birth, the church, or judgment—evaporates into happened-also-to-
believe-or-not-believe tenets; and culture can be redeemed by the efforts of
humans and the political process apart from, and even against, the Christian
theology of salvation and new birth. Kingdom work becomes altogether
the act of humans. Furthermore, the church plays absolutely no role except
insofar as it supports Jane Addams's social activism. The location of God's
work is in the *world*. In essence, the church gets replaced by Washington,
DC, and the ethic of Jesus is translated into Western liberalism's noble
ideals. Kingdom work, then, is when good people do good deeds in the
public sector for the common good.[12]

These are some harsh words, but they are not meant to devalue the noble
life of anyone who works hard for justice and peace in our world.[13] What

they are meant to do is to lay before us an example of indisputably good activism and to ask one question: Did Jane Addams do kingdom work? I believe many today would say yes, inasmuch as she was doing good, just, and peaceful work. I say no, however, and in the following pages I will show why, and we will see why getting clear what we mean by kingdom and kingdom mission makes a huge difference in what we devote ourselves to.

Skinny Jeans folks understand kingdom as social activism that is for the common good and accomplished in the public sector. Pleated Pants folks, in contrast, have reduced kingdom to "redemptive moments," which are sometimes seen in the inner heart, in healings of all sorts, and also in the public sector. But first let's see how the Pleated Pants folks explain themselves.

2

PLEATED PANTS KINGDOM

Bible scholars and theologians and many pastors—the Pleated Pants crowd, which includes males and females—have produced shelves of books examining what the Bible teaches about kingdom. Listening to this crowd makes one wonder if they are ever looking at the same Bible! For the Pleated Pants crew, two theoretical questions have risen to the front of this three-century-old discussion:

When does the kingdom arrive?
Where is the kingdom?

A little more completely, their questions are: Is the kingdom already here, or is it still in the future? And is the kingdom a dynamic rule of God or the realm over which God rules—that is, a nation or a people or a territory, such as the kingdom of Denmark? What kingdom mission or kingdom work looks like, if those directions are even pursued among this crowd, flows from answering these two sets of questions. We can summarize the Pleated Pants crowd's answers to these questions in two statements: the kingdom is both present and future, and the kingdom is both a rule and a realm (over which God governs).[1] Not very exciting conclusions, I agree, especially when compared to what the Skinny Jeans adherents talk about and do.

Kingdom as Both Present and Future

Instead of providing a lengthy list of Bible verses, I will give two statements of Jesus for kingdom as present and kingdom as future. Here the kingdom is present:

> After John was put in prison, Jesus went into Galilee, proclaiming the good news of God. "The time *has come*," he said. "The kingdom of God *has come near*. Repent and believe the good news!" (Mark 1:14–15)

> Once, on being asked by the Pharisees when the kingdom of God would come, Jesus replied, "The coming of the kingdom of God is not something that can be observed, nor will people say, 'Here it is,' or 'There it is,' because the kingdom of God is *in your midst*." (Luke 17:20–21)

Here the kingdom is future:

> "Truly I tell you, I will not drink again from the fruit of the vine until that day when I drink it new in the kingdom of God." (Mark 14:25)

> While they were listening to this, he went on to tell them a parable, because he was near Jerusalem and the people thought that the kingdom of God was going to appear at once. (Luke 19:11)

No matter how you cut your bread—lengthwise or crosswise or just nip off the crusts—these texts indicate with clarity that the kingdom of God, that long-awaited promise, was *already present* and at the same time *still in the future*. It is reasonable, then, to argue—and the Pleated Pants folks mostly agree on this—that for Jesus the kingdom was both present and future. It was, to use the terms of the arch-Pleated Pants scholar George Eldon Ladd, "present without consummation." This is a profound truth, but the Pleated Pants scholars have made the kingdom so theoretical and abstract, peppered at times with French and German terms, that church people cry out for clarity. To say, as they often do, that the kingdom is "eschatological existence" or "living between the times" or "dwelling in the tension between the now and the not yet"—frankly, that might work in some lecture hall, but when it comes to kingdom mission or to kingdom work, we want to know *what kingdom looks like in ministry*. What is kingdom mission? Is it worship? Social activism? Evangelism? Family life? Culture making? What is it in the concrete realities of this world? Is this crowd's habit of not taking us to the next level, to the level of church life itself, an example of turning kingdom study into what Karl Barth called "blowing bubbles"?[2] Yes, this is precisely what sometimes (maybe oftentimes?) happens.

Pleated Pants folks have delicate egos, so I want to put this issue about the timing of the kingdom into a theoretical epigram: *to the degree that the kingdom has been inaugurated, it can be realized in our world today.* The kingdom has invaded this world in and through redemption in Christ, and to the degree that the kingdom has been inaugurated, it can make us new people. The kingdom *now* is not the perfect kingdom of the *not yet*, and that means kingdom citizens are not yet perfect, not yet fully loving, not yet fully holy, not yet fully just, and not yet fully peaceful. But Jesus' redemptive lordship is at work in the now, so kingdom citizens are to reflect that lordship. We must now move on to a second question at work in the kingdom according to the Pleated Pants thinkers.

Kingdom as Rule and Realm

If one simply combs through the Old Testament with a concordance and looks up the word "kingdom," one can see it used to describe both the realm over which someone rules (a nation, a people, a territory) and the active rule of a king. A few verses exemplify this.

> "You will be for me a *kingdom* of priests and a holy nation." These are the words you are to speak to the Israelites. (Exod. 19:6)

Here the words "kingdom" and "nation" and "Israelites" are parallel, and clearly "you" means a people, so the word "kingdom" clearly refers to a "people governed by a king." This is even clearer in the next text.

Then Moses gave to the Gadites, the Reubenites and the half-tribe of Manasseh son of Joseph the *kingdom* of Sihon king of the Amorites and the *kingdom* of Og king of Bashan—the whole land with its cities and the territory around them. (Num. 32:33)

We've got a king and a land and cities, making it clear that "kingdom" is a "people governed by a king." This is clear in the Psalms when it says, "They wandered from nation to nation, from one *kingdom* to another" (Ps. 105:13). Here "nation" and "kingdom" are parallel. Or how about these cosmic-governing-of-God texts from the Psalms?

> Your throne, O God, will last forever and ever;
>   a scepter of justice will be the scepter of your *kingdom*. (45:6)

> The Lord has established his throne in heaven,
>   and his *kingdom* rules over all. (103:19)

These texts prove beyond doubt that "kingdom" in the Old Testament refers to both realm and governing (or ruling), sometimes emphasizing one and sometimes emphasizing the other, but always having a sense of both.

Somewhere along the line, someone in the Pleated Pants crowd argued that the Hebrew word "kingdom"[3] meant "rule" or "reign" or "sovereignty" but not "realm"; the final bell was wrung, the game was over, and they retired to a sitting room to chat and enjoy evening drinks with not a few of them smoking expensive cigars. Nearly everyone (but not all) fell in line, and a consensus arrived: kingdom meant "rule" and not "realm."[4] Since God as King is also Savior of Israel (Ps. 74:12; Isa. 33:22; 44:8), the kind of rule God brings is a saving, redeeming rule. The shift in meanings was heard throughout the land: the word "rule" became the word "redemption."

But any reading of the verses that I cited above, or of the many others that could be registered, makes it abundantly clear that the word "kingdom" means *both rule and realm*. Think about it: you can't have a realm without someone to rule it, and anyone who rules has to have a realm over which he or she rules, and it is unfair to the Bible to force us to choose. George Ladd forced the choice when he argued over and over for "rule" and that "kingdom" did not therefore mean "realm." The result of this sort of conclusion is that the word "kingdom" has come to mean God's *redemptive rule and power at work in the world.* Here are Ladd's famous words: "The Kingdom of God is the redemptive reign of God dynamically active to establish his rule among men, and . . . this Kingdom, which will appear as an apocalyptic act at the end of the age, has already come into human history in the person and mission of Jesus to overcome evil, to deliver men from its power, and to bring them into the blessings of God's reign."[5]

The fundamental idea at work here is that the kingdom of God is *the dynamic redemption of God in Christ.* The word "kingdom," then, is not a place or a space or a realm or a people with boundaries and kings and a temple. No, "kingdom" refers to the abstract dynamic that God is now at work redeeming individuals in Jesus Christ in this world, and this rule in Jesus Christ will be completed and universal at the eschaton when the kingdom arrives fully. For Ladd, then, it is fair to reduce kingdom to a *redemptive-rule dynamic.*[6] But what does this mean?

Kingdom as Purely Religious, Everywhere, Nowhere, Everything

Here we come to a rather amazing conclusion and, if I may, to a rather good case for "blowing bubbles": the location of the kingdom for the Pleated Pants crowd is *nowhere and everywhere at the same time!* It is wherever redemption is occurring, and of course "redemption" can shift its meaning from the spiritual to the social without so much as notifying us. The great German scholar Rudolf Schnackenburg, in his influential study *God's Rule and Kingdom,* pinned his thesis onto a public broadside in these words: "The salvation proclaimed and promised by Jesus in this reign and kingdom of God is *purely religious in character.* Jesus entirely excluded the national and the politico-religious elements from his *basileia* [kingdom] concept and, in so doing, repudiated the widespread hope of a splendid Messianic kingdom of Israel."[7]

Schnackenburg leaves a window open that will let the rains soak the floor when he admits that the Jewish world at the time of Jesus clearly understood kingdom in sociopolitical terms. He's right: to speak of kingdom for a Jew was to speak of Israel, nation, land, law, and a king in Jerusalem. But, for Schnackenburg, that was all denied by Jesus when he used the term. For Jesus the kingdom was "purely religious." That is, the kingdom is a redemptive reality.

But what kind of redemption? For some, kingdom-as-redemption throws open every window in the house. I take one example, John Stackhouse, who says this of the kingdom: "We see the marks of the Kingdom of God, then, wherever light penetrates darkness, wherever good makes its way against evil or inertia, wherever beauty emerges amid ugliness and vapidity, and wherever truth sounds out against error or falsity."[8]

I confess to being troubled by John's "wherevers" in this sentence, but he expresses precisely what many believe: kingdom is God's big will, and wherever anything like God's big will appears, there is kingdom. Much later in his book he makes it clear exactly what he means:

> When someone asks, therefore, "What are you doing for the Kingdom?" we might well reply with any of the following:
>
> - I'm mowing the lawn.
> - I'm washing the dishes.
> - I'm making a puzzle with my three-year-old.
> - I'm paying the bills.
> - I'm composing a poem.
> - I'm talking with my mother on the phone.
> - I'm teaching a neighbor child how to throw a ball.
> - I'm writing the mayor.
> - I'm preaching.
>
> Everything. Everywhere. Every moment. That is the scope of God's call on our lives, and that is the dignity our lives enjoy.[9]

When this is what "kingdom" means, "kingdom" means nothing because it means everything. I doubt that when Jesus said the "kingdom has drawn near" he was talking about mowing the lawn or washing the dishes! But Stackhouse speaks for the majority today—every "redemptive" moment is "kingdom." One sees the same view at work in N. T. Wright's many statements about kingdom work today.[10] I too used to think more along these lines, but confidence in this orientation to kingdom tiptoed out of my mental home, and when I woke up one day I knew there had to be a better way.

I complained about the Pleated Pants group not caring enough about concrete realities and kingdom mission,[11] but some have moved beyond this abstract, nowhere-and-everywhere redemptive-rule dynamic to practical ministry and into political influence. So this redemptive-rule dynamic becomes a living reality, showing itself, for example, in the following two ways:

In *ordinary evangelism*, when someone calls others to surrender to the redemptive rule of Christ. In this sense, kingdom is almost synonymous with surrendering to God or to "salvation."

In *power evangelism* or *power deliverances*, when someone sees a healing or an exorcism or a mighty act of God as "kingdom ministry."[12]

For the Pleated Pants crowd, then, kingdom has been boiled down to specific redemptive moments, moments when God's redemptive reign breaks in to save, to restore, to reconcile, to heal. Our brief thumbnail definition above, that kingdom refers to "a people governed by a king," is reduced by the Pleated Pants crowd to the word "governed," and the word "governed" has become the word "redeemed" or "saved." Because this way of defining kingdom is so pervasive and so abstract and so lacking in concrete realities, I turn to the words of Marilynne Robinson, who said, "This is an instance in which a theory that explains everything really does explain nothing."[13]

There is, however, a third way that this dynamic redemption is emerging in our context today, and it almost joins hands with the Skinny Jeans folks. This third way is to see "redemption" in cultural and political and global and political terms. In other words, kingdom work describes *public activism*.

The Pleated Pants Get Activist

At this point we could enter into the long conversation the church has had regarding how to relate the "church" to "culture" and to the "state." To avoid complicating this current study on what the Bible says about kingdom, I have moved that discussion to two appendixes at the end of this book. Here, two observations will reveal how significant this redemptive-dynamic idea of the kingdom is for (so-called) kingdom mission. First, for many this conversation about the redemptive dynamic of the kingdom has shifted toward culture making, cultural transformation, and cultural influence. Transforming culture is kingdom work, so it is claimed. A few notable and recent evangelical names[14] will illustrate what I'm saying. Carl Henry, as editor of *Christianity Today* and in his public voice, proposed balanced but "socially aggressive" Christian posturing in the public sector, including setting up shop directly across from the White House. Andy Crouch taps into how Christians can influence and reshape "culture" through a variety of strategies, and, from a different angle, James K. A. Smith contends for cultural liturgies shaped by what we love and worship and the importance of embodied practices. Miroslav Volf frames public engagement of the faithful in a global context; Os Guinness pleads for global civility, tolerance, and soul liberty; and James Davison Hunter contends that the best Christian "strategy" is to be "faithful witnesses."[15] Tim Keller, in his usual peacemaking way, seeks commonality between various approaches.[16] Probably the best sketch of this approach is found in John Stackhouse's proposal of a new kind of Christian realism. Stackhouse expresses his theory with an almost wry expression: "making the best of it."[17]

But from within this entire approach comes a warning. Hunter's study reminds us all of fundamental issues at work in any attempt to change culture. He argues that culture changes from top down and not from bottom up; that evangelicals on the Left and Right do not have enough social and cultural capital to change culture; that culture is resistant to any intentional change; that most Christian groups today are *too politically activist in grasping for power*; and that the gospel does not valorize power but loving service. He offers a deeper understanding of the world, and he concludes that the wisest approach for Christians is to back away from public agitation and to move into what he calls "faithful witness." In essence, Hunter's strategy of "faithful presence"—to each other, to our vocations, and within our spheres of influence—calls into question the transformation and liberation models that dominate Christian activism today.[18]

A second observation: not only have our efforts at culture's transformation far underachieved the goals (except on paper), but this word "culture" seems to be replacing the Bible's word "world."[19] Put less discreetly, just

sprinkle some baptismal water on "world" and we can now call it "culture."
In this sense "culture" becomes the redeemed elements of the world, but
often with the connotations of world dismissed. Why say this? Because
the word "world" does not come off so well in the New Testament. Notice
these potent lines from the Gospel of John:

> "Light has come into the world but people loved darkness instead of light
> because their deeds were evil." (3:19)

> "You are from below; I am from above. You are of this world; I am not of
> this world." (8:23)

> "If you belonged to the world, it would love you as its own. As it is, you do
> not belong to the world, but I have chosen you out of the world. That is why
> the world hates you." (15:19)

> "I pray for them. I am not praying for the world, but for those you have
> given me, for they are yours. . . . They are not of the world, even as I am
> not of it." (17:9, 16)

> "My kingdom is not of this world." (18:36)

This selection of texts from the Fourth Gospel represents the New Testament posture toward the "world" as the unredeemed realm of human
affairs, a realm into which Jesus is sent and out of which he saves his own.
The point I am making, then, is that Jesus didn't come to make the "world"
a better place or to "influence" or "transform" the world. He came to
redeem people out of the world.[20] Trying to make the world a better place
is a species of worldliness, and "worldliness," to quote Hauerwas and
Willimon, "is a hard habit to break."[21]

To be sure, the world is (or was) God's good creation, but in the fall the
world becomes unredeemed, corrupted, and chaotic, including humans in
all our sinfulness and systems. To quote Chris Wright, "It is simultaneously
the wonderfully good creation of God and the horrendously wicked theatre
of human and satanic rebellion against God."[22]

"World" in the New Testament isn't neatly balanced between the good
and the bad because, to quote John Howard Yoder,[23] in the New Testament

17

it is mostly the "creaturely order in the state of rebellion." Or, "The 'world' is neither all nature nor all humanity nor all 'culture'; it is *structured unbelief*, taking with it a fragment of what should have been the Order of the Kingdom."[24] And Stanley Hauerwas created a near marvel of expression when he said the first task of the church "is to be the church and thus help the world understand itself as world." He clarifies: "For the church to be the church, therefore, is not anti-world, but rather an attempt to show what the world is meant to be as God's good creation."[25] But this makes the church God's mission *to* the world *for the sake of* the world so the world will become what it is meant to be. When we reverse this posture the church ends up serving the world, or, as Hauerwas poignantly put it, we end up "running errands for the world."[26] Eugene Peterson, in *The Message*, in an apparent gloss on Paul's words to the Ephesians, has "The church, you see, is not peripheral to the world; the world is peripheral to the church" (at 1:23).

A Way Forward in the Kingdom Discussion

A first-year college student once approached me at the end of a lecture, looked both left and right to make sure absolutely no one but me heard what she wanted me to hear, got just to the edge of my private-space comfort zone with her mouth close to my left ear, and then revealed to me what was on her heart: "Never wear black shoes with navy blue pants unless you work for United Airlines." She rocked back a foot or so, looked me in the eye, winked like she had divulged a secret in life, and then marched out of the room. I don't remember telling anyone what went through my head when she said it, but I'm sure it wasn't pretty. But now I'm about to lay down a new rule: never use the word "kingdom" for what we do in the "world."

These two approaches to kingdom, one focusing on social activism through the public, political process and the other focusing on redemptive moments, reveal important truths about the kingdom in the Bible. There is no kingdom that is not about a just society, as there is no kingdom without redemption under Christ. Yet I'm convinced that both of these approaches to kingdom fall substantially short of what kingdom meant to Jesus, so we need once again to be patient enough to ponder what the Bible teaches.

18

To borrow words from Marilynne Robinson, what these two approaches provide "is a straight-edged ruler in a fractal universe."[27] It will take more than a few chapters to get this "fractal universe" called "kingdom" in view.

My wife, Kris, and I found ourselves on a clear, beautiful Saturday in Vancouver, British Columbia, so we chose to spend it walking around Stanley Park, the world's largest urban park. Stanley Park is almost entirely surrounded by water, and our experience was that it is a place where God smiles big. We were near a beach of rocks when I spied a crow that had, in Barbra Streisand's words when speaking of Andre Agassi, "evolved beyond its linear years." The crow had nabbed a clam and wanted to eat its juicy innards, but crows aren't designed by God to hammer on a shell as a woodpecker could. So, instead, the crow was flying just over the top of the rocks and dropping the shell onto the rocks hoping to crack it. As we watched, the crow went back and forth three or four times but had not yet found the magic spot of cracking through the clam's tough carapace. We needed to catch the bus, so we didn't see the end of this story, but I have no doubt the crow flew back and forth until it got what it wanted.

In what follows I will do the same: flying low over the Bible and the world of Jesus with a clam called "kingdom" and dropping it on the rocks of the Bible's books. I am confident that this shell will break open and that by the time we are done—before the bus comes or before you throw me under the bus—we will nab some juicy kingdom meat from the Bible and have a banquet together. So, one drop after another, I proceed now to various elements of the kingdom, and I have to admit we will need to talk about words and bring to them what the American poet Christian Wiman calls a "fury of clarity."[28] Words have to be studied in order to understand the kingdom. I agree, then, with Marilyn Chandler McEntyre and against Maria Edgeworth, the latter of whom once said, "Above all things, shun definitions; they will prove fatal to you." But McEntyre gets it right in her splendid Stone Lectures at Princeton, published as *Caring for Words in a Culture of Lies*: "Precision begins with defining terms."[29] She also said one page later, "If your verbs are precise, I tell students, if they get at who did what to whom in what way as specifically as possible, your writing will improve by 50 percent." She continues with a side note: "I made up the statistic, as I also tell them. I'm precise with words. Numbers are another

19

matter." I shall attempt to do both, including getting the numbers precise when they matter.

Where, then, do we begin in this fury seeking clarity? We should begin with what gives kingdom its meaning and context: Israel's story. Here we will discover a kingdom dressed up in a tunic and a turban.

3

TELL ME
THE KINGDOM STORY

Kingdom's first word is "story." Proverbs says, "Without a story [or vision directing one's plan in life] the people perish" (29:18, paraphrased). Israelites made sense of life through the story they learned to tell themselves. So Bible scholars today are searching for the best way to tell the Bible's story. For the Pleated Pants approach to kingdom, since it focuses on the redemptive-rule dynamic, the Bible's central story is about individual persons whose crisis is their sin and its consequences, and the resolution is the atoning work of Christ that both ends the consequences of their sin and offers them a new life and hope for the kingdom. This approach to the Bible's story clearly has all the necessary elements of a story: characters, events, tension, and resolution. The Skinny Jeans story is about participating in the direction of our world by lending a hand so the world will become a better place. Life's theme, then, is about being significant, and significance is usually wrapped up in things like justice and peace. What we know is that both the Pleated Pants and Skinny Jeans approaches lead to a mission: the first leads to evangelism and to church while the second leads to social activism and a better world. Kingdom story creates kingdom mission, but it leads us beyond evangelism and social activism.

It all hangs on *which* story we tell. I lay down an observation that alters the landscape if we embrace it—namely, we need to learn to tell the story that makes sense of Jesus. Not a story that we ask Jesus to fit into. No, we need to find the story that Jesus himself and the apostles told. To use common idiom, If Jesus was the answer, what was the question? I suggest that if we leave it at that, the "question" can roam across the entire Christian theological spectrum. So I want to narrow that idiom to this: If Jesus was the answer, and the answer was that Jesus was the Messiah/King, what was the question? This answer changes the question, and that question leads to the right story.

Elizabeth Achtemeier's Witness

Yes, Bible scholars are working on the Bible's overarching story, but many today ignore the Bible or attach themselves to only one element of that story while others attack the Bible in a variety of ways. I need to emphasize a point that drives this book: *I believe in the Bible, and I believe the only theology worth giving ourselves to is a theology shaped through and by the Bible.* Whether it is on my blog or in public speaking, I find myself routinely muttering these questions under my breath: "Do people not care about the Bible? How do these people claim any authority for their ideas if they do not permit their ideas to be formed by the Bible's story?" Or, more often, I find myself muttering, "Yes, yes, I know that's your view, but what does the Bible say? Or does it matter?"

I want to give a good example of someone who has done the kind of work this book is seeking to accomplish. Her name is Elizabeth Achtemeier, and she was an Old Testament and preaching professor at Union Theological Seminary in Virginia (along with her husband, New Testament scholar Paul Achtemeier). Her story is the story of letting the Bible shape a life. It begins with her devout mother.[1] "Through discipline and regularity, through teaching and example, Mother gradually instilled in me the necessity of the church in my life, and through that channel of grace I came to know my heavenly Father and his Son Jesus Christ, whose Spirit has accompanied my life ever since."

Because she is a woman, Elizabeth opens her memoir with a discussion of the church and women, and she expresses a kind of feminism not always well accepted. Her defense is that she's a Bible woman, and without that there's no genuine Christian feminism. She observes that by "not using women to the fullest, the church for years impoverished itself." But she finds radical feminism falling wildly short and says, "When the radical feminists claim they are 'victims,' and when they attack the core of the Christian faith by rejecting the Bible and its witness to the nature of God, they undermine the very church they think to improve." She claims she rarely experienced discrimination and confesses, "I have to attribute my unhindered work in the church not to my own ability but to the power of the Word of God of which I am merely a student and servant." She pushes back against unbiblical politicized feminism with a question: "What sort of God do the radical feminists offer me to replace the Father who has guided me my whole life long?" And yet another confession: "My attempt has been to be simply an evangel of the gospel that I know is true."

Elizabeth Achtemeier is a witness to the significance of the Bible for her own life and for the life of the church, and her many books reveal her passion for the Word. In a very clever turn of phrase, Brandon McKoy suggests that to discover the kind of life Elizabeth Achtemeier had, we need to move from the debate about "inerrancy and errancy" to the commitment to "inheritancy."[2] This is precisely what I mean by a kingdom-story approach to Scripture: its story becomes ours through soaking ourselves in it—that is, by inheriting this story and passing it on to the next generation.

A kingdom theology must be rooted in Scripture so that we form a genuinely biblical concept of the story. Which leads us to the question: What is the kingdom story of the Bible? Until we can articulate the Bible's kingdom story, we can't do kingdom mission.

The Two "Stories" in the Kingdom Story

There are actually two stories at work in the kingdom story, one of them seen in part in the Skinny Jeans view and one of them seen in part in the Pleated Pants view. The two have been separated and need to be brought together, but when we bring them together—as we will in this chapter—the kingdom story will transcend both the Skinny Jeans and the Pleated Pants approaches. The two stories are the narrower C-F-R-C story and the more complete A-B-A' story.[3]

C-F-R-C

The C-F-R-C story is the story of salvation in the Bible. It goes like this:

- God is the author of *Creation* (the C) and made all things good. Humans were designed by God in his own image and likeness, and they lived an innocent and good life in the Garden of Eden.
- Adam and Eve chose to go their own way, sinned against God, did the very thing God said not to, and this led to the *fall* (the F) of humans into sin. There are plenty of debates about how pervasive or infecting that sin is, but most Protestants accept some kind of "original sin" although not all accept "original guilt." At any rate, to quote James Thurber, it's the "day confusion got its foot in the door."[4] What also needs to be accepted is that the "fall" is the paradigm for all because each of us attempts to assert total control. As Karl Barth put it in the era before inclusive language, "Man would like to break free from God, to make himself independent of him, to posit himself absolutely."[5]
- Next comes R, which stands for *redemption*. God in his grace makes a covenant with Abraham, elects Israel for his own people, and works his mission for the world through Israel. Israel fails to be faithful to God and the covenant, so God sends the perfect Israelite to make full redemption. That perfect Israelite is Jesus Christ, and his redemptive work in his life, death, burial, resurrection, and exaltation on the cross establishes in the here and now a beachhead for the kingdom.
- Redemption will only be completed at the second coming (or eschaton), when God will usher in the full kingdom of God, called the new heaven and the new earth, with a new Jerusalem. This will be the *consummation* (the final C) of redemption.

Kingdom mission is only kingdom if this redemption dynamic courses through the entire story kingdom people tell. Anyone who reads the Bible finds the story of God as Creator, the fall of humans, and the need and provision of redemption, as well as a future, final, and gloriously eternal redemption in the kingdom.

Questioning this age-old way of reading the Bible is like sticking my finger into your coffee to see if it is warm enough, but I shall because there are three significant problems with the C-F-R-C story: (1) it has taken over how people read the Bible because (2) it is a reading of the Bible that resonates with humans personally. Therefore, (3) it is a narrow or inadequate reading of the Bible. There's so much more. Those who read the Bible solely through the C-F-R-C plot have an annoying propensity to read Genesis 1–3 to get their *C* and their *F* in place, but then they skip all the way to Romans 3 or to the crucifixion scenes in the Gospels to get to the *R*. This skips 99.5 percent of the Old Testament. Some, too, tend to omit any serious discussion of Israel or church or the people of God as the locus of what God is doing in this world.[6] Why? Because the focus of the C-F-R-C story is on personal salvation, it is also a focus on the salvation of the *individual*. By all means, the Bible tells the story of redemption, and each of us needs to be saved, and the C-F-R-C tells us how that happens. That's good. But when the Bible's story is reduced to the redemption story, we lose much of the story.

Please put down your smartphone. In fact, turn the thing off, listen to this claim, and take the time to judge if it is right. The most decisive text in the whole Bible for knowing how to read the Bible is the succinct summary of the gospel in 1 Corinthians 15:3–5, and we can reduce it to four points.

For what I received I passed on to you as of first importance:

1. that Christ died for our sins according to the Scriptures,
2. that he was buried,
3. that he was raised on the third day according to the Scriptures,
4. and that he appeared to Cephas, and then to the Twelve.

The gospel is a story about Jesus, and because it is about Jesus, it is about us. To make the story first about us, or first about me and my salvation, is to reduce the story and to rob Jesus of the glory of being the central actor. Once I was speaking on a topic at a conference—a topic I was asked to address, and a theological topic at that—and when I finished, a person came up to me with this demanding question: "Tell me, professor, what does this have to do with *me*?" I said rather straightforwardly, "Maybe nothing. But it is about what the Bible says." The response saddened me:

"Then I'm not interested." As the person walked away I thought about what happens when we turn the Bible's story into the story about and for "Me." So I'll say it again: the gospel is the story about Jesus. The gospel announces that *Jesus is Messiah, Jesus is King, Jesus is Lord, and Jesus is Savior.* This is not an either-or: either about me or about Jesus. But the order tells us if we are making the story about Me or about Jesus. First Jesus, then you and me. That's the gospel order.

Now a bigger claim to consider (while your phone is off): if 1 Corinthians 15:3–5 is the goal of the story, we need to learn to tell the Bible's story as the story about Jesus, or about God. That is, *until we find the story that leads us to the gospel claim that Jesus is the Messiah, we don't have the Bible's story right.* The most accurate Bible story is the story that leads us from Genesis 1 to Jesus as the Messiah, to Jesus as the one true King, to Jesus as the Lord of the universe, to Jesus as the one who redeems us so we can enter into the kingdom. The C-F-R-C story tells us about "Jesus as the one who redeems" but not about Jesus as the Messiah, not about Jesus as King, and not about Jesus as Lord. And often enough it does not tell us about the kingdom. So we need a story that swallows the C-F-R-C into a larger story, and a good example of someone who is telling this story is N. T. Wright.

Refocusing the Story

Tom Wright, in his well-known book on Jesus called *Jesus and the Victory of God,* frames the kingdom story with this observation: for Jesus to "say 'the kingdom of god is at hand' makes sense only when the hearers know 'the story so far' and are waiting for it to be completed."[7] The story at work can be found in Tom's book *The New Testament and the People of God.*[8] There he did the important work of proving that the "story" at work with Jesus was not simply what happened in Israel's history, like creation and the exodus and the exile, like the figures of Abraham and Moses and David, and like the comedies and tragedies of kings, prophets, invasions, captivities, economics, politics, family life, international relations, and times of peace. Those are elements in the story, but they are in turn part of a worldview—made of story, symbols, and praxis—that sets the people and events into a meaning-making story.

26

Tom's way of framing all this is worth a brief retelling because it anticipates what we will see below. The story begins with the Creator God and the fall, then the calling of the patriarchs and the exodus redemption-as-liberation under Moses, a story that becomes the paradigm story in Israel. Then the conquest sets up the story of David. His successors failed, however, and their failure leads to the exile in Babylon. This sets up the hope for another (new) exodus and the return to the land, and yet—and this is foundational to Wright's understanding of the story—even that return doesn't seem to bring together all that was expected. Here is one way Tom puts it: "The great story of the Hebrew scriptures was therefore inevitably read in the second-temple period as a story in search of a conclusion." Wright's magical expression of this is that Israel is still "living in exile," and what Jesus announces is the "end of exile." Kingdom and end of exile, then, are ways of telling the grand story. That Wright focuses on end of exile as the way to read the story at the time of Jesus has been criticized,[9] but I would contend that Wright's expression emerges organically from the expectations of Israel's prophets and leads us more directly to a storied understanding of kingdom. In some ways, then, "end of exile" means "kingdom has come." What Wright's proposal does perhaps most is put before us a series of questions that were being asked at the time of Jesus, and he provides a series of answers first-century Jewish thinkers were giving. In this context, then, the kingdom story of Jesus flourishes. Here are Tom's questions and answers:[10]

1. Who are we? We are Israel, the chosen people of the creator god.
2. Where are we? We are in the holy land, focused on the temple; but, paradoxically, we are still in exile.
3. What is wrong? We have the wrong rulers; pagans on the one hand, compromised Jews on the other, or, half-way between, Herod and his family. We are all involved in a less-than-ideal situation.
4. What is the solution? Our god must act again to give us the true sort of rule, that is, his own kingship exercised through properly appointed officials (a true priesthood; possibly a true King); and in the meantime Israel must be faithful to his covenant charter.

This set of questions, I think, reorients our "story" approaches, and it clearly surpasses the C-F-R-C approach. But I want to suggest that even

Tom Wright's story could be focused less on the benefits of the story (exile is over) and more on the king of the story. I suggest the A-B-A′ story does just that.

A-B-A′

When Jesus declared, "The time has come. The kingdom of God has come near. Repent and believe the good news," the average Jewish listener didn't say, "Finally, someone to tell me how to get saved." Instead, what first came to mind when Jesus spoke this way of the arrival of the kingdom were thoughts about "David" and "king" and "messiah" and "temple" and "Jerusalem" and "Kick the Romans out!" and "justice." Kingdom makes no sense in the New Testament, from Jesus to Paul and to the Apocalypse, until you understand the *specialized* story kingdom is telling. I propose that the following A-B-A′ story is the one driving the kingdom story and that the C-F-R-C story is a theme within the A-B-A′ story. Most important, the A-B-A′ story will lead us squarely to focus on the gospel declaration that Jesus is Messiah, Lord, and Savior.

PLAN A

Plan A extends from Adam and Abraham to Samuel. The period is marked by one major theme: *God rules the world through his elected people, but God is the one and only King.* God is the Creator—that's how the Bible's story begins. As Creator, God is King, but God does something amazingly radical: he shares his rule with Adam and Eve. However, sharing the rule is not enough for them, as the fall story in Genesis 3 makes clear. But the A-B-A′ story asks us to adjust the F part of the C-F-R-C story. In classical Christian thinking, we say Adam and Eve "fell" and now are marked by original sin. So the problem to be solved by redemption is disobedience and original sin. So far so good, but that explanation is just not enough. The problem to be solved by redemption is the *kind* of sin Adam and Eve committed *in light of their assignment.*

Back up now to Genesis 1. Adam and Eve are *eikons*, God's appointed ruling image-bearers (Gen. 1:26–27) in God's cosmic temple.[11] What are image-bearers to do? They are appointed to rule for God, or under God. The "fall" is from this task. That is, Adam and Eve decide they want to rule "like God" instead of ruling "under God," which means Adam and Eve are *usurpers*. The sin they commit is the sin of wanting more than the responsibility of governing on God's behalf; the sin they commit is made clear in the words of the scumbag serpent in Genesis 3: "For God knows that when you eat from it your eyes will be opened [in a *Pleasantville* sort of way], and [here it comes with full force] *you will be like God*, knowing good and evil" (3:5, emphasis added). *The story of sin in the Bible is the story of God's elect people wanting to be God-like instead of god-ly, of ruling instead of sub-ruling and being ruled.*

To end the mutiny of humans against God, and at the same time to forgive and bond humans to God according to Plan A, God *elects* one solitary man and cuts a covenant of grace with him, calling him and his people to rule for God. This begins the *R* in the C-F-R-C story. That man's name is Abraham, and the principal texts of this part of the story can be found in Genesis 12, 15, and 17. Abraham's descendant is Jacob, or Israel. This story will march on from the patriarchs and Joseph to Egypt, and then we get Moses, who develops the *R* theme into a theology of atonement and sacrifice and forgiveness and purity. Then comes Joshua, and then the distressing cyclical stories of the judges, until we get to Samuel. It's all about God ruling through Israel. There is no human king because a human king is, *by definition*, a usurper.

Plan A has four characteristics:

- God alone is King.
- Humans, from Adam and Eve to Abraham, are to rule under God.
- Humans usurp God's rule.
- God forgives the usurpers and forms a covenant with Abraham.

Plan B

The story of Israel ruling this world under and for God has a most unusual development, one that is almost always neglected in kingdom discussions.[12] In fact, it's so neglected that I need to dust off the story so we can see it again. Samuel, who was not a king in name, toys with turning his own rule into a dynasty by appointing his own sons to rule after him (1 Sam. 8:1). But his sons are moral failures as leaders. Samuel then comes to God in 1 Samuel 8 to announce that some arrogant Israelite "elders" would like to have a king (instead of his sons). Their request is more or less the sin of Adam and Eve. Furthermore, their request is precisely the option Gideon refused (Judg. 8:23). The words of the arrogant elders to Samuel in 1 Samuel 8:5 concern his age and what will happen if his knucklehead sons rule when he is gone: "You are old, and your sons do not follow your ways; *now appoint a king to lead us, such as all the other nations have*" (emphasis added).

Samuel's displeasure (1 Sam. 8:6)[13] is met by a revelation from God that provides one of the secrets to understanding kingdom. In YHWH's revelation to Samuel, YHWH explains what is really going on in the minds and hearts of those who want a king like the other nations. We learn from YHWH that Israel doesn't want to rule *for* God in this world but wants to be like the world and rule *like* God.

> And the LORD told him: "Listen to all that the people are saying to you; it is not you they have rejected, *but they have rejected me as their king.* As they have done from the day I brought them up out of Egypt until this day, forsaking me and serving other gods, so they are doing to you. Now listen to them; but warn them solemnly and let them know what the king who will reign over them will claim as his rights." (1 Sam. 8:7–9, emphasis added)[14]

From Adam and Abraham to Samuel, God is King. It's a theocracy. God rules Israel in a decentralized manner and often through a leader marked by nothing more than God's call. But from this event recorded in 1 Samuel 8—that is, from Saul forward—*a king* rules (1 Sam. 8:10–18). *A human king for Israel is Plan B in God's eyes.*

Plan B, or in more generous terms, the rest of the Old Testament story, is the story of David.[15] This is highlighted in Chronicles, where there is a simmering undercurrent running throughout the whole narrative: David was a good king, the current kings are far less than David, and we look forward to a new Davidic king. Read these verses from the Chronicler to catch just a glimpse of how important David was to the plan (B) of God:

> "I will set him over my house and my kingdom forever; his throne will be established forever." (1 Chron. 17:14)

"Of all my sons—and the LORD has given me many—he has chosen my son Solomon to sit on the throne of the kingdom of the LORD over Israel." (28:5)

So Solomon sat on the throne of the LORD as king in place of his father David. He prospered and all Israel obeyed him. (29:23)

"Praise be to the LORD your God, who has delighted in you and placed you on his throne as king to rule for the LORD your God. Because of the love of your God for Israel and his desire to uphold them forever, he has made you king over them, to maintain justice and righteousness." (2 Chron. 9:8)

"And now you plan to resist the kingdom of the LORD, which is in the hands of David's descendants. You are indeed a vast army and have with you the golden calves that Jeroboam made to be your gods." (13:8)

In Plan B God has focused his plan on David as the king whose descendants will be the rulers in Israel, and their "kingdom" is "the kingdom of God." Perhaps nothing could be clearer than the clause in the last cited text: "you plan to resist the kingdom of the LORD, *which is in the hands of David's descendants*" (emphasis added). David, then, is the center of Israel's story.

So there are six elements in Plan B:

- God alone is (still) King.
- Israel is to rule God's created world under God.
- Israel wants to usurp God's rule.
- God accommodates Israel by granting it a human king.
- The story of the Old Testament becomes the story of David.
- God continues to forgive Israel of its sins through the temple system of sacrifice, purity, and forgiveness.

A human king on the throne, even David, was still Plan B.[16] But that's the story of the Old Testament from the time of David on. God did not want a human king on Israel's throne, and lusty Solomon is but one good example of why. Kingship meant dynasty and empire and kings thinking they were God. Under a (bad) king Israel became a temple-state, and taxes blanketed the land like manna; theocracy, God's rule, was gone, and monarchy had arrived; treaties became vogue. YHWH the King became a distant memory, yet the memory lingered of the days when YHWH alone ruled.

That memory morphs into hope during Plan B, hope that God will someday rule once again. This hope is anchored in David and the future David, but this hope also responds to and takes shape in the midst of failure after David,[17] and so from Amos on there is hope for the right kind of king and kingdom, often expressed in the hope for a remnant (see Isa. 4:2–4; 10:20–22; 37:30–32). It is not accidental that James quotes Amos in Acts 15, but these are the words from Amos 9:11, which in the context of Amos 9 combine potent judgment with remnant, end of exile, and the restoration of the Davidic throne:

> In that day "I will restore David's fallen shelter—
> I will repair its broken walls
> And restore its ruins—
> And will rebuild it as it used to be."

Tom Wright's focal energy on exile in his book *Jesus and the Victory of God* moves us yet closer to seeing just how significant the A-B-A′ story is.[18] The southern tribe, Judah, was sent by God into exile to Babylon as discipline for unfaithfulness. In Babylon the ideas of ending their exile and returning to the land converged into a story of hope. Some seventy years later the exiles returned, but *not all of the promises were fulfilled* when they returned. So Tom Wright argues that even though the children of Israel were back in the land, the exile had not yet completely ended. When would it end? *When God once again sat on the throne and ruled the land.* The exile will only truly end when God rules, when the glowing words of Isaiah 40–66 are more than glimpsed in the realities in the land, when—in other words—*the damage of 1 Samuel 8 is undone and redeemed.* Until Jerusalem is ruled by God and God alone, the exile is still on. The template for how God will rule, it must be emphasized, is the rule of God through David.

But there's more to this exile theme. With exile is bound up a new development in the *R* portion of the C-F-R-C story: Israel's exile ends when, or because, Israel's sins are forgiven, and surely one of the most evocative sets of images for this atonement is found in Isaiah 52:13–53:12.

Here the Servant—a term that signifies at once Israel in exile, Israel's faithful leader, and Jesus as its anticipated Davidic and messianic king and redeemer[19]—suffers on behalf of the whole nation in order that forgiveness can be granted, the exile can end, and the exiles can return to the land. The *R* now becomes a single representative person, the Servant King. This is a development in the kingdom story of Israel, for there is no kingdom story until it wanders through the redemption of the exodus under Moses, and the "second exodus" and return seen in Isaiah 40–66. We must note this: on the basis of these chapters in Isaiah, Jesus builds his kingdom vision.

Here is where we now stand in explaining how to put the big picture together. Plan A is God's will for the world: God rules with Israel governing under God on God's behalf. But because Israel wants a king like other nations, Plan A takes a divine detour in Plan B, where God accommodates Israel's selfish desire. During Plan B arises the memory and a hope for the return to Plan A, to God's rule in Israel with no human king. As this hope moves forward, a Servant King who redeems by way of suffering and who rules by way of redemption comes to the fore. In Isaiah, then, A-B-A′ swallows up C-F-R-C into a kingdom story. What not even Isaiah expected came to pass, and what came to pass completely determines the meaning of both kingdom and kingdom mission. (You might now be tempted to think the C-F-R-C way of reading the Bible is simpler and therefore to be preferred. Hang on, because once we grasp the big themes, the Bible's story falls into place.)

PLAN A REVISED

Plan A was God ruling through Israel; Plan B was ideally David and then also an Israelite king ruling (and usually not very well because humans don't "do" God right). Under Jesus, Plan A takes on a new form. How so? God returns to Plan A because in Jesus God now rules once again.[20] So when Jesus declares that the "kingdom of God has come near," we need to pause for a moment to see something very special in the "of God." This is not the kingdom of Moses or Samuel or David or Solomon or any other of the kings of Israel and Judah. This is the kingdom *of God* as it was before Samuel's fateful request and God's accommodation to Israel, and yet this new King will be modeled on David. Jesus is announcing that God *once again has established divine rule in the land.*

Attentive Bible readers will know that the Gospel of Matthew prefers Jesus using "kingdom *of heaven*" over "kingdom *of God*," as in Matthew 4:17 (where Mark 1:15 has kingdom "of God"). For over a century most scholars, including the present author, have repeated the conclusion that "of heaven" replaces "of God" out of reverence. That is, Jesus said "of heaven" in order not to mention God directly because of his reverence for God. But a recent study by Jonathan Pennington has argued persuasively that "of heaven" is not so much about reverence but instead about the *contrast* between what God wants and what humans are doing. So kingdom *of heaven* was Jesus' way of saying that God's rule is invading the land and challenging the corrupted rule of human kings.[21] As such, this confirms the point I am making about Plan A Revised.

Jesus, reaching back into Israel's deep history and into the more recent visions of Israel's great prophets, announces that God is back in charge. The ideal Davidic king has now arrived. But we shouldn't skip from the last of the prophets over centuries of life and development and visions to Jesus. There's a history there that involves all sorts of permutations on kingdom ideas, like removal of sicknesses and defects, like the inclusion of gentiles and at the same time the defeat of occupying forces like those of Rome, like a climactic period of tribulation, and like graphic expectations of destruction. That history matters and influences the teachings of Jesus and the earliest Christians. So I agree that we need to ponder Jesus in his Jewish context, but we will do that in the next chapter.

Here, then, is Plan A Revised: in Jesus, who is called Messiah (which means king), who is also called Son of God (which also means king), *God establishes his rule over Israel one more time as under Plan A.* Here are the major elements:

- God alone is King.
- God is now ruling in King Jesus.
- Israel and the church live under the rule of King Jesus.
- Forgiveness is granted through King Jesus, the Savior.
- This rule of Jesus will be complete in the final kingdom.

Jesus is all of Israel's major leaders, and more: he's a new Moses and especially a new David and a new Solomon and a new Servant and a new Son of Man and a whole new redemptive order. Joseph and Mary name him *Yeshua* because he will "save his people from their sins" (Matt. 1:21). The story is that in Jesus God now rules, and God's kind of ruling is saving, rescuing, atoning, justifying, and reconciling. The cross and the resurrection redefine kingdom in all directions: Israel is not the same, obedience is not the same, love is not the same, peace is not the same, and justice is not the same. In other words, to say the kingdom has drawn near is to make a christological claim; it is to say the kingdom is now present in Jesus. As Luke's Gospel puts it, "The coming of the kingdom of God is not something that can be observed, nor will people say, 'Here it is,' or 'There it is,' because the kingdom of God is *in your midst*" (Luke 17:20–21). While some have suggested—indeed, banked on and written books about this—that "in your midst" means "in your soul" or "inside you," the far more persuasive interpretation is that Jesus means "the kingdom of God is standing here among you, and I am it!" The always-worth-quoting Karl Barth says it well: "What is meant in the New Testament by the presence of the kingdom of God? . . . What is meant is the center, the whence and whither, the basis, theme, and content of all the New Testament sayings, namely, the history of Jesus Christ. . . . 'The kingdom of God is at hand' means 'the Word was made flesh and dwelt among us' (John 1:14)."[22]

When Jesus said "the kingdom of God has drawn near," he announced a new day in an old story, and that story, I propose, is the A-B-A' story that includes and modifies the C-F-R-C story into the kingdom story. It is first and foremost the story of God as King, and God is King in King Jesus, so the story begins right there—just as the one and only gospel reveals: it's a story about Jesus, the Lord, the King, the Messiah, and the Savior. He is those titles now, and he will be those titles in full display when the kingdom is fully established, when we see on earth the new heaven and the new earth and the new Jerusalem, where Jesus will be the light and the lamb and where God will dwell with his people. That is the story that alone makes sense of Jesus' choice of the word "kingdom" to explain the mission of God in this world.

Kingdom Mission and the Kingdom Story

If kingdom means a story is being told, then kingdom mission means at least the following: we are to enter into that story as the one true story of the world through conversion, and we are to deepen our participation in that story through discipleship; but we need to be reminded that conversion and discipleship are only *partial* as we live in the now before the fullness of the not yet.

Conversion

First, kingdom mission requires conversion into the story. If the A-B-A′ story tells the Bible's larger story, a redemptive story for individuals must also be included, so my focus here will be individual conversion. Adam and Eve, as Paul makes abundantly clear in 1 Corinthians 15:21–22 and Romans 5:12–21, were not a one-off event unlike anything else in the history of the cosmos. Adam and Eve are Everyman and Everywoman; they represent us all, and their story is our story. That means their sin is ours, and the consequences of their story are ours. This is how Paul states it: "For since death came through a man, the resurrection of the dead comes also through a man. For as in Adam all die, so in Christ all will be made alive" (1 Cor. 15:21–22).

Romans 5:12–21, the Pauline lines to which we turn first when discussing Adam and Christ, does not appreciably advance the argument of 1 Corinthians. Adam and Eve sinned; they died. Sin leads to death. The sin they committed was the sin of usurping, of wanting to be God-*like* instead of god-*ly*. They died for the sin. We, too, are usurpers. From the moment we become conscious to the moment we die we want to be in charge, we want to control, and we want to rule our life. That is the sin of Everyman and Everywoman.

If the kingdom story is the true story, then we are summoned by it to surrender our pride and our desire to rule, to lay them before the One who died our death, who was buried, who was raised, and who is now exalted at the right hand of the Father as the King. We are to turn from our own ruling to the ruling of the King. In the grace of this surrender we are converted by the power of God's new creation Spirit.

36

We cannot enter into this story without surrendering. Why? Because if Jesus is the one and only King, we must surrender to Jesus as the King. There is no kingdom mission apart from submitting to Jesus as King and calling others to surrender before King Jesus. This is where the Pleated Pants approach gets it right and where too often the Skinny Jeans approach falls short. Too often the Skinny Jeans approach reduces kingdom to justice and then secularizes justice and peace so as to achieve a common ground for a common good. It is good to seek the common good, but not at the expense of personally surrendering to King Jesus. If the kingdom story is the true story, in fact, *there is no good for the common good until humans surrender to King Jesus.*

Discipleship

Second, kingdom mission means an ever-deepening discipleship into the story. It is far too easy for Bible scholars and pastors to reprimand lay folks for not knowing the Bible. If we had the schedule that many have, including parents with young children clamoring for attention, who often struggle to cope with their demands, perhaps we'd be more sympathetic. Furthermore, not everyone is a reader, so any suggestion that the true Christian should constantly be grabbing a concordance to check a word, or a Bible dictionary to find a geographical site, or a commentary to sort out interpretations, or a theology book that synthesizes it all into a new package—any suggestion that this is the norm simply isn't fair to the Bible or to Christians.

So, this is not about becoming Bible students. But it is about *the simultaneous act of being both mastered by the Bible's story and mastering that story for ourselves.* It is my conviction that if pastors and preachers and teachers do their job on Sunday mornings and in Sunday school classes or Bible study groups, the average Christian should be exposed every three to five years to the whole Bible story. In the course of a life a person converted prior to age twenty-five should encounter the breadth of the Bible's story at least ten times—that is, if the local church takes seriously its task of reading the Bible and teaching the Bible in light of the kingdom story. I'm confident that a reasonable number of Christians know the C-F-R-C story, or most of it, and can with some probing come up with its central elements without having to check some teachers' notes. But the larger A-B-A′ story is not as well known because it is not as personal and not as much about Me. Hence, the church has done well in teaching and catechizing the basics of the salvation story. Why can't it now meet the challenge of the larger kingdom story of the Bible?

How can we do this? I suggest three kingdom mission practices in our discipleship. First, we need to preach from the whole Bible and not just our pet passages (and this from someone who travels from church to church preaching on a very limited number of passages and topics because I'm asked to speak about books I've written!). Perhaps the safest and wisest approach here is to preach from the lectionary, often called the Revised Common Lectionary. The lectionary is a tool developed very early in the church, by the second century, of public readings from the Old Testament, the Psalms, a New Testament lesson, and then the gospel (a passage from one of the Gospels). The Revised Common Lectionary, if used completely, will take the reader through almost all of the Bible every three years. But we are talking here about public reading of the Bible, so I make this observation: if we use a lectionary, the church will be exposed to the grand themes and the kingdom story every week, and to parts of the whole Bible every three years.

Second, we need to encourage everyone in the church to *read the Bible regularly*. Some people try to read the Bible every year; others every other year. To read the Bible every year, read about four chapters every day; cut that in half for every two years. Others read the Bible according to other plans—one book from the Old Testament, then one book from the New Testament. Some read one chapter from the Old and two chapters from the New. *How* we read the Bible isn't what matters; what matters is *that* we read it. But here is where we have to raise an issue. Some read the Bible "devotionally," and by that I mean they read it quietly, slowly, and do so listening for a word from God directly to them. This practice, sometimes called *lectio divina*, is fine, but it is not what I'm talking about. I'm talking about reading the Bible the way we read any other book *so that we will learn what it says and be reminded of what we have forgotten*. We can do this without neglecting devotional practices.

Third, I am convinced that far too many of our church catechism programs teach the content of our creeds, or the substance of our statements of faith and confessions, and not the Bible's kingdom story. To think that we have catechized our children because we have gone line by line through the Nicene Creed or our church's doctrinal statement and then added some Bible verses before having them stand up and say, "This is what we believe" just won't do. But if we use the Creed as a window onto a much larger reality, supplementing where it is deficient—after all, it never was meant to cover everything—we will do well. How do we supplement the Creed? Return to the previous paragraph: we have to read the Bible, front to back, over time, to master that story and be mastered by that story. We can only do this by reading the Bible. Well, that's not completely right.

If you are fortunate enough to grow up in a place like San Gimignano, outside Siena, Italy, and attend weekly services at its famous cathedral, you will encounter how teachers and preachers and priests and theologians taught the church when ordinary folks could not read. From right to left all the way around the church is one fresco after another in chronological order of the major events of the Bible. It's not very good art; the images are flat, and the artists did everything they could to get as many details on one fresco as possible. But I stood amazed as I peered at each fresco in turn and took in all that the artists had painted into the scene. What I'm saying is that you can grab the kingdom story if you enter into the world of this kind of art on a regular basis. I don't live in Tuscany and you probably don't either, so about the only way you can learn the kingdom story is to (1) read the Bible for yourself, and (2) pay attention to the public reading of Scripture.

Eschatological Hope

Finally, kingdom mission admits that inaugurated kingdom means conversion and discipleship are incomplete until the final kingdom. We gladly announce that the kingdom has drawn near; we also gladly announce that someday the kingdom will be fully established. In these two announcements we confess that we live between two times, but we also confess that redemption and holiness and love and peace are only partly realized in the now. To return to an earlier statement: *to the same degree that the kingdom has been inaugurated in Jesus, the kingdom can be realized among us.* Something follows here: *to the degree that the kingdom has not yet been realized, it cannot be lived out in the present.* We cannot expect perfection, though some Christian groups have sought that perfection, and they ended in dismal disappointment.

Individual Christians will be both saints and sinners; local churches will be both profoundly formative and sometimes mind-bogglingly disappointing. This is what Dietrich Bonhoeffer was talking about when he exhorted his seminary students to slay their idealizations of the present church. Here's how he put it:[23] "Those who love their dream of a Christian community more than the Christian community itself become destroyers of that Christian community even though their personal intentions may be ever so honest, earnest, and sacrificial."

We soon discover that our admired saints are less than we expected and our local church fails "to deliver" what we hoped for. This is where we are given the opportunity to embrace the inaugurated reality of the kingdom: we are to embrace ourselves and our fellow "saints" as those in need of grace and forgiveness and love. As Bonhoeffer completes the thought, "The bright day of Christian community dawns wherever the early morning mists of dreamy visions are lifting."

We are, then, both disappointed and reminded of our own sinfulness when we encounter sin in our fellow saints. We are disappointed because the kingdom is at work; we are reminded of sinfulness because we still await the full redemption of the kingdom of God.

I recall the day I entered The Bookstore in Grand Rapids, Michigan, to see a stack of just-off-the-press copies of George Eldon Ladd's *A Theology of the New Testament*.[24] I was a college student and had been anticipating reading this book carefully before seminary. The summer before seminary, Kris and I moved back to our hometown of Freeport, Illinois, to live with our parents so we could work and save money for seminary. I worked at the local street department, painting lines on the street. For much of that summer, every break I got at work, every opportunity in the evening (though often dog-tired from working in the sun all day) and on weekends I read, studied, and pondered Ladd's *Theology*. It was a transformative book in my life, partly indicated by the number of underlinings and comments I registered in the margins.

I'm not alone. In 1984 Mark Noll did a survey of evangelical professors and found that most fell into three major groups: the Evangelical

Theological Society (ETS), the Institute for Biblical Research (IBR), and the Wesleyan Theological Society (WTS). One of his questions was about who was most influential in their thinking. The ETS group listed first John Calvin and second George Ladd; IBR members listed George Ladd first and F. F. Bruce second.[25] Within ten years Ladd's *Theology* had exercised a profound influence on major segments of evangelicalism. When I went to seminary I read that book again because it was assigned reading in our New Testament classes. When I began teaching at Trinity in 1983, I assigned Ladd.

I mention this because the story of George Ladd is the story of a man who both taught and *lived* an inaugurated kingdom. While I was a professor at Trinity, a colleague of mine who had once been a colleague of Ladd's told me one day at lunch that Ladd had struggled much of his academic career. He didn't tell me any more, nor did I hear what Ladd's struggles were all about until I read the fair but revealing study of Ladd by John A. D'Elia.[26] Ladd's own career began with a less than acceptable degree, so he struggled for intellectual acceptance while being inspired by the vision established by Carl Henry in his famous *The Uneasy Conscience of Modern Fundamentalism*.[27] Henry called evangelicals to get PhDs from the best institutions and to prove that evangelicalism was intellectually respectable, which Ladd did with a dissertation at Harvard. Ladd then became a heavyweight, intimidating, and influential professor at Fuller Theological Seminary. The unwritten story was that George Ladd struggled mightily with, and often lost to, a major evangelical taboo, alcoholism, and this on top of being a less than admirable father, given to being an impatient and obsessive workaholic, struck with emotional instability that led to acidic comments to friends and colleagues, and having a marriage that was less than expected of leaders. D'Elia says Ladd's marriage was in name only for the later years of Ladd's life. I tell Ladd's story only to say this: *the kingdom has only been partly realized, our redemption is not yet complete, and even those who best understand this theology can struggle mightily to become holy and loving.* Yes, I was profoundly grieved when I learned these facts about Ladd's life, but Bonhoeffer's words have stayed with me since I read them even before I read Ladd: we are not yet fully redeemed, so we must slay our idealizations of others and the church and learn to live into the story of an inauguration of the kingdom that awaits consummation in the future. Ladd, we might say, illustrates his theology of only the *inauguration* and not yet the fulfillment of kingdom realities in this world.

You know stories of influential Christians whose moral or inner life had turbulent crosscurrents and whose exterior was calm and powerful. I could have told of the sickening revelations about John Howard Yoder's so-called sexual experiments,[28] or of Karl Barth's long-term relationship with Charlotte von Kirschbaum[29]—what many think was nothing less than bigamy, while others would say we don't really know—none of which needs further elucidation. What I am saying is that we should be both shocked and not shocked by the sinfulness of Christians. Christians live, on one hand, after the inauguration of redemption, so they should be Christlike; but on the other hand, they live in a time when they are not yet fully outfitted for eternity, so they will bear the marks of the flesh. Kingdom theology leads to this very conclusion.

KINGDOM MISSION IS ALL
ABOUT CONTEXT

The stories that shaped Israel's memories and hopes were not time-less. They were like Charles Dickens's *A Christmas Carol* and Flannery O'Connor's "The Lame Shall Enter First," which were shaped to speak into a specific context. In Dickens's case, the combination of a liberal and humanitarian Christmas story took dead aim at the Poor Laws, and in O'Connor's case, Southern, conservative Christianity was held up to the scathing heat of a cross- and grace-shaped gospel for one and all.

What makes a story come alive is its capacity to evoke perspective, memory, and hope *for a specific people in a specific context.* This is what Jesus did with the kingdom story. His story was not timeless "biblical theology." His kingdom story took the Bible's A-B-A' plot and aimed it directly at Herod Antipas and the temple priests and Caesar in Rome. The last thing he was worried about was the popularity of his ideas. Front to back his message was countercultural and subversive of the powers of the age. When he spoke into that context, standing next to him were ordinary folks, the poor and the marginalized and the faithful who, in Jesus' kingdom vision, were beginning to tap to the beat of an old song that was sounding brand new. Jesus' kingdom vision worked on their memory, and on their hopes, and suddenly they knew where they were and where they were headed. The old story had new life.

Before I take another step, I want to say something about mission today. If kingdom mission flows out of the kingdom story, and if Jesus' kingdom theology was shaped by his context, then his mission was also for that context—fair enough for Jesus and undeniable for us too. Kingdom mission today only works when *tied to our context as we seek to live out Jesus' kingdom vision in our world.* Kingdom mission was, is, and always will be shaped by a context and for a context. To illustrate how *timely* Jesus' own kingdom mission was, I bring to the table the research of James D. G. Dunn, but I begin with something about Rembrandt.

Reading for the Original Context: Rembrandt, Aristotle, and Homer

Over my desk in my office at Northern Seminary is a cheap copy of a painting by Rembrandt van Rijn called *Aristotle, Bust of Homer*. Here we have Rembrandt's attempt to show how Aristotle sculpted, or perhaps only admired, the bust of the famous Greek storyteller Homer. Homer's bust is monochromatic in the painting, a mix of tans and some darker shadowing and shading that gives one the sense of an ancient bust so familiar in museums. Rembrandt's depiction of Aristotle, however, is the focus of the picture, not only because "Aristotle" is in the title of the painting, but because he occupies more space and is nearer to the center. Furthermore, he's more colorfully attired. Aristotle, in fact, is dressed up like a contemporary prince of Rembrandt's own time. His beard is full, his cap is fashionable, he is draped with billowy sleeves and a sparkling, golden sash, and unless my cheap image is inaccurate, he wears what appears to be a ring on his small finger between the fingernail and the first knuckle.

Why talk about Rembrandt? Why here? This painting tells us far more about Rembrandt than it does about Aristotle; Aristotle, one could say, looks like Rembrandt. To adapt biblical language of critique: he's made Aristotle in his own image, while he's left Homer to his own time.

I tell this because this is what has happened so often in biblical interpretation, and the impulse of the Protestant movement is that *we must return to the text in its time* over and over in order to hear the message

44

of the author and the inspired text. Often we will hear confirming words about our views; sometimes we hear the voice of challenge. I believe the kingdom message, when heard in context, is that challenging voice. We are tempted, like Rembrandt, to make "kingdom" in our own image, so that we are told what we want to hear and what will prop up our own agendas. We want to turn it into a basis for social activism or to tone it down to redemptive moments anywhere and everywhere. But if we will do what Rembrandt did to Homer and first let the text be a text for its own time, we will once again hear the Bible say what it wants to say. Jimmy Dunn is a master at letting the Bible speak a message in its time, and what he has done is provide a way of shedding the clothes of Rembrandt in order to find the original Aristotle for us. So, to Dunn we go to hear what the original kingdom message sounded like in its context.

Kingdom Vision as Timely

Where do we begin? Dunn says we must begin with the story context: "It will have to be the context of Israel's memory of its own monarchic past, of Jewish current experience under the kingship of others, and of the hopes of the faithful regarding God's kingship for the future."[1] He begins with three simple observations and then drenches those three points in a powerful display of evidence from Judaism of the various nuances at work at the time of Jesus. His three simple observations are these: (1) God was King over all the earth (Ps. 103:19); (2) only Israel acknowledges God's kingdom, and that means Israel's king (when they have one) is specially related to God the King; and (3) this universal kingship of God will someday, perhaps soon, expand over the whole earth. The integral features in the big story of Israel are these: God is King, Israel is God's people and as such is God's kingdom, and God's kingdom will someday cover the globe. We can say the story has three nonnegotiables: the universal kingship of God, the covenant kingship of God with Israel, and a future universal rule.

These three nonnegotiable beliefs in the Old Testament and in the shaping of Judaism's story are rarely alone and almost never this abstract or theoretical. Instead they flow into very timely and contextualized expressions, and it is here that Dunn advances our discussion. When those three ideas were at work in real ways with real people in real contexts, they wore all sorts of attire, and Dunn lists fourteen different ways this basic story was told in various contexts:

- Return from exile
- Hope for prosperity, healing, or paradise
- A Messiah
- The renewal of the covenant
- Building a new temple
- Return of YHWH to Zion
- Triumph over, destruction of, and sometimes inclusion of gentiles
- Inheriting and expanding the land
- A climactic period of tribulation
- Cosmic disturbances leading to a new creation
- Defeat of Satan
- Final judgment
- Resurrection
- Sheol/Hades morphing into a place of final retribution

This list does not come from one Jewish source. Each of the themes has traces or footings in the Jewish Scriptures, the Old Testament. Each takes on either emphasis or de-emphasis depending on the author and circumstance. Each can be the entry through which the whole story of Israel can be told. It is not as if there are fourteen elements of the one story that we are called to tally up, making sure each gets represented in each retelling of Israel's future. When a Jewish boy or girl asked a father or mother what the kingdom would be like or what God would do to resolve Israel's problems, these are the sorts of things they heard. Had those same children asked their uncle or a neighbor, they may have heard the whole story another way. *When Jesus said, "The kingdom of God has come near," he made that announcement in the context of these other expressions.* Yes, there's something new in his retelling of the story, but mark my words: when he talked about the kingdom drawing near, these are the sorts of ideas that flashed across the memory screen of the ordinary Galilean.

But he had competition—in fact, fierce competition—that was unlike what we think of as competition in our day. The competition was over who could tell the *most compelling story and so convince Israel to embrace the story*. To show how integral the fourteen various elements of Jimmy Dunn's sketch were and to show the real context into which Jesus set the kingdom story and therefore his kingdom mission, I want to sketch the competition of Jesus' day. There were five basic competing stories in Jesus' context (a good reminder for us to learn the competing stories in our world), each bringing into the light of day the best way to be faithful, holy, and righteous.[2]

Five Competing Versions of Israel's Story in the World of Jesus

Jesus' kingdom story sets him over against

1. The eschatological battle of God found in the *Psalms of Solomon*
2. The Maccabean and Zealot strategy of holy warfare
3. The Essene strategy of holy withdrawal
4. The Pharisee push for greater zeal for Torah observance
5. The Sadducee strategy of realism by cooperating with Rome

In that Jesus contrasts with each of these, his kingdom vision takes on new contours, and the context is thrown into bold relief for us to comprehend all that was at work in Jesus' kingdom story.

Psalms of Solomon: *God's Messiah Goes to War*

One of the passages I wish all Christians would read before they pick up the Gospels or before they talk about Jesus' kingdom story is in a book not found in our Bibles, the *Psalms of Solomon*, chapter 17. The *Psalms of Solomon* is a Judean response to Rome's capturing of Jerusalem in 63 BCE by the Roman ruler who preceded Julius Caesar—namely, Pompey. Since this psalm 17 is unfamiliar, I will provide a sketch. Israel's God, in spite of Roman captivity, remains God (17:1), and the psalmist's hope in God remains (17:3). God chose David to be king over Israel and promised a Davidic king on the throne forever, "but (because of) our [Israel's] sins, [some of its own] sinners rose up against us, they set upon us and drove us out" (17:5). Israel's rulers usurped God's rule: "With pomp they set up a monarchy because of their arrogance" (17:6).[3] So God responded in discipline with Rome's might against the sinful leaders of Jerusalem. Of Pompey's defiling the sacredness of God's sacred space, the psalmist says, "So he did in Jerusalem all the things that gentiles do for their gods in their cities" (17:14), and the children of Jerusalem joined in his sinful ways. But some were faithful: "Those who loved the assemblies of the devout fled from them" (17:16). So Jerusalem became a pool of sin: "The king was a criminal and the judge disobedient; (and) the people sinners" (17:20).[4]

What to do? The psalmist announces that God will raise up a military Messiah to seize the temple, the holy city, and the land for God's own possession. His strategy was partly right, but the wrong part was so wrong that the strategy could not be the kingdom vision of Jesus. Here are memorable words that express the heart of what was probably the second most popular option at the time of Jesus:

> See, Lord, and raise up for them their king,
>> the son of David, to rule over your servant Israel
>> in the time known to you, O God.
> Undergird him with the strength to destroy the unrighteous rulers,
>> to purge Jerusalem from gentiles
>> who trample her to destruction . . .
> to smash the arrogance of sinners
>> like a potter's jar . . .
> to destroy the unlawful nations with the word of his mouth.
>> (17:21–24)

In its place, God will establish a righteous Jerusalem and a holy nation, and he will do this *through that military, victorious Messiah.*

> He will gather a holy people
>> whom he will lead in righteousness. . . .
> He will not tolerate unrighteousness (even) to pause among them,
>> and any person who knows wickedness shall not live with
>>> them. . . .
> [T]he alien and the foreigner will no longer live near them. . . .

> And he will have gentile nations serving him under his yoke. . . .
>   and their king shall be the Lord Messiah. . . .
> He shall be compassionate to all the nations
>   (who) reverently (stand) before him [this is a veiled threat]. . . .
> And he himself (will be) free from sin, (in order) to rule a great
>   people. (17:26–28, 30, 32, 34, 36)

The battle is God's, and he will wage war through the Messiah as the great warrior. The focus in this psalm is rule under the Messiah, a perfect Messiah, and the elimination of gentiles from the land so that Israel can live an undistracted holy life. This Messiah is much like Jesus, and yet so different. The terms for the kingdom in the *Psalms of Solomon* are not unlike the terms of Satan to Jesus in the temptation (Matt. 4:1–11). Jesus refused Satan and therefore refused the kingdom vision of the *Psalms of Solomon*: Jesus' kingdom vision knows the self-sacrifice of the Messiah himself on a cross and a resurrection to create new life, not the military might of a warrior messiah. The notion of a warrior messiah was popular at the time of Jesus, and this kingdom vision comes to concrete expression in various ways in both the Maccabees (prior to the *Psalms of Solomon*) and the Zealots (after the *Psalms of Solomon*), two warrior-messiah groups with expectations of a militarily-won kingdom.

The Maccabees and Zealots: Holy Warfare

Stuck at the end of the Old Testament in Roman Catholic and Eastern Orthodox Bibles are the so-called apocryphal or deuterocanonical books, books that are not fully recognized by the church but in one way or another are useful for the church. The two most well-known books are 1 and 2 Maccabees, which tell the dramatic story of Mattathias of Modein and his boys, Judah (the Hammer), Simon, and Jonathan Maccabeus. That story occurred on the far side of the middle of the second century BCE. In particular, the major battles occurred between 167 and 164 BCE. You won't find a more developed story of Jewish heroism, and this is why the major athletic contest in Israel today is called the Maccabiah Games. To make their heroic tale of courage, stamina, and old-fashioned providence short: when the Syrian overlords demanded that the Judeans cease following their "boundary markers" such as circumcision, the Maccabees resisted and revolted and for a period of three years plotted and fought to regain control of the temple. That victory is celebrated to this day as the Feast of Hanukkah. The Maccabees were notoriously courageous and, not to put too fine a point on it, quite willing to use violence and bloodshed to accomplish their goal of recapturing the temple and restoring the people to God. Their first-century successors were the Zealots, a group of feisty warriors perhaps most famous because Josephus blamed the destruction of Jerusalem in AD 66–73 on their relentless use of violence to accomplish what they thought was God's will.

This *holy warfare to bring in the kingdom* strategy was the rejected option for Jesus, and so we dare not ignore the presence of a Zealot in the circle of Jesus' twelve apostles. Simon is called the "Zealot" in Luke 6:15,[5] and one has to wonder about the violent proclivities of James and John, who are dubbed "sons of thunder" in Mark 3:17. Jesus shut down the pervasive desire on the part of the disciples to lord it over others (Mark 10:35–45). Jesus' strategy was dead opposed to holy warfare, because for him the way of "winning" was "losing," and the way to resurrection and kingdom was through love and through the cross. Kingdom cannot be connected to holy warfare; holy warfare destroys the kingdom. Jesus' words are not "Grab some swords and let's head for the hills surrounding Jerusalem" but "Take up your cross daily."

Essenes: Holy Withdrawal

The third most popular option at the time of Jesus was the way of withdrawal. Because of such things as temple corruption and a lack of precise Torah observance among the priests, a group of Essenes fled Jerusalem to set up holy shop on the coast of the Dead Sea, a place now called Khirbet Qumran. It was here that the Dead Sea Scrolls were discovered. The strategy of the Essenes was clear: pleading with leaders to follow the Torah fell on deaf ears, so a collection of devout Jews fled Jerusalem, formed a community of holiness where they lived out with rigor their vision of obedience under the watchful eye and vision of their leader, the "Teacher of Righteousness," and simply waited for God's holy wrath to act in order to launch the kingdom. As in the *Psalms of Solomon*, they waited on God;

but like the Maccabees, they sketched themselves onto the pages of history as mighty warriors who would do battle with the Romans (or *Kittim*) and win for God Almighty. Part of their strategy, then, was rigorous holiness and zealous commitment to the Torah and their interpretations of that Torah. Part of it also was planned military holy warfare.

For the same reasons Jesus refused the way of the Maccabees, so Jesus also refused the way of the Essenes. He did not withdraw to form a holy community, and he did not plan a military battle of the forces of darkness against the sons of light. Jesus' kingdom vision was not the kingdom vision of the Essenes.

Pharisees: Devotion to Torah Observance

We now come to the most popular option available in Jesus' context. No Christian wants to be called a "Pharisee," so it can shock modern Bible readers to learn that the Pharisees were good guys. They were the home Bible study movement in the land of Israel, the ones who wanted to interpret the Torah in such a way that everything was clear so everyone could follow the whole Torah. Their vision for Israel was to obey the Torah, to teach the Torah, and in so doing to stimulate a revival in the land and draw down the blessing of God, including the coming of the Messiah and the kingdom. The way to the kingdom, then, was through Torah observance. At some level you have to like what you hear about the Pharisees, and if we could wipe out all the criticisms of Jesus and the barnacles all over the Christian tradition about the Pharisees, we might find the Pharisees to be most like us. And this is the problem: they are perhaps "most" like us among the options, but they are also at odds with Jesus. It was undoubtedly a battle of how best to read the Bible, but I like to put it this way: the Pharisees taught love of the Torah, and were good at it, but Jesus taught a Torah of love, and he was good at it. That distinction made all the difference in the context of Jesus because Jesus and the Pharisees clearly went toe to toe on one issue after another.

Jesus' politics of love ran into direct conflict with the Pharisees' politics of observance. In particular, the Pharisees—not unlike many church traditions—*equated their interpretations of the Torah with the Torah itself* in such a way that not following their interpretations was not following the

Torah and therefore disobeying God. We have plenty of Pharisees with us today! The issue here is not to excuse ourselves but to see that Jesus' kingdom vision ran head-on into the Pharisees' kingdom vision regarding how best to read the Bible. His Bible and their Bible became two different Bibles. One more (not at all small) point: Jesus thought the story of Israel was coming to fulfillment in himself. Anyone who says, "Do not think that I have come to abolish the Law or the Prophets; I have not come to abolish them but to fulfill them" (Matt. 5:17) would not have sat comfortably in the Pharisees' home Bible study groups. Anyone who makes that claim thinks BC became AD when he was born. That, in essence, was at the core of why Jesus' kingdom vision was opposed by that of the Pharisees. He saw himself as the center of the kingdom story; they didn't.

Sadducees: Cooperation with Rome

The last and least popular option was the one least available to ordinary Jews: it was the way of the aristocrats and politicians. The Sadducees left no writings to us; what we know about them we know from others, and most of those others were not their friends. Some of them were priests, but the evidence suggests they were the landed aristocrats of Jerusalem. As such they were like Washington, DC, lawyers who knew everyone and everything, and their proximity gave them power. What Josephus tells us about the Sadducees is an exaggeration, perhaps at times bordering on the sort of thing we might read in *The Onion* about the Roman Catholic curia or about what happens behind the scenes in a megachurch, but Josephus does provide a general impression that offers glimpses of what they were like: they were often at odds with the Pharisees; they didn't believe in the resurrection; they liked to dispute theological ideas; and they were "men of the highest standing," but they could "accomplish practically nothing." The Pharisees, he says, were affectionate to one another, but the Sadducees were, "even among themselves, rather boorish in their behavior . . . as rude as to aliens" (Josephus, *Antiquities* 18:16–17; *Jewish War* 2.164–65).

Their kingdom strategy, if they had one, was to make the world a better place for themselves and others like them, and to make that happen they learned the gentle art of negotiating with Romans and other gentiles in order to keep the peace. They were realists. Jesus had little to do with them or with their beliefs, and so we can safely conclude that Jesus' kingdom vision had almost nothing to do with the Sadducees. In fact, he was most at odds with the Sadducees.

Summary

In summary, then, Jesus did not think the kingdom would come by violence; he did not think the eschatological doom and gloom of the *Psalms of Solomon* was a sufficient glimpse of God's future or the kingdom. Jesus also did not believe the way forward was the way of withdrawal. And Jesus wrangled with the Pharisees over the proper way to live God's will, and in particular opposed their interpretations and the importance of those interpretations for entering into the kingdom. Finally, Jesus and the Sadducees had almost nothing in common, and where they were perhaps most divided was their realism and cooperation with Rome. The way of the kingdom for Jesus would cut a new path in the land of Israel.

Jesus chose the word "kingdom" because that term provided a new way of thinking of what God was doing in and for Israel, and what God was doing was not exactly what the Maccabees or the Zealots, the Essenes, the Pharisees, or the Sadducees were thinking. Jesus' kingdom mission flowed from his kingdom story. We now know more about what that kingdom story *was not*, and that leads us to reflect on *what kingdom mission today is not*. We'll get to the positives beginning in the next chapter.

Kingdom Today

First, Kingdom Mission Is Not Returning to a Former Era but Is Done in a Context and for That Context

Kingdom mission remains contextual. Jesus spoke in his day, for his day, and to his day. We speak in our day, for our day, and to our day. This basic approach to reading the Bible—in context—and to working out how to "apply" it or, better yet, "live it out" in our day in a way that is contextually appropriate forms the core of all genuine kingdom mission. We are not to return to the first century and live like Jesus or like Paul or like Peter. Nor do we idealize one of the great movements in the history of the church, such as the days of the Nicene Creed, the best days of the Holy Roman Empire, the Reformation, the Great Awakening, the American revivals of the 1950s or the Jesus hippies of the 1970s, or the confident evangelicalism of the 1980s. Mission has a context and comes to life in a specific context. To be sure, a biblical approach to kingdom mission listens *first and foremost* to Scripture in order to be formed by the gospel story, but, once formed, the kingdom citizen *explores what kingdom means in our world in specific locations.*[6] Kevin Vanhoozer, in his big book *The Drama of Doctrine*, likens our task to learning how to "perform" the gospel's script in our world. Here's how he puts it: "The church is a company of players gathered together to stage scenes of the kingdom of God for the sake of the watching world. The direction of doctrine thus enables us, as individuals and as a church, to render the gospel public by leading lives in creative imitation of Christ."[7] Precisely! Kingdom mission embeds kingdom realities in context.

WAYNE GORDON

I'll let my friend Wayne Gordon, pastor at Lawndale Community Church, tell a story of contextual kingdom mission.

> When I moved to North Lawndale in 1975, my chief ministry goal was to lead others into a relationship with Christ. One night I had the opportunity to do just that with one of my football players. I assured him that Jesus had forgiven him of all the sins he had ever committed in his life.
>
> His response threw me for a loop. "Well, I don't think I've ever sinned before," he said. "I'm a pretty good kid."
>
> I asked him if he had ever cheated on a test in school.
>
> He said, "Yeah, I've cheated on tests. Everybody cheats on tests."
>
> I asked if he had ever had sex with his girlfriend, and again he said, "Yeah, but everybody does that."
>
> Before long I realized that "get saved" evangelism was designed for suburban folk. It had little meaning in an urban context. . . . People in the city are not encumbered primarily with feelings of guilt. Their deepest feelings are of hopelessness.[8]

If the Christ of the suburbs is the Christ of forgiveness, the Christ of the city is the Christ of hope.

TIM DICKAU

Here's a slightly thicker example of kingdom in context. Tim Dickau is the pastor of Grandview Calvary Baptist Church in East Vancouver, British Columbia.[9] The connection of "East" to "Vancouver" sends off signals to locals, but what it means for gospel ministry today is "don't expect much," and one friend told me it also means "you better have another job too." Dickau knows his context well—a postmodern context streaked and striped with isolation, fragmentation, and transience. When Dickau began his ministry at the church, the membership was dwindling and the building decaying. It was obvious that the neighborhood had both little connection to the church and little interest in the gospel. What to do? This congregation made some tough decisions, including commitments to moving into the community instead of commuting to church, working in the neighborhood, partnering in every way possible with the locals, and shopping at neighborhood shops. Perhaps most radical was that a number of folks decided to live together in community. We are not talking here about the transformation of a neighborhood from poverty into wealth or of a dying church into a megachurch. We are talking here about contextualized ministry where the good folks at Grandview Calvary Baptist engage neighbors in the issues of the neighborhood—in listening, in learning, and in linking in loving ways with those they happen to meet on the path of their journey.[10] The church remains "small" according to Western standards.

All of this is profoundly contextual—in some ways it can be transferred to other communities, but in many ways it is totally bound to East Vancouver. Dickau observes, "If you work in one place, shop in another, play in a third and 'go to church' . . . in a fourth, life becomes more fragmented. When you are part of a community that inhabits a neighborhood with a vision to be involved in its transformation, *life itself becomes more integrated and whole*" (emphasis added). He illustrates from his own life how contextually located and integrated a life can be.

One morning, as I was heading home from my exercise routine at the gym, I encountered John, a homeless man who struggles with addiction but manages to hold down a full-time job. Arranging for an "appointment" to meet with John is difficult, but when I saw him on the street at 7:30 that morning, I offered him a ride to the Skytrain station and we talked in the car for twenty minutes. After I had breakfast and prayers with my family, I went for coffee at my usual café, where the barista I was getting to know well asked me about my church (and showed up for worship the next weekend). As I sat down in my regular spot to review my day and pray, I saw a woman walk by and invited her in to continue a conversation we had begun two weeks previously. All this took place before I "started work" in the natural flow of my day.

The conclusion to this story is not yet written, of course, but what we have now is a community seeking to embody in contextually sensitive ways the gospel of the kingdom.

Some church leaders think they can convert all their ideas into practical programs that can then be exported into all locations. And, in spite of their critics, successful exportations often do take place. But genuine kingdom mission never becomes fully missional until it becomes fully contextual. Jesus used the word "kingdom" because it appealed to his audience; Paul didn't use that term very often and neither did Peter. John decided that "life" and "eternal life" and "light" and "darkness" worked better in his context. If *theology* is contextual, then certainly our *praxis must also be contextual.*

Second, Kingdom Mission Counters Ruling Stories at Work in Our World

Contexts always want to swallow the gospel for their own consumption. So being contextual comes to us both as temptation and challenge. Our world, as Tim Dickau has said, comes to us as fragmented and isolating and transient, so part of that church's challenge was gospeling into a living, breathing, life- and space-sharing community that witnessed to Jesus Christ as a new way of life. Jesus, too, countered context with an alternative kingdom vision. What emerges from simple readings of Jesus over against the options of his day can now be summarized as signposts for us to observe and follow today.

First, Jesus countered a culture that told the story that the way of God was the way of violence. That is, as his brother would later write, "Human anger does not produce the righteousness that God desires" (James 1:20).

56

When we are persuaded into the depths of our heart that what we believe to be true is the Truth, we want this for all others. When we want this for others, we are tempted for our witness to become coercive, manipulative, and sometimes to resort to violence. Jesus opposed the ways of the Maccabees and the Zealots and offered instead of the symbol of the sword the symbol of the cross. The way to "rule" was the way of service; the way to love was with the basin and towel. Kingdom mission must resist all temptations to use coercion and violence to accomplish God's will.

Second, Jesus countered the culture of withdrawal. There is a time for retreat, but permanent retreat is not the way of kingdom mission. Yes, Jesus withdrew at times: to Galilee when he heard of John's imprisonment (Matt. 4:12), when he heard others wanted to murder him (12:15), when he heard of John's reckless decapitation (14:13), and when he evidently needed to get away (15:21). But permanent retreat becomes isolation, and isolation denies the missional way of Jesus. The way of the Essenes was not the way of Jesus. We, too, are tempted to permanent retreat. Some—not all—send their children to Christian grade schools, middle schools, high schools, and colleges as forms of retreat from our culture; some find jobs that are insulated from the "world" in order to feel safe; others want to form Christian-only relationships for similar reasons. Kingdom mission is the way of engagement, integration, incarnation, involvement, and participation. It is the way of Jesus, the way of love, the way of "neighboring," and the way of living in the world without being of the world.

Third, Jesus countered the story of legalizing life. We must be careful in stereotyping the Pharisees and other law-based religious movements. The Pharisees were good people, but Jesus and the Pharisees differed on the Torah and therefore on Torah observance. Jesus knew the whole Torah was to be seen as loving God and loving others so that the *core of Torah for Jesus was love*. Jesus clearly perceived the Pharisees as not centering the Torah in love but seeing love as merely *one* of the commandments. But the commandments were *all* love for Jesus, so Jesus' criticisms were more than this problem of Torah of love versus love of Torah. Jesus opposed their multiplication of laws, called *halakah*. If the Torah says no work on the Sabbath, the Pharisees got busy clarifying what "work" meant, *and their rulings became tantamount to the will of God*.

Fourth, kingdom mission avoids the zealotry of adding to the will of God. I don't want to confuse this term "zealotry" with the Zealot use of force only. What I mean by "zealotry" is conscious zeal to be radically committed to the will of God so much that one goes beyond the Bible to prove one's radical commitment. Zealotry produces a sense of immunity: if I'm even more radical than the Bible, *I must be right* or *cannot be wrong.* Zealotry also leads to judgmentalism toward others, and thus it creates boundaries between the "good" (us) and the "bad" (others less committed). Here's an example: Missional people can get pretty excited about their contextual commitments and their own versions of being radical. Some folks in church communities like this become proud of their radical zeal to the point that they look down their nose at those who live in the 'burbs in single-family homes with garages and aesthetically decorated yards. Another example: The Bible teaches that intoxication is contrary to God's will; zealotry teaches that if one abstains totally from alcohol, one is even holier than those who don't abstain, and those who drink are less committed. At the core, zealotry does not trust the sufficiency of God's word to us, so it adds, adds, and adds and then sees its additions as God's word for us. Zealotry, then, becomes the far side of obedience, leading the zealous to self-righteous congratulations, blockading love, and creating subtle kinds of retreat and withdrawal instead of genuine engagement.

Finally, kingdom mission avoids the way of political power to accomplish God's will. James Davison Hunter, one of America's finest observers of evangelical culture, scored two major points in his recent book *To Change the World*.[11] First, he argued that the *only* way to change culture and the world is through the use of *political power*, but second, he argued that the Christian would be far wiser to use the "strategy" of *faithful presence*. We may all differ on what "faithful presence" means and what strategies express it, but in this Hunter tracks with Jesus' posture against the Sadducees. They cooperated with the Romans in unhealthy ways, and by "unhealthy" I don't mean just the implications for first-century Israel. I mean they engaged with the Romans and the powers in ways that made them all but Roman in their ways, and far from the kingdom ways of Jesus. Kingdom mission lives by faithful witness *regardless of its political potential, regardless of its possibility for cultural change, and regardless of its power to influence society.*

Confession time. When I hit the period at the end of the last paragraph, I saved the file and opened up my email. In my inbox was yet another message from someone asking me for a list of authors and books for someone's personal study. Of course, I often oblige their requests and send along a list, but something unusual happened this time, and I confess it as just the sort of thing kingdom citizens have to learn to resist. I didn't recognize the person's name, it became a small irritant to be asked to write up a short bibliography for someone when I'm already busy enough (in my own work), and I was about to hit delete out of impatience when I noticed the signature at the bottom of the email. The person worked for a senator in Washington, DC, and the *first thing* that came to mind was, "This person is important; this person is influential; oblige them with a little extra gusto!" I confessed my sin and did for that email what I do for the others: made a few suggestions, pointed to the top-ten lists on my blog, and moved back to write this confession! That person has no more value to God than any other person, and that person will not enable kingdom mission more than any other person; kingdom people live that out better than I did.

Third, Kingdom Mission Counters Our World as a Counterculture

Kingdom mission means countering alternative stories with an alternative politics.[12] Stories give us meaning; they locate us in this world and give us guidance and direction and hope. Stories abound. But the kingdom story is the one true story. We are to be vigilant and appropriately critical—not in a cynical way—of the stories that flourish in our world. To embrace the kingdom story is to let go of other stories. In the world of Jesus, the disciples embraced the story of Israel that is fulfilled in the story of Jesus. This is our starting point, and it means that stories denying Israel's story—as did Rome's story, as did Greece's story—or stories denying Jesus' story, which fulfilled Israel's story—as did the Pharisees and scribes and Sadducees and Essenes and Zealots—must be rejected. We must, then, counter the worldview stories of our culture.

Steve Wilkens and Mark Sanford, in their fine book *Hidden Worldviews*, mention these worldviews at work in our world, often in ways completely unknown to those who inhabit them: individualism, consumerism, nationalism, moral relativism, scientific naturalism, New Age, postmodern tribalism, and salvation by therapy.[13] Tim Dickau encountered idolatries in ministering in Vancouver, discussing these six: entertainment, internet surfing, workaholism, accumulation of private wealth, individualism/autonomy, and family. These idolatries are not so much focused on blocking personal spirituality, though that would be true as well, but instead they impede local church fellowship and mutual living.[14]

Each of these could be explored as countered by the kingdom mission story of the Bible. But instead I want to offer another worldview and idolatry at work both in the world of Jesus and in our world: *the worldview of power*. Recent biblical scholarship has become enamored with the ideology of brutal power and how the message of Jesus and the apostles countered empire ideology.[15] Jesus more than once looked empire in the face in the form of lethal observations and questions on the lips of his opponents. Here's one example:

> At that time some Pharisees came to Jesus and said to him, "Leave this place and go somewhere else. Herod wants to kill you."
>
> He replied, "Go tell that fox, 'I will keep on driving out demons and healing people today and tomorrow, and on the third day I will reach my goal.' In any case, I must press on today and tomorrow and the next day—for surely no prophet can die outside Jerusalem!" (Luke 13:31–33)

Herod Antipas, probably no more than a minor leader with a moderate impact on Galilee,[16] wants to bring Jesus down, and he can do so, probably risking only public resentment. Jesus responds with a caustic label—"fox"—and a parabolic indication of his own destiny at the hands of Roman imperial power—a death in Jerusalem.

A second instance is the famous question Jesus is asked by "some of the Pharisees and Herodians" (Mark 12:13–17): "Teacher, we know that you are a man of integrity. You aren't swayed by others, because you pay no attention to who they are; but you teach the way of God in accordance with the truth. Is it right to pay the imperial tax to Caesar or not? Should we pay or shouldn't we?"

When two disciples—James and John—came to Jesus and asked, at their mother's prompting (and their mother is, according to church tradition, the sister of Jesus' mother), to be given seats at the left and right of Jesus in the kingdom to come, Jesus' response reveals that his story crashed headlong into Rome's story.

> Jesus called them together and said, "You know that those who are regarded as rulers of the Gentiles lord it over them, and their high officials exercise authority over them. Not so with you. Instead, whoever wants to become great among you must be your servant, and whoever wants to be first must be slave of all. For even the Son of Man did not come to be served, but to serve, and to give his life as a ransom for many." (Mark 10:42–45)

Roman politics is about power and domination and might and force and coercion and the sword. The politics of Jesus is about sacrificial love for the other *even if that means death from the sword*. Lording it over others is the way of Rome; serving others is the way of Jesus. The lords of the empire are for Jesus lordless lords. Those are two stories at work in two politics, and the politics of Jesus counters the politics of Rome.

Jesus' approach is not theoretical. His was the naked encounter with Rome's might in the stranglehold of a political challenge in a context dripping with lethal implications. I think we can all agree that Jesus' response outstrips their cleverness twofold, if not more so.

> "Whose image is this? And whose inscription?"
>
> "Caesar's," they replied.
>
> Then Jesus said to them, "Give back to Caesar what is Caesar's and to God what is God's." (Mark 12:16–17)

We will also surely agree that Jesus is not endorsing Caesar but instead deconstructing the empire's power inscribed on a coin. True power is with God, the true King and Emperor, and Jesus will submit only to that God. Summing this up, then, we see that Jesus teaches—and the apostles carried on his teaching—that obedience to God is the one true allegiance; any claim of power and authority and might on the part of earthly rulers, from Herod Antipas to Pilate to Tiberius in Rome, is either sub-governing under God or outright idolatry and ideology. Rome was the latter, and Israel's story was the former, but there was now a new story: God had once again resumed his rule over the people of God in Jesus.

Power has always been a temptation, and I want to argue that *majority rule in America carries with it an empire temptation for many Christian citizens.* Those of us who know our American history might be tempted to say, "That's precisely the opposite of what our democracy, or representative democracy, stands for." True enough, at one level, because giving everyone a voice vastly surpasses anything less. But take any heated political issue, from abortion to same-sex marriage to national health care to free-market enterprise to nuclear build-up for security, and you may glimpse what I'm trying to say. The political left takes one posture on issues while the political right draws swords from another posture. If we step back we see that each side *seeks to impose its view on the minority.* This is ruling over the other. Now to a few questions.

Is this imposition of power over others consistent with following Christ? Do we ever wonder if the right to vote is the right to coerce and impose, the right to use the power of the majority against the minority?[17] Is the power of the majority that different from the power of King Charles when the pilgrims and Puritans left England to establish the "city on a hill"? We would all agree that empowering the people improved the conditions, but I want to ask another question: Does it make the political process of voting the source of seeking for power over others? What is the best Christian response to the drive for power?

I call this quest for power through the political process the "eschatology of politics"—that is, the belief that if we usher in the right political candidates and the right laws, then kingdom conditions will arrive. Every two years America goes through convulsions as one candidate after another promises (all but) the kingdom if he or she is elected. Every two years Americans go through the same convulsions as they lather up for the election because they believe if they get their candidate, not only will they win, but (all but) the kingdom will come. This is idolatry and yet another example of Constantinianism (see appendix 1).

The question we should ask is this: Where is our hope placed? In our elected candidates? In our country? To be sure, I hope our country solves its international conflicts, and I hope we resolve poverty and dissolve our educational problems and racism. And I hope we can create a better economy. But where does my hope turn when I think of war or poverty or education or racism? Does it focus on my political party? Does it gain its energy from thinking that if we get the right candidate elected, our problems will be dissolved? If so, I submit that our eschatology has become empire-shaped, Constantinian, and political. And it doesn't matter to me if it is a right-wing evangelical wringing her fingers in hope that a Republican wins or a left-wing progressive wringing her fingers in hope that a Democrat wins. Each has a misguided eschatology. The kingdom story counters the culture of politics as the solution to our problems.

You may be one who thinks the majority rule is better than tyranny, and you'd be right. The issue, though, is the story at work in the American political process and the participation of so many Christians in that story in ways that betray the kingdom story. Kingdom mission follows kingdom theology, and kingdom theology has a story to tell: the kingdom story. We are summoned by Jesus to enter into that story by submitting to King Jesus, to participate in that story by letting it permeate our entire life, to gospel that story to the world, and to challenge all idolatrous stories that seek to diminish the kingship of King Jesus.

In talking counterculture I am reminded of what Hauerwas and Willimon said in their smart little manifesto called *Resident Aliens*, for if our gospel is countercultural, then we as a community, as the church, are also to be countercultural—in all our ways. Here is how they put it: "The challenge of the gospel is not the intellectual dilemma of how to make an archaic system of belief compatible with modern belief systems." No, that is called modernizing the gospel, and it is all around us. Instead, they say, "The challenge of Jesus is the political dilemma of how to be faithful to a strange community, which is shaped by a story of how God is with us."[18]

The challenge, I agree, is for the church to be faithful to the kingdom story. We now turn to the focal point of my contention in this book: kingdom and church.

5

KINGDOM IS PEOPLE

When Jesus said, "The kingdom of God has drawn near," what word associations do you think his Galilean audience created? If we transport ourselves back to Roman Galilee, under Herod Antipas, with Israel's history centered in Jerusalem, and then use our imagination for ordinary folks and for Jesus himself (who matters the most)—if we then ask that question, I suggest there would be one of two words that would come to mind first: "David" (and by implication, "king") or "Israel" (and by implication, "land" and "law"). These terms are two of the many synonyms of "kingdom." The Skinny Jeans kingdom folks instinctively find their synonym in the word "justice," while the Pleated Pants fathers of this discussion say "salvation." Each has a place in this discussion, but I will show in this chapter that the words naturally connected to "kingdom" swim in different waters. The word Jesus used is "kingdom," so the first word-association uttered in Jesus' context would have been "Israel" as a people in a place—that is, in the land. Had Jesus announced, "The King has drawn near," then the first word would have been "David." Because so many today associate "kingdom" either with "justice" or with "salvation," we will need to dig into Scripture a bit more in this chapter to establish once and for all that kingdom in Jesus' world would have meant "a people governed by a king."

Israel and Land

So, let's begin right where they began, with Israel and the land. To say "kingdom" was to say "Israel" and mean the "nation of Israel" with all that a nation has been, is, and will be, and with all that it does to keep itself going. I am not a little confused by the number of very good thinkers who have managed to evade or avoid the term "Israel" or the word "land" when it comes to the term "kingdom." All it takes is a good read of major studies and you will see how far out of the picture those terms have become. To gain our bearings, let's remember that the word "kingdom" means a circumscribed area ruled by a king. This lands us square in the middle of the word "kingdom" with this: a kingdom means a *geopolitical people under a king.*

Our responsibility is to point our noses at the Bible to see what is there, to read it carefully enough to fashion an explanation that is rooted as much as possible in what it says. We are not supposed to invent our own ideas, then go to the Bible to find support, and then claim the Bible as the authority for our own inventions. This whole book is a nose-pointing exercise, then, one in which we are looking at what the Bible says about the kingdom. This pertains, now, to how closely the Bible connects the word "kingdom" to "Israel," including Israel's precious land. I have to emphasize this because so many in the Pleated Pants crowd have "de-landed" the kingdom and have turned it into something "purely religious" or "spiritual" or more generally into the "redemptive dynamic." Back when people were wearing tunics and turbans, though, kingdom and land could not be separated.

One can cite an abundance of verses on this geopolitical understanding of a kingdom for Israel, but the core of it can be found in the first promise of YHWH to Abram in Genesis 12:1: "Go from your country, your people and your father's household"—notice the geopolitical and people orientation here—"to *the land* I will show you." The first promise is the land. The blessings and curses of Leviticus 26 and Deuteronomy 28, two formative chapters for Israel's faith, are about dwelling in the land. The exodus is about getting into the land, the kings govern and protect the borders of the land, the exile is the discipline of YHWH from the land, and the return means Israel is back in the land. One can say that as the land goes, so goes Israel. Betsy Halperin Amaru, a scholar of Judaism, summarizes the Bible's perception of land: "Living in the land becomes a primary gauge of the quality of Israel's relationship with God."[1] Land was not just an indicator of blessing but even more a fixture in Israel's various hopes for its future. As David Frankel puts it at the end of his lengthy study of land in the Old Testament, "In spite of the great variety and complexity of theological views [in the various parts of the Old Testament], one never finds . . . a biblical conception of Israel's final destiny as a people *that does not somehow incorporate . . . national life in the land as the ultimate ideal.*"[2]

Perhaps the one section in the Old Testament that brings this together is Psalm 37. I quote here a string of verses in that chapter about the land and ask you to point your nose at these verses instead of skipping them:

> Trust in the LORD and do good;
> > dwell in the *land* and enjoy safe pasture. (37:3)

> For those who are evil will be destroyed,
> > but those who hope in the LORD will inherit the *land*. (37:9)

> A little while, and the wicked will be no more;
> > though you look for them, they will not be found.
> But the meek will inherit the *land*
> > and enjoy peace and prosperity. (37:10–11)

> Those the LORD blesses will inherit the *land*,
> > but those he curses will be destroyed. (37:22)

> Turn from evil and do good;
> > then you will dwell in the *land* forever. (37:27)

> The righteous will inherit the *land*
> > and dwell in it forever. (37:29)

Hope in the LORD
>and keep his way.
He will exalt you to inherit the *land*;
>when the wicked are destroyed, you will see it. (37:34)

This set of verses—yea, this deeply rooted dimension of Israel's faith in which God's favor and the blessings of numerous people in the land could not be separated—shapes what the word "kingdom" means for Jesus. Before we dig a little deeper in Israel's Scriptures, take this one blessing of Jesus (from a set of blessings that sound very much like Ps. 37): "Blessed are the meek, for they will inherit the *earth*" (Matt. 5:5). There are a number of things to notice about this verse. It is an explicit quotation of Psalm 37:11, where the Hebrew word means "land" and not "earth" in its cosmic sense. Not only did Jews like Jesus not give a fig about the land as the cosmic earth, but Jesus spoke in Aramaic, in which the term he would have used was "land." But these points aside, the fundamental orientation of kingdom language for Jesus emerged from the story of Israel in which *the land and dwelling in the land in peace, justice, love, and wisdom* were absolutely central. It is, then, well-nigh certain that when Jesus blesses the meek, the promise he gives them is that they will inherit the *land* (not the earth). Now we dig into the use of "kingdom" in the Old Testament.

Kingdom as a People Governed by a King

"A people governed by a king"—this is how the Old Testament uses the term "kingdom." Because this evidence in the Bible is evaded or avoided, we need to rattle off some Bible references to get this element of kingdom back on the table again. I begin with Genesis 20:9, where Abimelek[3] calls out to Abraham and says, "What have you done to us? How have I wronged you that you have brought such great guilt upon me and my *kingdom*?" Another gentile, Balaam, seeing Israel before him, says prophetically of God's blessings, "Water will flow from their buckets, their seed will have abundant water. Their king will be greater than Agag; their *kingdom* will be exalted" (Num. 24:7). Moses, before Israel enters into the land, gave to some tribes the "*kingdom* of Sihon king of the Amorites and the *kingdom* of Og king of Bashan" (Num. 32:33). Here "kingdom" refers to a "people governed by a king."

Israel is a kingdom. Moses legislates how a king in Israel is to behave: "When he takes the throne of his *kingdom*, he is to write for himself on a scroll a copy of this law" (Deut. 17:18). If he does this, that king "will reign a long time over his *kingdom* in [the land of] Israel" (Deut. 17:20). There are so many references like this in the Old Testament it will boggle the careful Bible student how anyone could reduce kingdom either to "salvation" or to "justice." The word refers to a people governed by a king—over and over and over. But to make this even clearer, I want to point out how often "kingdom" is connected in parallel expressions with "nation" or "city" or some other governmental unit.

> They wandered from nation to nation,
> from one *kingdom* to another. (Ps. 105:13)

> "I will stir up Egyptian against Egyptian—
> brother will fight against brother,
> neighbor against neighbor,
> city against city,
> *kingdom* against *kingdom*." (Isa. 19:2)

> "For the nation or *kingdom* that will not serve you will perish."
> (Isa. 60:12)

"If at any time I announce that a nation or *kingdom* is to be uprooted, torn down and destroyed . . ." (Jer. 18:7)

"And if at another time I announce that a nation or *kingdom* is to be built up and planted . . ." (Jer. 18:9)

"If, however, any nation or *kingdom* will not serve Nebuchadnezzar king of Babylon or bow its neck under his yoke, I will punish that nation with the sword, famine and plague, declares the LORD, until I destroy it by his hand." (Jer. 27:8)

"After you, another *kingdom* will arise, inferior to yours. Next, a third *kingdom*, one of bronze, will rule over the whole earth. Finally, there will be a fourth *kingdom*, strong as iron—for iron breaks and smashes everything—and as iron breaks things to pieces, so it will crush and break all the others. Just as you saw that the feet and toes were partly of baked clay and partly of iron, so this will be a divided *kingdom*; yet it will have some of the strength of iron in it, even as you saw iron mixed with clay. As the toes were partly iron and partly clay, so this *kingdom* will be partly strong and partly brittle. . . .

"In the time of those kings, the God of heaven will set up a *kingdom* that will never be destroyed, nor will it be left to another people. It will crush all those *kingdoms* and bring them to an end, but it will itself endure forever." (Dan. 2:39–44)

Over and over, the word "kingdom" in the Old Testament refers to a people governed by a king. Any suggestion, then, that "kingdom" means only "ruling" or "reigning" cannot satisfy what the Bible explicitly affirms.

The preeminent kingdom of the Old Testament, of course, is Israel and Judah. So now we will look at a few verses that show that when Jesus said "kingdom," his contemporaries thought "Israel." In 1 Samuel 15:28 we get some sad, tragic, Bart-Giamatti-to-Pete-Rose-like words of history-rattling significance. Samuel tells King Saul that his days are now eclipsed, that God is removing him as king. Saul admits he has sinned, but Samuel tells him God is still removing him as king. Saul begs Samuel not to make this happen, but Samuel announces, "The LORD has torn the *kingdom* of Israel from you today and has given it to one of your neighbors—to one better than you."

In this passage we see two grieving leaders—Samuel over what has happened to Israel, and Saul over his own failures—but the deeper grief is not found until the last verse of the chapter: "The LORD regretted that he had made Saul king over Israel" (1 Sam. 15:35). What I wish to call our attention to is this: Saul was king over the *kingdom* of Israel. The nation of Israel is a kingdom.

So too was Judah, the "state" composed of two tribes, Judah and Benjamin. Rehoboam, the successor to Solomon in the two southern tribes, fortified cities in both Judah and Benjamin and found support in the priests, which makes sense since the temple was in Judah. But the Bible tells us in 2 Chronicles 11 that the northern kingdom's ruler, Jeroboam, was unfaithful to the covenant with David, so some priests and their assistants, the Levites, jumped ship, moved into Benjamin or Judah, and entered into an alliance with Rehoboam. The Chronicler sums it all up with this: "They strengthened the *kingdom* of Judah and supported Rehoboam son of Solomon three years, following the ways of David and Solomon during this time" (2 Chron. 11:17).

Again, notice that Judah is called a *kingdom*, a people governed by a king.

Solomon was a king over a kingdom, though the NIV 2011 slightly obscures the translation by using the Pleated Pants idea in its translation: "So Solomon sat on the throne of his father David, and his rule [or *kingdom*] was firmly established" (1 Kings 2:12). Near the very end of his life David summoned all the leaders of Israel to hear him out, and he explained two things. First, he wanted to build a temple, but God denied the request by revealing that it would be Solomon's mission. Second, he said, "Of all my sons—and the LORD has given me many—he has chosen my son Solomon to sit on the throne of the *kingdom of the* LORD over Israel" (1 Chron. 28:5). Again, it is David's kingdom and then Solomon's kingdom, but in hindsight that kingdom was ultimately YHWH's kingdom. Even in the mess of turbulent leaders and sinful behaviors, the "*kingdom* of the LORD [was in] the hands of David's descendants" (2 Chron. 13:8).

The overarching belief in Israel and in Judah was that though God had voluntarily surrendered kingship to human kings when Samuel revealed the desires of the people (1 Sam. 8), YHWH was still in some sense the ruling King. One of the more panoramic visions of God's rule over all can be found in Daniel 4:32: "You will be driven away from people and will live with the wild animals; you will eat grass like the ox. Seven times will pass by for you until you acknowledge *that the Most High is sovereign over all kingdoms on earth* and gives them to anyone he wishes" (emphasis added). But perhaps nothing expresses this better than the beautiful Psalm 47, a hymn shouted aloud from the courts of the temple and the heart of the nation.

> Clap your hands, all you nations;
>   shout to God with cries of joy.
> For the LORD Most High is awesome,
>   the great King over all the earth.

He subdued nations under us,
  peoples under our feet.
He chose our inheritance for us,
  the pride of Jacob, whom he loved.
God has ascended amid shouts of joy,
  the LORD amid the sounding of trumpets.
Sing praises to God, sing praises;
  sing praises to our King, sing praises.
For God is the King of all the earth;
  sing to him a psalm of praise.
God reigns over the nations;
  God is seated on his holy throne.
The nobles of the nations assemble
  as the people of the God of Abraham,
for the kings of the earth belong to God;
  he is greatly exalted.

Though 1 Samuel 8 reveals the underbelly of Israel's choice to have a king, at the heart of Israel's faith was the belief that over even the king was YHWH, "the King of all the earth," who "reigns over the nations" from "his holy throne" in the temple of Jerusalem.

It would take us too far afield to examine how "kingdom" is used in various Jewish sources from Daniel to the rise of the rabbinic literature, but an example or two must be given. Josephus, a rough contemporary of our New Testament, was a Jew who wrote in Greek and used the term "kingdom" (*basileia*) almost five hundred times. In almost every case the word refers to a "people governed by a king." On the cusp of the ministry of Jesus, the sons of Herod (the king) were the talk of the town because Herod wanted his sons put to death. When Herod arrived in Caesarea, the administrative center, "everyone at once began to talk about his sons, and the kingdom was in suspense as people waited to see what would be done" to the sons (*Antiquities* 16.373). "Kingdom" here refers to the people of Israel, governed by King Herod. Later the Pharisees refuse to swear allegiance to King Herod, and Herod fines them as punishment. The wife of his brother, Pheroras, pays their fine, and this leads to their prophecy of the future. Here are the words as reported by Josephus: "By God's decree

Herod's throne would be taken from him, both from himself and his descendants, and the *kingdom* would fall to her and Pheroras and to any children that they may have" (*Antiquities* 17.43). Here "kingdom" refers to a new king and his queen wife and their rule over the people of Israel. One more event is worth mentioning. Herod's ambassadors are dispatched to Rome, and in his deep anxiety over what could happen, Herod makes his will, "giving the kingdom to his youngest son [Antipas] because of his hatred of both Archelaus and Philip" (*Antiquities* 17.146). Never mind that both the Pharisees were wrong and that Herod later changed his mind; the point here is how the word "kingdom" is being used.

We could give example after example, but this yet again shows that "kingdom" refers to a people governed by a king. It is noteworthy that Antipas, who ruled Galilee during the time of Jesus, is often described as ruling over a kingdom (*Antiquities* 17.188, 227, 229; *Jewish War* 2.20, 94). Most notably this text witnesses to the yearning for a kingdom by Herod's sons and Caesar's final decision, which impacts every page of the Gospels:

> Caesar, after hearing both parties, dismissed the assembly. His decision was announced a few days later: he gave half the kingdom to Archelaus, with the title of ethnarch, promising, moreover, to make him king, should he prove his deserts; the other half he divided into two tetrarchies, which he presented to two other sons of Herod, one to Philip, the other to Antipas, who had disputed the *kingdom* with Archelaus. (*Jewish War* 2.94)

I have belabored this evidence for a reason: for nearly a century, far too many have reduced the word "kingdom" to the word "rule," as if it refers to only the dynamic of ruling or what I have called the "redemptive dynamic" and not the people over which the king rules. For instance, D. A. Carson, in a recent editorial in *Themelios*, lays down the observation, "In no instance is kingdom to be *identified* with church, as if the two words can on occasion become tight synonyms. Even when there is a referential overlap, the domain of 'kingdom' is reign, and the domain of 'church' is people."[4] But this mistaken and reductionistic, if not simplistic, conclusion comes at the expense of ignoring text after text in the Old Testament and Judaism where "kingdom" does refer to people, which formed the context of usage for Jesus and Paul. So the linguistic domain of "kingdom" cannot be reduced to "reign" but includes "people." Gerhard Lohfink, a German scholar, pushes against this all-too-common conclusion in these memorable words: "A king without a people is no king at all but a figure in a museum."[5] He's right. To say "kingdom" is to speak of a people governed by a king. To say that kingdom is "reign" is to tell half a story.

By registering this evidence above, which far outweighs the number of texts where an emphasis is reduced to the dynamic of ruling, I am making an appeal that we learn to see the word "kingdom" in its fullness: it refers to a people, to a people ruled, and to a people ruled by a king. There are, then, at least three elements of the word "kingdom,"[6] and it makes no sense to reduce these to just one. I now rest my case: kingdom refers to a people governed by a king. This has colossal significance for mission, and in one stroke challenges the most common reductions to justice or to the redemptive-rule dynamic. (To return to our crow who was dropping the clam to break the shell, we have now cracked the shell.)

This establishes a most important point when it comes to Jesus' kingdom story and to kingdom mission: *the kingdom of which Jesus speaks is a people governed by a king.* An array of shifts will occur when Jesus becomes King over a people, but the word "kingdom" cannot be reduced either to justice or salvation without doing serious damage to the story that animates the word "kingdom." When Jesus said the kingdom has drawn near, he meant we are about to see a new king governing a new people—that people will be marked by salvation and justice, but it is a people first and foremost.

Kingdom's Synonyms

As indicated above, for a first-century Jew like Jesus to say "kingdom" was to evoke "Israel" and "David ruling over Israel" and "liberated Israel (or Judeans or Galileans)," but the word always evoked Israel. I began this chapter asking what words came to mind to Jesus' contemporaries when he said "kingdom." We have now established the case that "kingdom" refers to a people governed by a king, which means that its closest synonyms will be terms and metaphors having to do with people. So we will explore briefly a variety of terms Jesus uses for his people or his followers, words that evoke the people-centeredness of what Jesus was all about. Bible readers discover a databank loaded with metaphors about peoplehood used by Jesus for those connected to him. In the most important study on this topic ever, Paul Minear found no less than ninety-six different images of the church in the New Testament, though one could say just as accurately that he found ninety-six images of the people of God, of which "church" is one.[7] I will focus on metaphors that lead us to see the people of Jesus as a fellowship or community, as a people marked by an ethic, and as a people having leaders. These terms are synonyms or word associations with "kingdom," and each of them reveals that Jesus was forming a community when he spoke of the kingdom of God.

First, I begin with terms that evoke fellowship and community, and any reading of the Gospels will find such terms: vineyard, branches and vines and wine, a "nation," a fellowship at table, a "people," and "Israel"; they are also a flock, and they are "one," friends, children of God, a brotherhood, and a family. These terms help define the meaning of the word "kingdom." We cannot enter into these terms in detail, but notice what we can see in pondering the vineyard and branches and vines and wine. Jesus is the vine, and Jesus' kingdom citizens are the vineyard, the branches, and the wine squeezed from the grapes on the branches (Mark 12:1–12). "I am the true vine," Jesus says (John 15:1), but his Father will remove branches that don't bear fruit. "I am the vine," he repeats, "you are the branches. If you remain in me and I in you, you will bear much fruit" (15:5). Vineyard, the vine, branches, and now grapes. Jesus tells a parable in which he says, "And no one pours new wine into old wineskins" (Mark 2:22). It is not entirely clear what Jesus has in mind. Is the new wine the kingdom message, the king, or the redemptive power now at work in the kingdom? Or is this new wine of the kingdom the new people who cannot be contained by the old wineskins? Probably yes to each and a little no to each too. However we read the new wine, there is a notable image at work for Jesus, and at each juncture we hear the message that Jesus is forming a kingdom *people*. "Vineyard," "vine," "grapes," and "wine" are terms Jesus uses for the kingdom.

Second, there is a sense at times that Jesus has set apart his kingdom people, and I think here of Matthew 17:24–27:

After Jesus and his disciples arrived in Capernaum, the collectors of the two-drachma temple tax came to Peter and asked, "Doesn't your teacher pay the temple tax?"

"Yes, he does," he replied.

When Peter came into the house, Jesus was the first to speak. "What do you think, Simon?" he asked. "From whom do the kings of the earth collect duty and taxes—from their own children or from others?"

"From others," Peter answered.

"*Then the children are exempt*," Jesus said to him. "But so that *we* may not cause offense, go to the lake and throw out your line. Take the first fish you catch; open its mouth and you will find a four-drachma coin. Take it and give it to them for my tax and yours." (emphasis added)

This passage hangs on one word: "we." If worldly kings exempt citizens, certainly the Father exempts his children. Jesus identifies himself and Peter with the children of the Father. Jesus has just distanced himself from both Roman and Galilean/Judean citizens by claiming that he and his followers are citizens of the Father's kingdom and, as such, are free from taxation as a duty. They are no longer worldly citizens but kingdom citizens who operate on a different basis. They pay taxes not as duty-bound citizens but as kingdom citizens voluntarily choosing loving acts of charity. Instead of claiming a right not to pay, as he could have done, Jesus surrenders rights to the charitable deed. As Jesus was the sovereign Son of God but chose in his freedom to enter into the human condition and to die and be raised for us, so we are "free" but choose to enter into the conditions of our society for its redemption (Phil. 2:5–11).

Third, a kingdom implies a king, a rule, a people, a land, and a law. So we are not surprised to see that Jesus reveals to his followers the will of God for kingdom people who want to live in the kingdom. Three sorts of terms come to the surface: Jesus calls people to *believe* in him, he calls people to *follow* him, and he calls people to *witness* to new kingdom realities. The entire Gospel of John, on the one hand, is shaped by the response of faith, which is an entire life of dependence upon the life of God available in King Jesus. Those who received Jesus have the authority to become the "people" or "children" of God (John 1:12). It is disciples of Jesus who believe in him (2:11, 22). The Synoptics, on the other hand, emphasize discipleship, or following Jesus, more. No saying of Jesus expresses this more clearly than Luke 9:23: "Whoever wants to be my disciple must deny themselves and take up their cross daily and follow me." As believers and followers, they are also witnesses. The word "witness" encompasses a fullness. The Father witnesses to Jesus, the Son witnesses to the Father, the Spirit witnesses back, and the disciples are to re-witness or echo-witness the witness of the Father to the Son and the Son to the Father and the Spirit to the Son. To witness, then, is to enter into the Story of God in this world. "When the Advocate comes, whom I will send to you from the Father—the Spirit of truth who goes out from the Father—he will testify about me. And you must also testify, for you have been with me from the beginning" (John 15:26–27).

Finally, if "kingdom" implies a king and a king ruling, then we are not one bit surprised to discover Jesus speak of himself as leading, judging, and ruling his kingdom people, though it is clear he appoints others to "rule" under him. Notice this stiff warning—one that evokes Adam and Eve, Babel, and 1 Samuel 8:

> But you are not to be called "Rabbi," for you have one Teacher, and you are all brothers. And do not call anyone on earth "father," for you have one Father, and he is in heaven. Nor are you to be called instructors, for you have one Instructor, the Messiah. The greatest among you will be your servant. For those who exalt themselves will be humbled, and those who humble themselves will be exalted. (Matt. 23:8–12)

That's the kingdom vision of Jesus: a people ruled by God who appoints Jesus as King. His apostles are but under-rulers. But what we need to draw out is this: *if there are leaders among the kingdom people, it is because the kingdom people are a new kind of fellowship, a new community, a new people of God.*

Simmering under the surface of this entire chapter has been another question: Who is this people? Asked from another angle: Is this people the church? To this question we now turn, and only after we have established the relationship of the kingdom to the church can we ask what kingdom mission means now. I contend this is the most significant discovery we can make for sorting out what kingdom mission means today. Everything changes if this next chapter's conclusion is sound, including changing what we mean by kingdom and what we mean by mission.

But before we do that, we should pause to consider a very typical use of "kingdom" versus "church" language. For a century or more a meme in the church is that the church and the kingdom are totally at odds with one another and that we need to get into the kingdom and say our good-byes to the church.[8] The whole posture of talking like this had at least a predecessor in the famous French skeptic Alfred Loisy, who once quipped—and I paraphrase—that Jesus preached the kingdom, but unfortunately it was the church that showed up![9] A recent example comes from a pastor intent on showing how small the church is when compared with the kingdom.

> Though the church and its activities can fit into the Kingdom, you *cannot squeeze the Kingdom into the Church.* When we try to fit the Kingdom into our church-box, *we create church people, instead of Kingdom people!* And there is a huge difference between the two:
>
> - Church people—have reduced ministry vision and can't see past church-bound categories for ministry (i.e., usher, greeter, children's worker, inviter-of-lost-friends, etc.).
> - Kingdom people—have Kingdom vision to think/dream/act outside the box (read church here). They want to heal the wounds in their neighborhood, workplace, and community (fatherlessness, addictions, marriages).
> - Church people—see the gospel in terms of good news about the afterlife (it's how you can be sure you're going to heaven after you die).
> - Kingdom people—see the gospel in terms of good news about Kingdom life (it's about life in God and with God, both now and forever).
> - Church people—understand discipleship as primarily about enjoying a closer relationship with God that grows me to spiritual maturity.
> - Kingdom people—understand discipleship as the call to lose their life for Christ's sake so they can participate in His family for His mission.
>
> The Kingdom is *not a means to a bigger church*; the church *is a means to demonstrating the Kingdom!*[10]

That set of observations pits kingdom against the church, with the former the mighty good guy and the latter the little punk.

Instead of a direct engagement with this kind of comparison, which is intent on minimizing church and maximizing kingdom with almost no attention to eschatology, and which is irresponsible but also quite commonly heard in coffee shops, I will move straight to a discussion of how kingdom and people and church need to be brought into close proximity. I will contend that you can't be kingdom people without being church people.

6

No Kingdom
outside the Church

Here's a simple rule: whenever you hear someone say they are doing "kingdom work," ask yourself if "church work" would communicate the same message. As in this: "My friend is in Africa doing kingdom work, building water wells for the poor." Would anything change if you said, "My friend is in Africa doing church work, building water wells for the poor"? Or, as many in both the Skinny Jeans and the Pleated Pants crowds claim, is kingdom work bigger than church work? My proposal will lead us to ask if one can call it "kingdom" work if it is clearly not "church" work. People are groping for words that sanctify and justify and legitimate and, if I may use the term, spiritualize good work like building water wells because people want their efforts to have transcendent significance. If our previous chapter is accurate, we need to think about whether the word "kingdom" is the right word to use in describing those actions and, perhaps more important, whether those who use it are cutting out the heart of the word "kingdom" when they do so.

"The Church Is Not the Kingdom": Pleated Pants and Skinny Jeans

Pleated Pants and Skinny Jeans thinkers are agreed on this: the church isn't the kingdom. One of the more common claims made by New Testament scholars is that the church and the kingdom are not the same thing. George Ladd can speak for the Pleated Pants crowd.

> If the dynamic concept of the Kingdom is correct, it is never to be identified with the church. The Kingdom is primarily the dynamic reign or kingly rule of God, and derivatively, the sphere in which the rule is experienced. In biblical idiom, the Kingdom is not identified with its subjects. They are the people of God's rule who enter it, live under it, and are governed by it. The church is the community of the Kingdom but never the Kingdom itself. . . . The Kingdom is the rule of God; the church is a society of women and men.[1]

Ladd's claims are representative, for at the core of this way of thinking is some kind of nervousness about equating church and kingdom. The one certainty is that the two are not the same. Old Testament scholars often make the same claim. So, for one example, John Bright states, "There is no tendency in the New Testament to identify the visible church with the Kingdom of God. . . . The Church is indeed the people of the Kingdom of Christ, but the visible church is not that Kingdom."[2] Just exactly how they can be "the people of the Kingdom" without being "that Kingdom" is not spelled out, and one must wonder what's left, but I must move on to others. Theologians join hands with the Bible scholars. H. Richard Niebuhr, whose book *Christ and Culture* has shaped the discussion of this book's topic, strongly denied too close of a connection between church and kingdom. Here are his words from his later book *The Purpose of the Church and Its Ministry*: "The Church is no more the kingdom of God than natural science is nature or written history the course of human events. It [the church] is the subject that apprehends its Object [the kingdom]."[3]

Kingdom is the big, final, ultimate topic, and the church is the smaller, temporary, and penultimate topic. Yet Niebuhr probes a little deeper.

> Several things are implied in this understanding of the Church: negatively, the Church is not the rule or realm of God; *positively, there is no apprehension*

of the kingdom except in the Church; conversely, where there is apprehension of, and participation in, this Object there the Church exists; and, finally, the subject-counterpart of the kingdom is never an individual in isolation but one in community, that is, in the Church.[4]

Niebuhr, then, expresses the widespread confidence that kingdom and church are not the same, but the moment he clarifies this claim, he creates ambiguity with his "no apprehension" statement. Niebuhr concludes that the church is the *only manifestation* of the kingdom today, but he opens more ambiguity when he continues with this:

What seems important is the distinction of the Church from the realm and rule of God [and this next statement leads to the "common good" approach to kingdom today] . . . *the recognition of the primacy and independence of the divine reality which can and does act without, beyond and often despite the Church*; and the acceptance of the *relativity* yet indispensability of the Church in human relations to that reality.[5]

He seems to think kingdom is an immaterial, spiritual reality—what we call the "redemptive dynamic"—while the church is a material, visible reality. But, as I have already indicated, this compares apples and oranges. (What about the already-realized dimension of the kingdom? Is that the same as the church?)

Biblical scholars and theologians, then, often reduce kingdom to the "redemptive dynamic" of God in this world. The same is found among those who focus on spiritual formation. Take, as an example, Dallas Willard. Here are his most significant words about kingdom: "Now God's own 'kingdom,' or 'rule,' is the range of his effective will, where what he wants done is done."

By narrowing kingdom to "the range of his effective will," Willard sides with the "redemptive dynamic" view I have already mentioned. The kingdom is about God's rule. But in the next sentence Willard opens the door to wide-ranging possibilities: "The person of God himself and the action of his will are the organizing principles of his kingdom, *but everything that obeys those principles, whether by nature or choice, is* within *his kingdom*" (emphasis added).

Whether Willard means the kingdom is found outside the church or outside faith in Christ is not clear here, but his statement sounds like John Stackhouse's "everywhere" cited above. What I'm sure of is that many readers will see in his words a kingdom operating outside the church.

> Accordingly, the kingdom of God is not essentially a social or political reality at all. [In addition,] the kingdom of God is not *primarily* something that is "in the hearts of men." . . . By relying on his word and presence we are enabled to reintegrate the little realm that makes up our life into the infinite rule of God. . . . The reality of God's rule . . . is present in action and available with and through the person of Jesus.[6]

Willard's approach to kingdom is through the discipline of spiritual formation, and for him kingdom is the ultimate, spiritual reality of God at work in this world to transform God's people into Christlikeness. But for our context this approach to kingdom has an important corollary: for Willard the kingdom is not a people or a political reality but a spiritual reality. It is a personal, inner-transforming redemptive reality.

Often enough behind this Skinny Jeans approach are themes drawn from the social gospel or from liberation theology (see appendix 2 for more). The major voice in liberation theology has been Gustavo Gutiérrez, who *overtly declared that the church had to be decentralized to make room for kingdom liberation*. Gutiérrez throws the weight on social praxis instead of the church, or, better yet, he redefines church as an instrument of economic liberation for the poor where the primary action is political process: "Social praxis is gradually becoming more of the arena itself in which the Christians work out—along with others—both their destiny as humans and their life of faith in the Lord of history."[7] This social work for him is salvation: "To work, to transform this world, is to become a man and to build the human community; it is also to save."[8] The church, he says, needs to be decentered from God's saving plan: "The perspective we have indicated presupposes an 'uncentering' of the Church, for the Church must cease considering itself as the exclusive place of salvation and orient itself towards a new and radical service of people."[9] There is a history here, a history of how salvation was divorced from poverty, of how the Catholic Church formed alliances with oppressive powers in Latin America. There is also a history of local and specific contexts that led to the "preferential option for the poor," as well as the history of political thought—in particular, Marxism—that sought answers to serious poverty in Latin America. All this history must be respected in order to hear what this architect of liberation theology was saying.

Any suggestion that liberation theology totally disconnected itself from the church is, however, a mistake. One element of liberation theology is the revolutionary small group movement, called Christian Base Communities, that sought to break away from hierarchy and institutionalism in the Roman Catholic Church to form fellowship groups of the poor and for the poor.[10] These communities offer a genuine alternative to the Roman Catholic Church of Latin America and in some ways mesh with what I am arguing for in this book: connecting kingdom mission to local church mission. However, my own reading of liberation theology in its Latin context leads me to think that these local expressions are the exception rather than the rule. The fundamental location for activism for liberation theology is the political and the public rather than the local church. So I want to frame it all with this question: Is the primary locus of redemption in society or in the local church? Or, to put the question to the Pleated Pants crowd, is it in the individual or in the local church?

Here's where we are: there is a widespread "consensus" that kingdom and church are not identical, but everyone knows there is some connection between the two. One might be tempted to side with the diversity and breadth of voices that make the strong claim that kingdom is not the church, but consensus on this one deserves to be challenged. The oddity of this seeming consensus is that there is a widespread lack of attempting to articulate the relationship of church and kingdom other than by way of denying they are identical. We need to explore the relationship more carefully, and the place to begin this discussion all over again is to point our noses once again at the Bible. The crucial text is found in the classic statement of Jesus to Peter about the church.

Let Jesus Have the First Word

As I have just indicated, those wanting to understand the relation of the church and the kingdom frequently set off in the wrong direction because the relationship is turned into either ethics or moments of redemption. But if "kingdom" necessarily means "people," then the relationship of the kingdom to the church is first and foremost a question about people. Our questions should be about who is in the kingdom and who is in the church. That is why we need to begin with Matthew 16:16–19.

> Simon Peter answered, "You are the Messiah, the Son of the living God."
>
> Jesus replied, "Blessed are you, Simon son of Jonah, for this was not revealed to you by flesh and blood, but by my Father in heaven. And I tell you that you are Peter, and on this rock I will build my church, and the gates of Hades will not overcome it. I will give you the keys of the kingdom of heaven; whatever you bind on earth will be bound in heaven, and whatever you loose on earth will be loosed in heaven."

Peter is the first to penetrate into one of the mysteries of the kingdom: the identity of its true king (Jesus). What Jesus divulged to Peter inside the mystery is this: First, this kind of knowledge is kingdom knowledge that can be known only because the kingdom is breaking in—this is the implication of the eschatological force of "blessed" (see Matt. 13:16–17). Second, this kind of knowledge derives from the Father's revealing graces. Third, Peter's confession that Jesus is King leads to a special privilege for Peter: "You are Peter" (*Petros*) and "on this rock" (*petra* in Greek) Jesus will himself build *the church*.[11] At a minimum this means Peter will be a founding apostle in the church, and Paul says much the same in Ephesians 2:20 when he says the church is "built on the foundation [synonym to "rock"] of the apostles and prophets." Fourth, Jesus reveals to Peter, and undoubtedly to the other apostles listening in and perhaps already beginning to feel some envy, that the "gates of Hades will not overcome it [the church]." The church is under battle from the cosmic forces, but God's sure promise is eternal, not unlike God's promises to Abraham in Genesis 12 and 15 and to David in 2 Samuel 7. Now to the final revealing promise to Peter: Jesus will give to Peter the "keys of the kingdom of heaven." Keys have one purpose: to open and to lock gates and doors. Peter's locking and unlocking privileges are now defined as granting access to and exclusion from the kingdom. Peter's actions are done while on earth but endure in the presence of God, and here "heaven" touches on the future kingdom of

God. Anything less than these observations doesn't cover the ground . . . but some ground it is!

What has to be observed, and some of us may have to read this over and over to catch the power of the connection, is that Jesus connects the *present church* (a people) to the *future kingdom* (a people). He connects *what Peter does now in the church* to what *God will do then in the kingdom*. Protestants and Catholics have gone to battle over these verses and in the process have turned a glorious reality into a buffer zone. What is revealed here by Jesus is that church and kingdom are indissolubly connected; what goes on in one goes on in the other! I want to ramp this up one notch: if kingdom is a people and the church is a people, then it follows that the church people are the kingdom people. *The church, then, is what is present and peopled in the realization of the kingdom now.*

Other New Testament references make a similar connection. Paul says God "has rescued us from the dominion of darkness and brought us into the kingdom of the Son he loves" (Col. 1:13). One must think here that the redemption of God is to usher people "into" Christ so they can be "in Christ" and brought "into the kingdom of the Son," and that these are variants of "church." Paul mentions three chapters later "co-workers for the kingdom of God" who are working for the church of Jesus Christ (4:11). The apostle John in the book of Revelation says that God has "made *us* to be a *kingdom* and priests" (Rev. 1:6, emphasis added). We are a kingdom, and the "we" is the church—specifically, the seven churches to whom John writes. This same John says that he is their "brother and companion in the suffering and kingdom and patient endurance that are ours in Jesus" (1:9). Here "kingdom" is something in the here and now, the people of the Lord Jesus. Like Jesus' words to Peter in Matthew 16, cited above, John says God has "made them to be a kingdom and priests to serve our God, and they [the people of Jesus, the people of the kingdom] will reign on the earth [in that kingdom]" (5:10).

With one sentence, now, I pull the rope taut: *there is no kingdom now outside the church*. You will perhaps wonder if I'm pulling the rope too taut. I shall answer back by quoting E. B. White, who once said, "A writer, like an acrobat, must occasionally try a stunt that is too much for him."[12] Acrobat on a taut rope or not, I contend kingdom and church need to be seen as much closer than most see them today.

Church

I have made what some will think is a preposterous claim in connecting kingdom so closely to church. Admittedly, most of us think of kingdom as a future glorious reality with only a glimmer of expression in our world while we see the church in mostly earthy and rather mundane terms—with almost no future! When we use the term "church" most of us think of a local church, like the Lutheran church across the street, or the Presbyterian church around the corner, or the Evangelical Covenant church down the road a bit, or the Evangelical Free church down a different street. In other words, we think of brick-and-mortar and tangible realities, and we can tell stories about each. But we are comparing the not-to-be-compared: the future kingdom of glory with the present church of mundane, messy realities. We need to compare like to like, and we will do that now.

Israel Expanded for Gentiles

But what does the church look like if we examine it in the full scope of the New Testament? We might be surprised. Israel's story provides the first theme: God chose Israel as his possession and covenant partner. We must begin with Israel and God's inviolable covenant promise to be faithful to Israel—forever. Once we begin with Israel as the beginning, the church naturally will be seen as the "Israel of God" (Gal. 6:16). But there's even more here: in Romans, when this issue of God's faithfulness to Israel is on the line and when church seems to be too many gentiles and not enough Jews, Paul shatters many of our preconceptions when he refers to the gentile believers as "wild olive shoots" grafted into the tree trunk called Israel (Rom. 11:17–21).

> If some of the branches have been broken off, and you [gentiles], though a wild olive shoot, have been grafted in among the others [faithful Israelites] and now share in the nourishing sap from the olive root, do not consider yourself to be superior to those other branches. If you do, consider this: You do not support the root, but the root [Israel] supports you. You will say then, "Branches were broken off so that I could be grafted in." Granted. But they were broken off because of unbelief, and you stand by faith. Do

not be arrogant, but tremble. For if God did not spare the natural branches, he will not spare you either.

The image is clear, and we need to embrace it if we want to understand what church means. Paul did not say that God chopped down the original tree trunk (Israel) and planted, nurtured, and caused a new tree (church) to grow. Yet that is what so many Christians believe: they believe God has put paid to Israel and pushed them off the cliff. This makes God unfaithful. No, God's promises are not obliterated, nor are they forgotten: they are up front and central to *how Paul understands the church*. The unfaithful of Israel are clipped from the same tree trunk called Israel, and gentile believers are grafted onto that tree trunk called Israel.

For this reason it is wise to see the church as "Israel Expanded" and not as "Israel Replaced." Those who are most sensitive to the Old Testament are also sensitive on this issue, and a good example is Christopher Wright: "It is a totally false and misleading reading of the Bible to imagine that God had a Plan A (Israel), which failed, so he replaced that with Plan B (the Christian church). The Bible never talks of the *replacement* of Israel with the church, but rather of the *expansion* of Israel to include the Gentiles."[13]

Any reading of the apostle Paul reveals that Paul strives to incorporate gentiles into the people of God, into one unified fellowship.[14] In places like Romans 11:25 he calls God's plan to expand Israel with gentiles the "mystery." But perhaps the place to camp out on this theme is Ephesians. Here are the texts to ponder:

> He made known to us the mystery of his will according to his good pleasure, which he purposed in Christ, to be put into effect when the times reach their fulfillment—*to bring unity to all things in heaven and on earth under Christ.* (Eph. 1:9–10, emphasis added)

> Surely you have heard about the administration of God's grace that was given to me for you, that is, the mystery made known to me by revelation, as I have already written briefly. In reading this, then, you will be able to understand my insight into the mystery of Christ, which was not made known to people in other generations as it has now been revealed by the Spirit to God's holy apostles and prophets. *This mystery is that through the gospel the Gentiles*

are heirs together with Israel, members together of one body, and sharers together in the promise in Christ Jesus. (3:2–6, emphasis added)

Although I am less than the least of all the Lord's people, this grace was given me: to preach to the Gentiles the boundless riches of Christ, and to make plain to everyone the administration of this mystery, which for ages past was kept hidden in God, who created all things. (3:8–9)

Already we have a firmer connection to kingdom since kingdom is so connected to Israel. The church is the kingdom called Israel now expanded to include gentile believers.

Church: What the Word Means

What is perhaps most notable is that the apostle Paul chose a term, "church," from among a myriad of possibilities in his day. First, the Greek word behind our "church" is *ekklesia*, and since Paul grew up reading the Old Testament, he also used the Hebrew word *qahal*. This term in Hebrew referred to Israel's public gatherings.[15] Paul chose this word "church" because it perfectly described what the church was all about: public but local gatherings of Jesus' followers. (Yes, in Paul's later writings, like Colossians and Ephesians, the term "church" also means the worldwide "church" in an all-inclusive sense.) Thus, our first observation winds down to this: "church" refers to local gatherings of Israel Expanded in specific locations in the Roman Empire.

But there's a second usage of the term "church" that reveals a tighter connection to kingdom. In the Greek world of Paul the word "church" (*ekklesia*) referred to local political gatherings of citizens and leaders. While the first context for the early Christian usage should be the Jewish evidence, discussed in the previous paragraph, this second sense of the term could not have been avoided by Paul. In fact, the Jewish use of *ekklesia* also had political and social overtones. So we have to conclude that when Paul and the earliest Christians began to call their gatherings and themselves the "church," they were making a powerful claim. Their claim was this: they were Israel Expanded and were gathered locally as a sociopolitical fellowship under King Jesus. Now to set this into the context of this book:

both "kingdom" and "church" are, then, sociopolitical terms describing the people of God.

Third, this term "church" (*ekklesia*) refers to Israel Expanded throughout the Roman Empire, now gathered *out of the world and over against the world.* The term "fellowship" (*koinonia*) refers to the inner life that creates unity of life in the *ekklesia* in the world. The term "church," then, defines a community under the God of Israel and King Jesus, over against those who are not part of that people of God. In his exceptional study of the church as a family, Joseph Hellerman compares early Christian churches with other options in the Roman Empire—with professional and domestic and religious associations, with philosophical schools, and with the Jewish synagogue—and he observes that the Christian church offered more dimensions of life than any of the other options. In particular, it countered the corruptions of the Roman Empire, summoned its participants into an exclusive allegiance, and, most important, created a family kind of life.[16]

Since kingdom requires a king and a people and a land and a law, we are led to questions such as: What about land? What about Torah? We cannot resolve these questions in depth, but I would like to make a fourth observation: the land promise is not done away with by the mystery of bringing gentiles into the people of God. God's promise remains, though I want here to distance myself from some Christian speculations about land and modern-day Israel. It seems to me, in light of Jesus as the temple and the Christians as temples of the Holy Spirit (1 Cor. 3:16–17; 6:19; 2 Cor. 6:16; Eph. 2:21; 1 Pet. 2:4–9), that we should see local churches as the land promise taking root in gentile territory, or as the land promise expanding into the Roman Empire. This fourth observation gives way to a fifth point: What about Torah? King Jesus gives the Sermon on the Mount as the Kingdom Torah for kingdom citizens. As the apostles continue to teach how to live as kingdom citizens, we encounter new themes, but they are all variants on what we might call Kingdom Torah: we get life in the Spirit, the fruit of the Spirit, and the gifts of the Spirit. We have, then, the makings in the church of a kingdom—a king, a rule, a people, a land, and a law. Now the happy crow will observe that the clam is about to crack wide open.

Church as Now and Not Yet

There is one fundamental observation that changes the whole perception of what church is, and once we see it we will be able to compare church and kingdom more accurately. You will recall that the New Testament does not teach that the kingdom is totally here. Instead, it teaches that the kingdom is both now and not yet, that the kingdom is inaugurated in Jesus and in the Holy Spirit's special presence in the church. That is, the kingdom is an eschatological reality and phenomenon. The important observation is this: the church is also an eschatological reality. The futurity of the church is often ignored.

THE CHURCH NOW

For the church now we think of Paul's constant struggles with his churches, and who can ignore Corinth and the back-and-forth letters and travels all over morality and theology and division and . . . well, the church at Corinth was a mess. The same messiness is found in all other churches. The church now is the church gathered in broken leadership, broken fellowship, broken holiness, broken love, broken justice, and broken peace. Every page of each of Paul's and Peter's and John's letters and of the books of Hebrews and Jude leads to the same observation: the church now falls short of the church not yet. What does the New Testament say about the church not yet?

THE CHURCH NOT YET

For the church not yet I think not only of the promises that the church will inherit the kingdom (Matt. 16:17–19; 1 Thess. 2:12; Rom. 8:17; Eph. 1:18; Phil. 3:20) but even more of Ephesians 5:25b–27, where you can see the church not yet in full glory: "Christ loved the church and gave himself up for her to make her holy, cleansing her by the washing with water through the word, and *to present her to himself as a radiant church, without stain or wrinkle or any other blemish, but holy and blameless*" (emphasis added; see also Col. 1:22).

Notice the terms Paul uses of the church not yet: "radiant," "without stain or wrinkle," without any "blemish," "holy and blameless." These terms do not describe the church now except in part; they instead describe what the church will be. When? When the kingdom's fullness arrives or, to use now completely appropriate terms, when the church's fullness arrives. I think, too, of Revelation 21–22, especially of the long, beautiful passage about the church as the bride of the Lamb descending in full glory into the new Jerusalem in the new heaven and the new earth, proving once and for all that the church, like the kingdom, is an eschatological reality with a now and a glorious not yet. I quote Revelation 21:9–22:5, and I am asking you to read this carefully.

One of the seven angels who had the seven bowls full of the seven last plagues came and said to me, "Come, I will show you the bride, the wife of the Lamb." And he carried me away in the Spirit to a mountain great and high, and showed me the Holy City, Jerusalem, coming down out of heaven from God. It shone with the glory of God, and its brilliance was like that of a very precious jewel, like a jasper, clear as crystal. It had a great, high wall with twelve gates, and with twelve angels at the gates. On the gates were written the names of the twelve tribes of Israel. There were three gates on the east, three on the north, three on the south and three on the west. The wall of the city had twelve foundations, and on them were the names of the twelve apostles of the Lamb.

The angel who talked with me had a measuring rod of gold to measure the city, its gates and its walls. The city was laid out like a square, as long as it was wide. He measured the city with the rod and found it to be 12,000 stadia in length, and as wide and high as it is long. The angel measured the wall using human measurement, and it was 144 cubits thick. The wall was made of jasper, and the city of pure gold, as pure as glass. The foundations of the city walls were decorated with every kind of precious stone. The first foundation was jasper, the second sapphire, the third agate, the fourth emerald, the fifth onyx, the sixth ruby, the seventh chrysolite, the eighth beryl, the ninth topaz, the tenth turquoise, the eleventh jacinth, and the twelfth amethyst. The twelve gates were twelve pearls, each gate made of a single pearl. The great street of the city was of gold, as pure as transparent glass.

I did not see a temple in the city, because the Lord God Almighty and the Lamb are its temple. The city does not need the sun or the moon to shine on it, for the glory of God gives it light, and the Lamb is its lamp. The nations will walk by its light, and the kings of the earth will bring their splendor into it. On no day will its gates ever be shut, for there will be no night there.

The glory and honor of the nations will be brought into it. Nothing impure will ever enter it, nor will anyone who does what is shameful or deceitful, but only those whose names are written in the Lamb's book of life.

Then the angel showed me the river of the water of life, as clear as crystal, flowing from the throne of God and of the Lamb down the middle of the great street of the city. On each side of the river stood the tree of life, bearing twelve crops of fruit, yielding its fruit every month. And the leaves of the tree are for the healing of the nations. No longer will there be any curse. The throne of God and of the Lamb will be in the city, and his servants will serve him. They will see his face, and his name will be on their foreheads. There will be no more night. They will not need the light of a lamp or the light of the sun, for the Lord God will give them light. And they will reign for ever and ever.

We are at a crucial juncture in our argument. "Kingdom" describes the people governed by King Jesus. All we see of that kingdom now is an inauguration creating a tension between kingdom now and kingdom not yet. But "church" describes the very same realities: the people of God, Israel Expanded to be sure, is an eschatological reality, a people of God that has a now and a not yet. C. K. Barrett, a leading New Testament scholar of the former generation, called the church an "eschatological monster, a prodigy." And he defines the church as "the people of the interim."[17] He's right: the church is now and not yet, partially redeemed and on its way to full redemption. So, what is said of the kingdom in the New Testament is also said of the church in the same New Testament: both have a now and a not yet. In their "now" condition they are the same; in their "not yet" condition they will be the same. To quote Bonhoeffer in support: "The church according to Paul's understanding presents no essential difference from Jesus' ideas [about the kingdom]."[18]

If we want to make comparison, we need to compare kingdom now and church now or kingdom not yet and church not yet. To compare, as so many do, church now with kingdom not yet is not fair to the church (or the kingdom). A notable scholar, Rudolf Schnackenburg, after directly observing that the church too is an eschatological reality with a now and a not yet, then fails to follow up with the natural conclusion. Instead of saying that the present church needs to be compared with the present kingdom realities, he slides into, "It is not the Church but the kingdom of God which is the ultimate goal of the divine economy of salvation and redemption in its perfect form for the whole world."[19] Had he been consistent, Schnackenburg would have said that the future can be expressed *either* as kingdom *or* as church—as the book of Revelation makes clear. The mistaken notion that *only* the kingdom is the final form of God's redemptive community drives the current inability to see the important overlap of kingdom and church today. If kingdom is the future perfection and church the modern mess, then kingdom and church are not comparable. (I'm repeating myself, I know, but these points must be said over and over if we are to absorb their importance.)

Kingdom mission flows directly out of the kingdom story, but once we see the people focus of kingdom and church, kingdom mission now has a whole new focus.

Kingdom Mission and the Church

Here is where we are in understanding kingdom mission: kingdom mission is entering into and participating in the kingdom story, a story that sees Israel's story (the A-B-A' story) being fulfilled in the story of Jesus. Furthermore, that story contradicts the world's stories that dominate our culture. So kingdom mission means not only telling the kingdom story but also countering the world's stories. At the very heart of kingdom mission are the kingdom people, the church of King Jesus. In one short expression, then, *kingdom mission is first and foremost church mission.*

Especially in a day when an increasing number jettison the church in order to do kingdom work and who also find little reason for the church, we need to wrap our minds around this most pregnant of statements by Jesus: "You are Peter, and on this rock [Peter and his confession] I will build my church, and the gates of Hades [death itself] will not overcome it" (Matt. 16:18). To Peter "the keys of [i.e., into] the kingdom of heaven" (16:19) are given. Jesus only uses the word "church" twice according to the Gospel traditions, the other being Matthew 18:17, which refers to a local gathering. But this first use of the term clearly reveals a dramatic connection between church and kingdom. The two may not be identical, but one can say they are the same people governed by the same King living out the same law under the same kingdom redemptive powers.

This is where I have to lay down what is perhaps the strongest conclusion of this book: *kingdom mission is church mission, church mission is kingdom mission, and there is no kingdom mission that is not church mission.* This conclusion might die at the hand of a dozen nuances—I don't mean "institutional church," I don't mean Roman Catholic Church or Eastern Orthodox Church or the Anglican Communion or the Southern Baptist Convention or the particular church in your neighborhood or a church that suppresses women or excludes others on the basis of race or gender or status, and yet I do! Many see the kingdom exclusively in utopian terms and the church in all its rugged messiness, so they toss dust in the eyes of anyone who gets the two too close. But this fails at the most basic level of exegesis. The kingdom in the New Testament is not just a future glory but a present rugged reality struggling toward that glorious future. That is, the kingdom is only partly realized; it is only inaugurated in the here and now. So the kingdom today is a rugged mess no less than the church is also a utopia, as I outlined in an earlier chapter. The church's future, when church morphs into kingdom in its fullness, will be a grand, glorious display of holiness and love and justice and endless fellowship. So one might wonder how the present kingdom could even be called the "church" if one thinks of the church's future. No, instead we are to see the inaugurated kingdom of the here and now and the inaugurated church of the here and now as the one people of God that journeys toward, but has not yet reached, the perfect eschatological people of God. Once we overlay inaugurated eschatology on top of kingdom and church, there is simply no barrier to seeing the kingdom as the church today.

This means *all true kingdom mission is church mission.* For many today it is far easier to be committed to social justice in South Africa, to the restoration of communities on the Gulf Shore following Katrina, to cleaning up from the devastating tornadoes of the Plains, or to fighting sexual trafficking in any country than it is to be committed to building community and establishing fellowship in one's local church. I hate to put it this way, but I must: it is easier to do the former because it feels good, it resolves some social shame for all that we have, it creates a bonded and encapsulated experience, it is a momentary and at times condescending invasion of resources and energy, and it is all ramped up into ultimate legitimation by calling it kingdom work. Not only that, it is good and right and noble and loving and compassionate and just. It is more glamorous to do social activism because building a local church is hard. It involves people who struggle with one another, it involves persuading others of the desires of your heart to help the homeless, it means caring for people where they are and not where you want them to be, it involves daily routines, and it only rarely leads to the highs of "short-term mission" experiences. But local church is what Jesus came to build, so the local church's mission shapes kingdom mission.

What do I mean at the concrete level? I'll tell you exactly. It's the difference between our energies being focused on a local church community embodying the inaugurated kingdom and a group of local Christians going to the city council or to Washington, DC, joining with others in some kind of good activism in order to bring about more peace or justice. A beautiful example of what I'm talking about is Lawndale Community Church in Chicago, Illinois. The founding and lead pastor is Wayne Gordon.[20] A white man, Wayne learned at a young age to cross racial boundaries as an expression of the gospel. Wayne graduated from Wheaton College, began teaching at Farragut High School in the city of Chicago (a man in Iowa called him a "damn fool" for considering a life in the city), became a football coach, and eventually had enough impact on some young men (mostly black) to begin a Bible study. The study led to a church, which led to his being the pastor of Lawndale Community Church (LCC), where he is now going into his fourth decade. It's been gloriously messy and full of kingdom realities. Everyone calls Wayne "Coach."

The core of LCC is a worshiping, fellowshipping, praying, serving, loving, Bible-reading, preaching church. For all the magnificent good done by the good folks at LCC, this is a church-centered ministry. The Spirit's new creation life at work in the church leads LCC folks to love on their neighbors and to listen to their neighbors well enough to be able to create ministries that meet their needs. The church began with a laundromat; then it developed health facilities and ministries to help with drugs and addictions and economic development; then it built a gymnasium and housing for those in

need; then came a hip-hop ministry and an arts ministry and a pizza joint
. . . and I could go on. Lawndale is a church that establishes care for one
another—when Wayne's home was burglarized some dozen times in his
first few years as a pastor, the church folks resupplied his home—and that
transforming love spills over into caring for the community. The impulse of
LCC is not to get the city of Chicago to donate funds for what LCC wants
done but to *be the church in Lawndale* and, on the foundation of being
the church, to cooperate with the city in common aims. Their recreation
and medical facility is now state-of-the-art. All of this has developed right
in the middle of one of the most devastated communities in the United
States—where some 120,000 jobs have left the house since the 1960s and
1970s white flight.

Take Randy Brown. He grew up in Lawndale and, like many young
African American males, focused on basketball in Lawndale's gymnasium.
Someone at LCC invited him to the Bible study, and that led to his attend-
ing church on Sunday. A year later he was baptized in Lake Michigan. He
went off to college to play hoops, and then—what came as a surprise to
LCC—returned to Lawndale upon graduation to become director of the
gym ministry in a gym used seven days a week. Randy teaches Christian
living to those who participate in this ministry. The local high school kids
love Randy because he loves them and gives himself to them.

What one sees, then, is holistic ministry: Gordon writes, "Christian
community development, virtually by definition, is wholistic ministry that
seeks to meet physical, spiritual, emotional, and social needs in the name of
Christ"—and notice the stinger at the end of this long sentence—"*without
concern for which is most important.*"[21]

Kingdom mission is local church mission.

7

KINGDOM MISSION
AS CHURCH MISSION

The question I asked to close the opening chapter was whether Jane Addams, in her marvelous activism, was doing kingdom work. One can ask the same of Gandhi. We answered this question when we discovered that the Bible speaks of the kingdom as the people who are governed by King Jesus. Kingdom work is what kingdom citizens do under King Jesus. We will look below at what we are to call Jane Addams's noble work and how we are to "act" in the public sector, but for now I want to make the claim that kingdom mission cannot be defined until we've defined kingdom. The kingdom is the people who are redeemed and ruled by King Jesus in such a way that they live as a fellowship under King Jesus. That is, there is a king (Jesus), a rule (by Jesus as Lord), a people (the church), a land (wherever Jesus' kingdom people are present), and a law (following Jesus through the power of the Spirit, something I consider in chap. 10). Kingdom mission is about creating and sustaining that kingdom community, the church. With this definition I want to sort out what kingdom mission looks like in nine observations.

A Dwelling Place for God

First, *kingdom mission means the local church is first and foremost a dwelling place for God*. I begin with the general idea for understanding kingdom mission. Revelation 21–22, when combined with other grand eschatological passages in the Bible, like 1 Corinthians 15 and Philippians 2:6–11, reveals that God's ultimate mission is to dwell among his people alongside the Lamb, and in that dwelling presence to rule the people of God in the heart of the world. If the ultimate mission of God is to dwell among the people of God, then *kingdom mission is to be the dwelling place of God in this world*. Kingdom mission is about *being* the presence of God in this world. If we connect kingdom people to church people, then we have also defined church mission as identical to kingdom mission.

Each local church, then, is to be a place fit for the presence of God, a place that mediates the presence of God to the people of God as a gift to the local community. Kingdom mission is the church's mission, and the only "place" in the world where this kingdom mission is found is in the church (as Israel Expanded). How does the church do this kingdom mission? Again, the fundamental mission of the church is *to mediate the presence of God in this world*. We do this when the kingdom mission, or church's mission, is seen as the prophetic declaration of the gospel, in the priestly mediation of grace and love and justice and peace and wisdom as embodied in the local church, and in the gentle, servant-like rule of King Jesus over us.

Church as Kingdom Politic

Second, *kingdom mission as church mission means the church is a kingdom fellowship, or a kingdom politic*. Both the word "kingdom" and the word "church" come straight from the world of ancient politics. These terms describe political assemblies, and we are wrong to think that the church is not political. The church is political from the inside out. What does that mean? Fifteen hundred evangelical pastors went political in October 2012 to make a point to the IRS that it was sticking its nose into the sacred space of the pulpit.[1] Freedom to preach what preachers think needs to be preached was their concern, and if freedom means they must denounce or endorse a given candidate on the basis of their faith, then they must have the freedom to say so. After all, if one reads the Old Testament, one constantly encounters the prophets of God taking direct aim at the king and the priests. The IRS law circumscribes what pastors and churches can do publicly to endorse candidates as a trade-off for tax exemptions, so the pastors were taking a risk when they chose to thump the boss in the chest. While many would sympathize with and defend their contentions, not to mention that one could easily point to both African American and mainline pastors who have been fundamentally political in their sermons for most of the twentieth century, my contention here is that this kind of politics misses the whole point of the "politics of Jesus" and seeing the church as a politic. To say the church is a politic is not to say the church needs to be more political by becoming more active and aggressive in the political process.

The kingdom is the people under King Jesus who fellowship with one another and form churches. These churches *are the politic of Jesus in this world*. That is, a local church embodies—or is designed by God to embody—the kingdom vision of Jesus in such a way that it tells the kingdom story. That is a politic, a witness to the world of a new worship, a new law, a new king, a new social order, a new peace, a new justice, a new economics, and a new way of life. Engagement at the pulpit level to endorse or denounce a candidate is a minor chord in God's masterpiece. Rather than spending our time with candidates, kingdom politics means we embody all that the country could be and far more than it is by living out what Jesus calls us to do. As John Howard Yoder has said, "If in society we believe in the rights of employees, then the church should be the first employer to deal with workers fairly. If in the wider society we call for the overcoming of racism or sexism or materialism, then the church should be the place where that possibility first becomes real."[2]

But Christians have failed to embody the church as an alternative politic and have instead opted for influencing and improving Caesar or transforming culture or using the political process to accomplish their wishes. Americans love politics, as do people all over the world. America is made up of lots of Christians, and this means many Christians get riled up in the political process. Many fall for what I called earlier the "eschatology of politics," the belief that the next candidate or vote can bring in kingdom conditions. Some give themselves to politics, and an increasing number have joined hands with the political process through social activism. To be blunt, many have abandoned the church and opted for the political process and are now calling it kingdom work.

In one simple sentence: what Christians want for the nation should first be a witnessed reality in their local church. Until that local church embodies that desire for the nation, the church's witness has no credibility. When it is embodied in the local church, that embodiment is the only activism the church needs. Put directly, fighting for justice means embodying justice in the local fellowship; striving for peace means striving for peace in the local church; opposing abortion means converting sexuality into a pure, loving, and family-honoring joy; contending for economic justice means living out the kingdom vision for all we own and have. But too many Christians have ignored the politic of the local church and bowed down to the politics of the world.

Politics is a colossal distraction from kingdom mission. Politics entails diminution of our kingdom message, because to speak well in the public forum means we have to turn our gospel-drenched message that focuses on Jesus, the cross, and the resurrection into acceptable, common-denominator language and vision. Instead of talking discipleship and a cruciform life, we talk about values and soak it in the pretentious "Judeo-Christian ethic." Politics entails energies and time that could be used more directly for kingdom mission tasks. Politics means seeking to influence the state in the direction of the kingdom, but in so doing it is asking the public and the state to put into law and policy the kingdom story. Politics sees victory when a candidate wins or when a law passes or a policy is reformed. I speak directly now: we kingdom people don't need the state, we don't need the majority, and we must refrain from equating victory in the world with kingdom mission. We have a story to live and to tell, and that story is the kingdom story (A-B-A'). The culture war story is not the kingdom story, and it is idolatrous when Christians equate the two.

Living under King Jesus

Third, *kingdom mission as church mission means learning to live under King Jesus*. The church is only the church to the degree that it lives under

102

King Jesus. We call Jesus "Lord," and that means he is our Lord and we are the Lord's servants as kingdom citizens. We are not "under the Lord" when we do our part as Christians—at home, in the church—but then "under Caesar" when acting as public citizens. If Jesus is Lord, he is always Lord—at home, in the church, and in the public. We don't have an ethic for our Christian life and another ethic for our public, worldly, secular life. We have one ethic because Jesus is Lord over all.

We confess Jesus is Lord, so

when we are faced with an economic decision, we look to Jesus;

when we are faced with a community decision, we look to Jesus;

when we are faced with a family decision, we look to Jesus;

when we are faced with an education decision, we look to Jesus;

when we are faced with a global decision, we look to Jesus;

and when we are faced with a political decision, we look to Jesus.

We look to Jesus because Jesus is Lord.

One of the more discouraging trends visible in the church today emerges when folks defend a given posture—from nuclear proliferation to same-sex marriage to women in ministry—on the basis of a constitutional sense of "justice" or "peace." More often than not we are hearing a defense of Western liberalism's understanding of both justice and peace, where the former refers to rights and freedoms and the latter to international relations noted by the absence of war or diminishing nuclear proliferation. I affirm these values myself, but the Christian does not look to the US Constitution, to the Declaration of Independence, to the Articles of Confederation, to Thomas Paine's *Common Sense* or his *Rights of Man*, or to Jean-Jacques Rousseau's *The Social Contract* or his *Discourses*. I could go on. Followers of Jesus define justice and peace on the basis of the Bible, where the will of God determines what is "just" and the same will defines what "peace" is. Only on that basis can a "Christian theory of justice/rights" be constructed, and until that is done, Christians will more or less parrot Western liberalism.[3]

Put now more boldly, the kingdom story defines justice and peace for us: justice is doing the will of God as taught by Jesus and establishing a kingdom society (the church) where that will is done; peace is the condition that flows from living under King Jesus, who defeats the foes through the cross and resurrection and creates peace with God, with self, and with others in the kingdom fellowship. The justice and peace offered by Western liberalism, which transcends in many ways the kinds of justice and peace offered in other cultures of other times, is a pale shadow compared to what is offered by the radical Galilean.[4] Kingdom citizens are committed to the Galilean, and all kingdom mission will be shaped by the Galilean's vision. We are under a new Lord, and the lordless lords of culture and world are no longer the voices to whom we listen.

A Local Church Fellowship

Fourth, *kingdom mission as church mission means forming and indwelling a local church fellowship.* The most political thing you and I as followers of Jesus can do, the most political thing we as kingdom citizens can do, the most political thing we as the church of King Jesus can do is to *gather together* in order to do things the church is called to do. Before listing what we are to do as a political body, we need to recall how the church has thought about what the church is when it is being church. (1) The Nicene Creed teaches us these four characteristics of the church: we are one, we are holy, we are universal (or "catholic"), and we are apostolic. Most of us are willing to say that these terms beg for clarification, so (2) the church has clarified them—with perhaps the most notable attempt coming out of the Reformation. These characteristics were then labeled "marks" of the church, of which the two primary marks—both focused on the "apostolic" term in the Creed—are "Word" and "Sacrament." That is, the church is only apostolic when it preaches the Word faithfully and offers the Sacraments as a means of grace to the faithful. (3) Rising for a little attention after Word and Sacrament is the call for the church to exercise "church discipline," which can be summarized as a local church, usually through the pastor or the elders, maintaining standards of holiness and purity for those who participate in that local church.

(4) As John Howard Yoder, the most influential Mennonite thinker of the last century, observed, these "marks" of the church are far more about

what "pastors" do than what the church does, so he proposed five "practices of the Christian community before the watching world."[5] Yoder gets us closer to what the church is and does when it is being the kingdom church. The crucial church practices begin with binding and loosing, which is all about a local church gathering to discern the will of God for that community in a given context.[6] Breaking bread together—which unfortunately Yoder reduces too much to table fellowship without sufficient attention to the sacrament of the body and blood of Christ—forms an important practice of the church. We share life with one another, especially at the table. Baptism is the plunging of the unconverted into the life, death, burial, and resurrection of Christ, the act whereby the convert publicly identifies himself or herself with King Jesus and kingdom citizens, and is marked as one who now lives in light of the cross in fellowship with others. As a fellowship, Christians live in the "fullness" of Christ, which means they are indwelt and empowered by the Spirit with fruit and gifts so they can live out a gospel-shaped life. A church is a people of the Spirit empowered by the Spirit to live in ways not attainable by ordinary means. Finally, Yoder sketches the "rule of Paul," which refers to the radical democratic vision of the gathered church having an "open conversation." That is, the world's hierarchy is turned upside down into a church where each person has a place at the table and a voice worthy of hearing.

If the Nicene Creed's four characteristics speak more about how to keep the Roman Empire's Constantinian church from fracturing, and the Reformation's "marks" were more about what pastors do in leading churches, Yoder's five practices focus on the inner life of a local church. I'd like us to step back to consider how the kingdom story frames kingdom mission and how the notion of kingdom as people reframes the so-called marks of the church discussion. Furthermore, once we factor in the kingdom story as a counter-story to the world, we open up some new space to consider kingdom mission as an alternative society. I suggest that kingdom mission means we work at forming churches shaped by the Creed's elements, the Reformation's summoning of us to the Word preached and the Sacraments distributed, as well as Yoder's practices; but they still leave us short. What most shocked the Jews living in Jerusalem when the earliest kingdom communities formed was not any of the above but was instead *the kind of community that became visible.* The people became a family.[7]

So we return yet again to those descriptions of the earliest Christian churches in Acts 2:42–47 and 4:32–35, and when we begin here, we see the following characteristics of church as fellowship and family:

- A fellowship formed by the apostolic gospel
- A family formed by fellowship with one another
- A fellowship formed by table fellowship, Eucharist, and prayer
- A family formed by the presence of God through the Spirit
- A fellowship formed by economic sharing
- A family formed by evangelism

Kingdom is people; church is people. A people under King Jesus begins to live into an alternative society that witnesses both to and against the world's system. Our world is marked today by isolation, fragmentation, transience, privacy, consumerism, power, complacency, alienation, suspicion, and a host of idolatries. The church, which is a kingdom fellowship under King Jesus, counters each of these stories with the story of new creation that becomes possible through the power of the Spirit and the life of Jesus. Kingdom creates a family called a church. Joseph Hellerman, who has spent his career studying family and church as family, spells out four characteristics of "life together in the family of God": (1) we share our stuff together; (2) we share our hearts with one another; (3) we stay, embrace the pain, and grow up with one another; and (4) family is about more than me, the wife, and the kids—it is about the people of God in this world.[8]

Kingdom mission cuts deep into our way of living. Instead of seeking to make the world a better place through the political process, kingdom citizens are called to live into the kingdom with one another. The features listed above are to describe our local churches where we seek to embody them. When someone needs help finding a job, the church pools its resources; when someone's income falls flat, we help one another. We share life with one another. In other words, we don't just stand for justice in the public realm; we embody justice in God's grand experiment, the church. We mock peace in the world if we don't first form a peaceful fellowship. We mock justice when the poor suffer in our midst and may choose, because of their discomfort among us, not to participate in our "kingdom" fellowship. We mock our defense of love when our own fellowships are marred by divorces and fractured relationships and lack of love for other kingdom citizens who don't have our theology. Our first focus is the condition of our fellow kingdom believers in our local church; our first commitment is to one another. Yes, the apostle Paul once told the Galatians, we are "to do good to all people." But he followed that up with a direct hit on kingdom mission when he added "especially to those who belong to the family of believers" (Gal. 6:10).

A Free People

Fifth, *kingdom mission as church mission means learning to live in the world as a free people.* Jesus knew the story of freedom, and that is why he told Peter that he was "exempt" or "free" from taxation. So we begin right here: those who live under King Jesus in the kingdom fellowship called the church are free from the dominating stories of their culture and free to do what God calls them to do—even if it means rejection, repudiation, and suffering. The following lines from the apostle Paul express the kingdom mission of freedom:

> Submit to one another out of reverence for Christ.
> Wives, submit yourselves to your own husbands as you do to the Lord. . . .
> Husbands, love your wives, just as Christ loved the church and gave himself up for her. . . . Husbands ought to love their wives as their own bodies. He who loves his wife loves himself.
> Children, obey your parents in the Lord, for this is right. . . .
> Fathers, do not exasperate your children; instead, bring them up in the training and instruction of the Lord.
> Slaves, obey your earthly masters with respect and fear, and with sincerity of heart, just as you would obey Christ. Obey them not only to win their favor when their eye is on you, but as slaves of Christ, doing the will of God from your heart. Serve wholeheartedly, as if you were serving the Lord, not people, because you know that the Lord will reward each one for whatever good they do, whether they are slave or free.

And masters, treat your slaves in the same way. Do not threaten them, since you know that he who is both their Master and yours is in heaven, and there is no favoritism with him. (Eph. 5:21–6:9)

There is something profoundly paradoxical in these teachings, often called the "household regulations." The paradox is the freedom one senses and the obligation one sees as radically absent. In each case, people in a given status in the Roman Empire are told to order themselves[9] according to their Roman status. But instead of teaching superiority and inferiority, or instead of teaching this ordering as right and a part of some kind of "creation order," the ordering is on the basis of living under King Jesus. Jesus told Peter precisely the same thing: the sons are exempt, but in order not to offend, go pay the taxes. Here we can see a radical exemption for Jesus' followers: kingdom citizens are set free from the world's ordering system, but they are to live an orderly life because they live under King Jesus and because in so ordering themselves they can witness to a new kingdom order.

There is something radical about this. Kingdom citizens in the United States are good citizens, not because they are Americans or patriots or citizens but because they listen to a King Jesus who calls them to goodness. When I was a little boy I was next to my bed, on my knees, saying my prayers. My mother walked into the room, listened as mothers do, and then said to me, "Scot, I can't hear you." Without a moment's reflection, I said back, "I'm not talking to you." OK, I was four years old and didn't have much theology at work, but perhaps we can see in that lighthearted experience the freedom we as kingdom citizens have under King Jesus. When the state's coercive powers come our way, as a result of discernment we at times might have to say, "I'm not listening to you. I listen to King Jesus." Kingdom mission indwells that freedom.

An Ordered Life

Sixth, *kingdom mission as church mission means an ordered life under King Jesus in the context of local church fellowship.* Kingdom mission means we don't listen to the world's stories but to the kingdom story, and part of that kingdom story is that Jesus is King and has appointed some under-leaders. We are summoned to do two things at the same time: we both serve Jesus *alongside* the under-leaders, and we listen to the under-leaders as those appointed by Jesus. This gets touchy and testy and some get twitchy, and there's not space here to enter into a lengthy debate about church leadership, but one can't read the New Testament without seeing the choosing finger of Jesus pointing to some as his chosen agents (apostles) to extend the kingdom mission and to other leaders (elders, deacons, teachers, etc.) whom he appoints through the under-leaders. Yes, I need to stand here with the many, and I'm thinking of women I know and have heard from who have been abused by church leaders, who have been manipulated by church officials, or whose spiritual life has been damaged—not to mention their gifts quenched and denied—by those who exercise authority in churches. And yes, sometimes the way to be most *faithful* to Jesus' vision for the church is to separate from churches dominated by such leaders. More needs to be said, and this is not the place for that, but I can't move forward until at least this much is said. Jesus created a church where leaders would be under King Jesus, and disciples are created by Jesus to live in that kind of ordered church.

Once again, we listen to King Jesus directly and also through Jesus' under-leaders. Westerners, even more so Americans, are driven by individualism. Our heroes are folks like Henry David Thoreau, his friend Ralph Waldo Emerson, and behind them individualists like Roger Williams who eventually believed so much in a church of purity that he could not fellowship with others—he became a church of one! Our individualism leads us to think that to "listen to Jesus" means we can add "alone" or "and to no one else." But this means we are actually not listening to Jesus, because Jesus—in calling the Twelve (Mark 3:13–19; 6:7), then informing them that they would govern the kingdom (Matt. 19:28), then sending them out to disciple others (28:16–20), and then through the Spirit commissioning more and more leaders (elders, deacons, teachers) to serve both under King Jesus and under the original under-leaders—made it clear (not to put too blunt a point on it) that he uses leaders. That means your pastor and your elders and deacons.

For leaders, the words of Paul to Timothy about how leaders are to live remind us that leaders are first followers and not just leaders:

Command and teach these things. Don't let anyone look down on you because you are young, but set an example for the believers in speech, in conduct, in love, in faith and in purity. Until I come, devote yourself to the public reading of Scripture, to preaching and to teaching. Do not neglect your gift, which was given you through prophecy when the body of elders laid their hands on you.

Be diligent in these matters; give yourself wholly to them, so that everyone may see your progress. Watch your life and doctrine closely. Persevere in them, because if you do, you will save both yourself and your hearers. (1 Tim. 4:11–16)

What to say? Leaders are to be examples "in speech, in conduct, in love, in faith and in purity." They are to be devoted to Scripture and to making it known through preaching and teaching. They are to grow—so noticeably that others will take note of progress. They are to see their calling as one that leads to redemption.

But leaders are not infallible, nor were the apostles. But Jesus was, and the Infallible One told us to listen to the fallible ones because through them we would hear from Jesus. I don't know any other way to put it. God sets up local churches with leaders so we will hear from Jesus as our leaders listen to Jesus and we listen to Jesus. The writer of Hebrews says, "Remember your leaders who spoke the word of God to you." He deepens what this remembering is all about: "Consider the outcome of their way of life and imitate their faith" (Heb. 13:7). They were to ponder how their leaders lived faithfully, obediently, and lovingly as servants and to see their lives as a pattern for their walk. Yes, of course, it's rather obvious: those who are bad examples are not in view here (so find a good example rather than an excuse to do what you want).

Kingdom mission means entering into and fostering the local church. This raises the question that percolates whenever kingdom and church are drawn to one another, and it is a question I am asked in every setting where I speak about this topic: "How then should we live when it comes to the public sector?" Sometimes I'm asked this question in a more accusing way: "Are you saying we should withdraw from the public sector?" Others push in a different direction: "Are you suggesting that only 'church work' is kingdom work, and if so, what about our callings or vocations? Are they not kingdom work?" Good questions, and I hope to indicate in what follows the direction of my thinking on this.

Doing Good Deeds in the Public Sector for the Common Good

Seventh, *kingdom mission as church mission means the kingdom citizen is compelled by love to "good deeds" or "doing good" in the public sector.* The most common criticisms of the connection between kingdom and church that I have argued for here, especially when combined with framing the "world" as structured unbelief, are these: you have withdrawn the church from society, you are sectarian, or you are a separatist.[10] These are superficial criticisms. To disconnect the biblical idea of kingdom from social activism and to claim that the location of God's work in this world is not the state but the church does not entail withdrawal. It is, to use the words of someone else, "leaving without departing."[11] But the church is the church, and the world is the world. Distinguishing the two, even radically separating them, however, does not mean withdrawal. Instead, when the church is the church it is fully engaged in loving everyone as neighbors. As such, the church becomes the most lovingly, compassionately, justly, peacefully engaged segment in all the world. And yet one more response to this charge: in contending that this approach is sectarian, the accuser unwittingly makes the world the dominant and determining category. That is, to say that the church withdraws from society means the society is the primary category into which the church must learn to fit. Or if the church is of no use to the world, the church is of no use. Au contraire! The church is the primary reality into which the world and society are summoned in order to be God's world and God's society.[12]

Once again, we need to point our noses toward the Bible to see what we can learn. The first place to go is the first Christian attempt to relate the church to the state, done by the apostle Peter, who established churches in the Roman Empire in the northern provinces of Asia Minor, in today's Turkey and roughly the areas south and east of the Black Sea. His churches had experienced redemption through the unleashed powers of the resurrection and were awaiting the fullness of that redemption at the parousia of Christ (1 Pet. 1:3–12). He urged the churches to be holy, to be loving, and to develop a life of fellowship with other Christians as the church became a living embodiment of God's redemptive work (1:13–2:10). At this point Peter consciously focuses on how to live in the Roman Empire, or the world, around them. Not only do Peter's words open the spine of a new book in history, they are dramatically significant for perceiving how the Christian relates to the world. Here are Peter's formative words: "Dear friends, I urge you, as foreigners and exiles, to abstain from sinful desires, which wage war against your soul. *Live such good lives among the pagans that, though they accuse you of doing wrong, they may see your good deeds and glorify God on the day he visits us*" (2:11–12, emphasis added).

These two verses are the thesis for 1 Peter 2:13–3:12, in which Peter works out these two ideas—holiness and "good lives"—for various groups. He mentions relations to government (the Roman Empire), slaves, wives, husbands, and the family of God, and this leads to reflections on suffering for "good lives" in this world. I want to draw our attention to one line: "Live such good lives among the pagans that, though they accuse you of doing wrong, they may see your good deeds and glorify God on the day he visits us" (2:12).

Peter is writing to marginalized kingdom citizens. Some read "foreigners and exiles" in 2:11 as language about life as a *spiritual* pilgrimage until heaven, but the more accurate reading is to see the *social* condition of the Christians. They really were exiles and temporary residents in the Roman Empire[13] and needed wisdom to negotiate their precarious location. Think of them as migrant workers. Peter's theory is simple: *be holy, be loving, and do good.* I focus on "do good" because it emerges out of the other two—that is, out of a loving, holy life. (We will talk about love and holiness in chap. 10 below.) Their "lives," or their "conduct" (Greek: *anastrophe*), were to be marked by moral excellence, virtue, and goodness. Their "good life" was to be shaped by "good deeds."

But what did Peter really have in mind? This is where Peter uses words that by and large are missed by most today. I will quote the verses and italicize the words that reveal what he means by "good deeds."

. . . or to governors, who are sent by him to punish those who do wrong and to commend those *who do right*. (1 Pet. 2:14)

For it is God's will that *by doing good* you should silence the ignorant talk of foolish people. (2:15)

But how is it to your credit if you receive a beating for doing wrong and endure it? But if you suffer for *doing good* and you endure it, this is commendable before God. (2:20)

... like Sarah, who obeyed Abraham and called him her lord. You are her daughters if you *do what is right* and do not give way to fear. (3:6)

For it is better, if it is God's will, to suffer *for doing good* than for doing evil. (3:17)

So then, those who suffer according to God's will should commit themselves to their faithful Creator and continue *to do good*. (4:19)

The word Peter is using is built on two words, "good" and "doing" (*agathopoieo, agathapoios, agathapoiia*), and it describes those who are marked by pleasing, good, and noble moral behaviors—kindness, generosity, compassion, obedience, and civic virtues. But there's more: this term was often used to describe Roman and Greek citizens who *acted benevolently in the public sector for the common good*. Bruce Winter, who has studied early Christian relations to the state, describes such acts of benevolence in concrete details, and this opens up for us what Peter had in mind with his terms cited above.

> Benefactions included
> supplying grain in times of necessity by diverting the grain-carrying ships to the city,
> forcing down the price by selling it in the market below the asking rate,
> erecting public buildings or adorning old buildings with marble revetments such as in Corinth,
> refurbishing the theatre,
> widening roads,
> helping in the construction of public utilities,
> going on embassies to gain privileges for the city,
> and helping the city in times of civil upheaval.[14]

Without explicit evidence (of which there is none) it would be hard to know what specifically Peter had in mind or what specifically those early Christians did in the public sector, but we can be confident they were encouraged to engage in public benefaction like this list if they were able. Two very important conclusions: first, Christians were expected to be good citizens by participating in the community, and second, Peter doesn't come close to describing benevolence as kingdom work. Like everyone else in the Bible, Peter saw kingdom as the realm of redemption and the redeemed, not what followers of Jesus did in the public sector.

The final observation from 1 Peter 2:11–12 is that good deeds solicit, inherently and unavoidably, the praise of the powers of this world because good deeds are unimpeachable. Peter says they will see your "good deeds" and "glorify God," and in this Peter sounds like Jesus, who said much the same about being salt and light (Matt. 5:13–16). These deeds aren't done *in order to* solicit their praise; they are done out of obedience and love, and their inherent goodness is *inherently praiseworthy*. Put in another way, Peter urges what Miroslav Volf calls a "soft" difference; strong, but not hard. This "soft difference is the missionary side of following in the steps of the crucified Messiah." He continues, "The softness which should characterize the very being of Christians—I am tempted to call it 'ontic gentleness'—must not be given up even when we are (from our own perspective) persuaded that others are wrong or evil."[15]

What Peter is urging here is what Jeremiah urged the exiles who lived in Babylon to do, which deserves to be read in its entirety once again in the context of this entire kingdom, church, and world discussion, but we can only include a clip of the most pertinent lines.

> This is what the LORD Almighty, the God of Israel, says to all those I carried into exile from Jerusalem to Babylon: "Build houses and settle down; plant gardens and eat what they produce. Marry and have sons and daughters; find wives for your sons and give your daughters in marriage, so that they too may have sons and daughters. Increase in number there; do not decrease. Also, seek the peace and prosperity of the city to which I have carried you into exile. Pray to the LORD for it, because if it prospers, you too will prosper." Yes, this is what the LORD Almighty, the God of Israel, says: "Do not let the prophets and diviners among you deceive you. Do not listen to the dreams

you encourage them to have. They are prophesying lies to you in my name. I have not sent them," declares the LORD. (Jer. 29:4–9)

Here is Jeremiah's wisdom: build an economically sustainable lifestyle; develop a family life; be good residents and help that city flourish; and be faithful to the covenant God made with them. That is, be good and be good citizens. That, too, is Peter's wisdom for the kingdom citizens of Jesus who dwelled in the Roman Empire. This is permanent wisdom for the Christian in the world. Peter no more thinks "good works" are kingdom work than Jeremiah thinks being good citizens is making Babylon Jerusalem. One is not the other, but not being the other does not mean choosing one or the other.

In arguing what I am arguing—that kingdom mission is church mission and that kingdom mission is not working for the common good—I am open to the criticism that I am not in favor of public action or social justice or compassion for the poor or feeding the homeless. But that can never be inferred from what I am arguing because I am 100 percent in favor of Christian engagement in social activism, an exceptional example of which is Lawndale Community Church and its clear social engagement.[16] What I am not in favor of is assigning the word "kingdom" to such actions *in order to render that action sacred or to justify that action as supernatural or to give one the sense that what she or he is doing is ultimately significant.* When we assign the word "kingdom" to good deeds in the public sector for the common good, we take a word that belongs in one place (the church) and apply it in another (the world). In so doing we run the risk of diminishing church at the expense of the world.

Missional in Vocation

Eighth, *doing good means disciples are missional in their vocation.* We now enter into a discussion that deserves at least a full book, if not two volumes, a book I am not the person to write. But I can indicate a few directions of how we can be missional in our vocation or how we can baptize our vocations into kingdom mission.

To begin with, our deep calling is to love God and to love others or, in the words of Jesus, to love our neighbor as ourselves. Jesus said this in

Mark 12:28–32, and the apostles worked it out in local church settings, first James (2:8–10), then Paul (Gal. 5:14; Rom. 12:10; 13:9), then Peter (1:22), and then John (throughout 1 John!). To be neighborly, then, is our calling, and I point you to the very clever yet demanding vision we find in Jay Pathak and Dave Runyon's book *The Art of Neighboring*, in which they provide a little map to be applied to your refrigerator on which you write the names of your eight closest neighbors.[17] Being missional can only begin when we turn bodies into neighbors.

We can intensify this when we expand neighboring into "faithful presence" in all the spaces we occupy. David Fitch and Geoff Holsclaw in *Prodigal Christianity* and Lance Ford and Brad Brisco in *The Missional Quest*,[18] to name two recent examples, speak of first, second, and third places—our homes and neighborhoods, our workplaces, and our casual-encounter places, like coffee shops. Each of these is to be seen as a place where we embody the kingdom vision of Jesus to those who are around us; that is, we become a faithful "witness" as a faithful "presence." These two observations are the foundation.

Now to vocation. The primary—let that word be given heavy emphasis— the *primary* drive of our "jobs" is *provision for ourselves and our family*. There is nothing wrong, in a capitalist world, with laboring in order to acquire sufficient funds for the sake of provision. There need be no more ultimate meaning in our labor than provision. Martin Luther, who created potholes everywhere he drove, but who also offered amazing insights about almost everything, has become a huge success for arguing that the common laborer's task is as much a vocation as the pastor's or the Reformer's. Nice idea, but it's like so much of Luther: an exaggeration with a nasty problem. Everyone today who talks about vocation seems to want to begin with Luther and then argue that we all have vocations and move on—what's the big deal?! Well, yes and no. Just because we turn ourselves (not necessarily our jobs) toward the kingdom and bathe everything we do in that kingdom—and don't forget that we have connected kingdom to church—doesn't mean every vocation is alike. Yes, every job can become a vocation when we turn it toward the kingdom and the church, but let us not think that this makes the "secular" job just as important as the "sacred" job. The first thing a job does for us is provide for us.

116

My opinion on vocation is that when our job is swallowed up by the kingdom/church mission, it becomes vocation instead of "just a job." I quote John Stackhouse with full approval: "Vocation is the divine calling to be a Christian in every mode of life, public as well as private, religious as well as secular, adult as well as juvenile, corporate as well as individual, female as well as male."[19]

Not all jobs are vocations, since not every person doing them is oriented toward the kingdom, no matter how much goodness is connected to that job. When the kingdom citizen orients himself or herself entirely toward Jesus, living under King Jesus, and when that kingdom citizen joins into the local kingdom fellowship as the embodiment of the kingdom in the here and now, that kingdom citizen can turn a job into a kingdom vocation. So to cut against the grain of Luther, one's job cannot be seen as vocation until that person turns to King Jesus. What one does for the common good, then, may or may not be a vocation.

What, then, does this have to do with "kingdom work"? Golden question. Only to the degree that a person has turned his or her focus in life from the world toward the kingdom/church is a person doing kingdom work. What's more, on the basis of a kingdom life being lived, only to the degree that a person is pointing others to live under King Jesus, guiding others into the fellowship of the kingdom called church, and encouraging others to follow the moral vision of Jesus is a person doing kingdom work. Vocation, then, is kingdom mission, as long as kingdom mission is seen as gospel-shaped church mission.

Yet something must be said about what Andy Crouch calls "culture making."[20] I have for a decade or more now pointed others to J. R. R. Tolkien's marvelous story about Niggle, who painted leaves.[21] His calling in life was to paint leaves, and after his death he discovered that the leaves he was painting imperfectly were revealed to be perfect leaves in the kingdom of God. Yes, what we do we are to do as well as possible—we are to master the art of coaching or selling or buying or building or connecting or surfing the internet or creating new technology or composing pieces of music or trimming trees or constructing someone's genealogy or serving customers at the local bank or local store. We do our best because God wants our best—and to the degree that we convert what we do toward

117

the kingdom, we are doing kingdom mission work. Andy Crouch defines culture as "what we make of the world" with the materials at hand, and he's right in saying we make sense of the world by the cultures or products we create. He's also right that "the only way to change culture is to create more of it," and I enthusiastically endorse this claim. I would argue, too, that the "more" we are to create begins with a culture called "church" (or "kingdom"). The same reorientation applies to his major conclusion: "Culture—making something of the world, moving the horizons of possibility and impossibility—is what human beings do and are meant to do. Transformed culture is at the heart of God's mission in the world, and it is the call of God's redeemed people. But changing the world is the one thing we cannot do."[22]

Now to put this all together: yes, humans are called to create culture. How? By entering into that special culture Jesus is creating—the church, the kingdom—and by entering we become people on mission, people with a vocation. One more way now: it is not so much *what* we do but *where what we do is headed* that makes our job a vocation. Is it headed toward the church? This is the most important question laborers today can ask.

Social Justice, Social Gospel, and Liberation Theology

Ninth, *kingdom mission means that social justice activism, the social gospel, and liberation theology are important paths for Christians to express love to those in need.* They are, to use Peter's words, forms of "doing good" or "good works."

This may sound like I don't think the social gospel or liberation theology are complete; that is precisely what I mean. In fact, I'm willing to sound the gong: the public sector and systemic elements of social activism are not kingdom mission but instead Christians "doing good" in the public sector for the common good. As such, this activism is good—very good and inevitable—but good works are not the same thing as kingdom work. Good works are the overflow of love toward those in need. Two primary expressions of this overflow today are the social gospel and liberation theology; both of these get to the heart of the Skinny Jeans approach to kingdom and social justice activism. I have reservations about each (see appendixes 1 and 2), but their fundamental orientation is inevitable for the kingdom citizen. Anyone who follows Jesus and gets swallowed into his kingdom vision will love others, and caring for the poor and the marginalized and working to remedy economic, systemic injustices are inevitable expressions of that love. Hence, an evangelical social gospel and an evangelical liberation theology are natural expressions of kingdom citizens.

In concrete terms, the civil rights movement that took root in American consciousness in a new and lasting way in the 1960s under the leadership of Martin Luther King Jr.—now carefully chronicled by Charles Marsh in his important book *The Beloved Community*[23] in terms of how faith inspired so much of what was going on—is how Christians should have (and much sooner should have) engaged racism in America. Why? Because kingdom citizens are tied not only to King Jesus, who was himself from the margins, but also because this same King Jesus taught and embodied compassion toward all, especially to those on the margins. Kingdom mission takes root in the church, I am arguing, and spills over into the public *because of the moral fellowship and vision created by King Jesus.* The fundamental problem of the civil rights movement was that many churches didn't catch on until it was established by law in the public sector. This is a shame to the church. The church should have shown the way, which it did at times (but not nearly enough). Multiracial and multiethnic churches today are good; they are tragically about two centuries late.[24]

But I want to explain this more. When a kingdom citizen, consumed as she might be by the vision of Jesus for a kingdom community, observes injustice in the public sector—whether racism, oppressive structures creating oppressed peoples, sexual trafficking, lack of water and toilets, or otherwise—that person's vision for what could be done is nearly always inspired by a kingdom vision. In fact, engagement is inevitable; not to engage makes a person complicit in the injustice. As Stanley Hauerwas expressed it, "What must be remembered is that Jesus came preaching a Kingdom *that makes it impossible for his followers to be indifferent to the injustices in their surrounding social orders.*"[25] The kingdom citizen is inspired by the kingdom vision to be a more loving person and to create a more just world. This is how we are to explain the social gospel and liberation theology, *and this kind of activism is entirely good.* But that doesn't make it kingdom work; it makes it good work.

Now a reminder: it is not good or just for the Christian to do this kind of social work *at the expense of striving for kingdom conditions in his or her local church.* I appeal first to Jesus, and to a text that will surprise many readers. In one of Jesus' most well-known parables, often called the parable of the sheep and the goats—that parable in which Jesus commends for eternal life those who show compassion to the "least of these"—Jesus identifies himself with the "least of these." His famous words are given in three moves (Matt. 25:35–40). First, Jesus says, "For I was hungry and you gave me something to eat, I was thirsty and you gave me something to drink, I was a stranger and you invited me in, I needed clothes and you clothed me, I was sick and you looked after me, I was in prison and you came to visit me."

But those destined to inherit eternal life in the kingdom are surprised that they had done such good works for *Jesus.* (They are not surprised they had done such good works.) "Then the righteous will answer him, 'Lord, when did we see you hungry and feed you, or thirsty and give you something to drink? When did we see you a stranger and invite you in, or needing clothes and clothe you? When did we see you sick or in prison and go to visit you?'" So Jesus clarifies that in doing this for "the least of these" they had done those good works *to him.* "The King will reply, 'Truly I tell you, whatever you did for one of the least of these brothers and sisters of mine, you did for me.'"

These verses are routinely taken to be about compassion for the poor in general, for the needy in general, or for random prisoners.[26] No one denies the importance or inevitability of genuine disciples showing mercy to those in need. But there is one important omitted factor in all of the above commentary. What Jesus says is not just "the least of these." He says "the least of these *brothers and sisters of mine.*" The Greek only has "brothers," but because it is generic, one can reasonably add in "and sisters." Leave that to the side and ask this question: in the Gospel of Matthew, and in the Gospels in general, to whom does Jesus refer when he uses the word "brothers"? The answer is "the followers of Jesus."[27] Notice, for instance, what Jesus says when someone informs him that his mother and brothers and sisters are at the door wanting to speak to him. "'Who is my mother, and who are my brothers?' Pointing to his disciples, he said, 'Here are my mother and my brothers. For whoever does the will of my Father in heaven is my brother and sister and mother'" (Matt. 12:48–50). Or this: "But you are not to be called 'Rabbi,' for you have one Teacher, *and you are all brothers*" (23:8). There is a long and noble interpretation in the history of the church that the parable of the sheep and the goats refers not to the needy in general but to the persecuted church, or to persecuted missionaries, or to persecuted followers of Jesus. One often appeals to Matthew 10:40–42 for a close parallel to this parable of Jesus.

> *Anyone who welcomes you welcomes me, and anyone who welcomes me welcomes the one who sent me.* Whoever welcomes a prophet as a prophet will receive a prophet's reward, and whoever welcomes a righteous person as a righteous person will receive a righteous person's reward. And if anyone gives even a cup of cold water to one of these little ones who is my disciple, truly I tell you, that person will certainly not lose their reward. (emphasis added)

Here solidarity with Jesus is expressed when one receives the missionary of Jesus. Even more important, notice that *Jesus extends himself in those whom he sends*, in his kingdom followers. Those sent are the presence of Jesus; reception of those sent is reception of Jesus. This is what is at work in the parable of the sheep and the goats, not general compassion for the poor (however important that might be).

I think the followers-of-Jesus interpretation is right for the parable, and it reveals the importance of showing mercy *especially* to those who follow Jesus *as an act of solidarity with King Jesus and his kingdom people*. Once again, we need not infer any sort of view that suggests I am not in favor of mercy to those who are in need. Rather, this text is not a good text to support that activism. That kind of support can be found in the "good works" tradition of Matthew 5:13–16 and especially in Peter.

Next I appeal to Paul in Galatians 6:10: "Therefore, as we have opportunity, let us do good to all people, especially to those who belong to the family of believers." Notice the order: first the church and kingdom, and then society and culture and world. When social activism decenters or replaces the church, it becomes a kind of idolatry in which our allegiance is no longer to Jesus and the kingdom but to the world. But when the kingdom citizen's activism in the local church spills over into the world, that is the "good work" about which Peter is speaking. This is the place—this "spilling over" of kingdom goods into the world—where social gospeling and liberation theology belong. If the activism is designed to make the world a better place, it is "good works," but it is not kingdom mission. If it is designed to make the church a better place, it is kingdom mission and not "good works." Social gospel and liberation theology activism, then, when assessed by kingdom mission, are measured by one criterion: *their impact on edification of the local church.*

Kingdom Protests

Finally, and something that cannot be developed in this context, we cannot avoid a reality: sometimes churches fail to embody the kingdom, and this means at times that perception of kingdom mission turns against the realities of church life. In other words, the kingdom sometimes protests the inadequacies and failures of the church. But we can reverse the terms: sometimes the biblical teachings about church sharply criticize the realities of church life now. Pastors and church people who abuse children are to be protested because the church is to embody the kingdom. Women must protest pastors and church authorities and structures that quench the gifts God's Spirit has given to women. I spoke recently to a large gathering of women about kingdom and church, and the single most telling criticism I heard (more than a few times) was this: "I can't go to church because it abuses me and the gifts God has given me." What is the solution here? The solution is not to think that parachurch organizations are adequate substitutions for the church, for they aren't. Instead, that woman is to work—slowly if necessary, respectfully always, but relentlessly—at informing the church of what the New Testament teaches and what God is raising up women to do. That is, in such situations the kingdom-as-church realities rise up in protest against the suppressing of gifts on the basis of gender—and I could say the same about race, about economic status, and about educational accomplishments—and let's add ageism to the mix. The kingdom of God reveals what God wants for his people in the church, and when the church falls short, the kingdom-as-church protests and calls us to God's mission for *all* of God's people.

I want now to sum up what kingdom mission is: kingdom mission flows from the kingdom story, and that story focuses on God at work in history as God brings that history to its focal point in Jesus as King. That kingdom story, then, focuses on God as King through King Jesus. That story counters all other stories, especially stories that make humans kings and queens and thereby become stories of idolatry. Kingdom mission always has been and always will be contextually expressed: there is no "universal" context-less kingdom or kingdom mission. This kingdom story tells the story of a kingdom; kingdom is a people, and that means kingdom mission is about forming the people of God. That is, kingdom mission forms a kingdom people and that kingdom people in the present world is the church. This means kingdom mission is all about forming and enhancing local churches as expressions of the kingdom of God in this world. Which leads us back to a central reality of kingdom theology: there is no kingdom without a King. We turn now to the King of the kingdom.

8

THE KING OF THE KINGDOM

W hen Jesus announced the arrival of the "kingdom" and then
said "*of God*," he evoked a myriad of possibilities for ordinary
Galileans. But surely they asked, "Who is king?" And then
asked, "Kingdom of *God*?" Yet one more followed: "How so?" Tom Wright
has driven his chariot loudly throughout the land of biblical studies for
two decades announcing that Jesus' message was that God was returning
to Zion, and eventually Wright settled on the formula that Jesus was God
become King.[1] Indeed, God is king, but God rules through his Son, the
Messiah, the Lord, King Jesus.

What does it mean, then, to say in Jesus' world that God was King?

God the King

A good text to remind us of the truth of God's dynamic dominion and
rule of the entire cosmos is Psalm 145:11–13.

> They [God's works] tell of the glory of your kingdom
>   and speak of your might,
> so that all people may know of your mighty acts
>   and the glorious splendor of your kingdom.

125

> Your kingdom is an everlasting kingdom,
>> and your dominion endures through all generations.

Here "kingdom" is surrounded by terms of God's dynamic rule: "glory," "might," "mighty acts," and "dominion." I hasten to add that when a first-century Jew heard this psalm read aloud, he or she knew that this was *Israel's* kingdom extending beyond her borders and reaching into the far corners of the empires of this world. But what strikes the hearer is that *God rules.*

In the twentieth century the Swiss theologian Karl Barth emphasized this element of the kingdom of God, not only speaking of God's assertion of rule over the "lordship of the lordless powers" but contending that "kingdom of God" means nothing more and nothing less than *God himself ruling.*[2] Barth's words about the kingdom as God's own coming to humans are worth repeating even if, as is typical when reading Barth, more than one reading is needed in order to take it all in! He wrote, "In coming he [God] illumines, establishes, asserts, and protects his questioned, obscured, and threatened right to man and therefore man's own right, his right to life, which is negated apart from God's own right as Lord and King."

Jesus, in calling it the kingdom *of God*, makes it abundantly clear that we are now dealing with God's own assertion of divine rule.

Kings Determine the Character of the Kingdom

God accommodated Israel with a king, we must remember from 1 Samuel 8. In accommodating Israel, though, God sets out what the ideal king is to be like, because the king is designed to represent God to the nation. Undoubtedly the leading baritone in this ideal choir of ideas is Psalm 72.[3] We should perhaps quote the entire psalm to keep it in mind, but I italicize the theme of justice to bring to the fore what kings are to be like.

> Of Solomon [added later].
>
> Endow the king with your *justice*, O God,
>> the royal son with your *righteousness*.
> May he judge your people in *righteousness*,
>> your afflicted ones with *justice*.

126

May the mountains bring prosperity to the people,
    the hills the fruit of *righteousness.*
May he defend the afflicted among the people
    and save the children of the needy;
    may he crush the oppressor.
May he endure as long as the sun,
    as long as the moon, through all generations.
May he be like rain falling on a mown field,
    like showers watering the earth.
In his days may the righteous flourish
    and prosperity abound till the moon is no more.

May he rule from sea to sea
    and from the River to the ends of the earth.
May the desert tribes bow before him
    and his enemies lick the dust.
May the kings of Tarshish and of distant shores
    bring tribute to him.
May the kings of Sheba and Seba
    present him gifts.
May all kings bow down to him
    and all nations serve him.

For he will deliver the needy who cry out,
    the afflicted who have no one to help.
He will take pity on the weak and the needy
    and save the needy from death.
He will rescue them from oppression and violence,
    for precious is their blood in his sight.

Long may he live!
    May gold from Sheba be given him.
May people ever pray for him
    and bless him all day long.
May grain abound throughout the land;
    on the tops of the hills may it sway.
May the crops flourish like Lebanon
    and thrive like the grass of the field.
May his name endure forever;
    may it continue as long as the sun.

Then all nations will be blessed through him,
and they will call him blessed.

Praise be to the LORD God, the God of Israel,
who alone does marvelous deeds.
Praise be to his glorious name forever;
may the whole earth be filled with his glory.
Amen and Amen.

This ideal-king psalm leads to one of the most important observations about kings and kingdoms: *kings determine what their kingdoms are like.* To make this more specific, titles for a king shape both how we understand that king and what that king's kingdom will be like. So a king's associated names will shape the kingdom's associations. Jumping all the way now to the first century, we make this claim: *What we call Jesus—his titles—determines what the kingdom is like.* If Jesus is Lord, the kingdom is composed of those who live under his lordship. If he is Son of God . . . if he is Son of Man . . . if he is Messiah . . . if he is Savior . . . if he is Rabbi . . . Each of these titles does three things:

• A title will interpret Jesus.
• A title will reveal something about the kingdom.
• A title will define our relationship to Jesus.

If I call Jesus "Lord," I interpret Jesus as the Lord; I imply that in his kingdom he exercises lordship; and I surrender myself to his lordship in that kingdom. In this chapter we will look at three titles: Jesus as Son of Man, Jesus as Son of God, and Jesus as Messiah. The first expresses Jesus' self-title; the second, the title of his spectators; and the third title, the interpretation of his disciples.[4]

Jesus as Son of Man: Self-Interpretation

Something went wildly wrong early on with the title "Son of Man," and ever since we've had to work our way around it like mowing around a big tree with wild roots in the yard. You heard it and I heard it, and it's almost completely backward: "Son of Man" refers to Jesus' humanity while "Son of God" refers to his deity.[5] This is simply wrong. Apart from one isolated use by Stephen in Acts 7:56, Jesus is the only one to use the title "Son of Man" in reference to himself. It is, then, Jesus' self-interpretive title. In this title we see what Jesus thought of himself.

The title "Son of Man" translates the Aramaic *bar enasha*, where *bar* means "son of" and *enasha* means "man." In the language of Jesus, a "son of" was a representative of a type, in this case "a son" who represents "man." Hence, the title means at some level "the Man" or "the Representative Man." The Common English Bible translates "son of man" as "the Human One." If we were to stop with the linguistic evidence, we'd have to agree with the widespread belief that "Son of Man" refers to Jesus as a human being—but we'd completely fail if we stopped there. There is a background to "Son of Man" that alters the entire story, and it is a background that illuminates what kingdom means and what it means to live as a kingdom citizen.

There are three senses to the title "Son of Man" in the Gospels. First, "Son of Man" sometimes means a Human One—that is, it refers to humans in general—and most point to Mark 2:28 and Matthew 12:32 to support this view. To paraphrase one view of these two verses: humans are more important than the Sabbath and what one says against humans is forgivable. A second usage of "Son of Man" is when Jesus refers to himself as the one who suffers (e.g., Mark 8:31). But I want to concentrate on the third usage.

On a number of occasions Jesus refers to himself as Son of Man when he is referring to his exalted status and his coming again. These sayings are so dramatic, and one must say egocentric, that they not only chase away the idea that "Son of Man" refers to Jesus' humanity, but they lead us to the genius of Jesus' own relation to the kingdom, to his profound lordship, and they brush up against a claim for deity.

> As they were coming down the mountain, Jesus gave them orders not to tell anyone what they had seen until the Son of Man had risen from the dead. (Mark 9:9)

> "If anyone is ashamed of me and my words in this adulterous and sinful generation, the Son of Man will be ashamed of them when he comes in his Father's glory with the holy angels." (Mark 8:38)

"I am," said Jesus. "And you will see the Son of Man sitting at the right hand of the Mighty One and coming on the clouds of heaven." (Mark 14:62)

"When you are persecuted in one place, flee to another. Truly I tell you, you will not finish going through the towns of Israel before the Son of Man comes." (Matt. 10:23)

"When the Son of Man comes in his glory, and all the angels with him, he will sit on his glorious throne." (Matt. 25:31)

"I tell you, whoever publicly acknowledges me before others, the Son of Man will also acknowledge before the angels of God." (Luke 12:8)

Briefly, the Son of Man—remember, this is Jesus talking about himself—is raised, will come again, and will judge from God's throne. Where did such an idea come from? Daniel Boyarin once observed that "the Son of Man is the name of a narrative and its protagonist."[6] That is, when Jesus uses "Son of Man," he's got a story in mind.

You can find it in Daniel 7, and what it records is nothing less than the plan of God in history when God restores his own rule over his people. Daniel sees four beasts emerge from the sea, beasts that are like a lion, like a bear, and like a leopard, and then a fourth that is without a "like," and so undefined, but terrifyingly powerful, with large iron teeth that it uses to crush its enemies. It has ten horns, one of which begins taking on a life of its own, becoming a horn full of egomania and boastful speech. God, here called the Ancient of Days, sets up judgment against the egomaniac. Then comes the one "like a son of man"—that is, like a human being. He came with "the clouds of heaven," and the Ancient of Days grants him "authority, glory, and sovereign power; all nations and peoples of every language worshiped him." The language that follows sounds like the promise to David: "His dominion is an everlasting dominion that will not pass away, and his kingdom is one that will never be destroyed" (Dan. 7:14). Daniel's son of man clearly is a king, a future David-like king.

Daniel watches it all, but his mental feet are suddenly wobbly, so an angel interprets the vision: the four beasts are four kings "that will rise from the earth" (7:17). Just who these beasts are is up for interpretation, but few

130

doubt that the fourth beast is Rome. Hence, the four beasts are probably Babylon, Medo-Persia, Greece, and Rome. By the time the vision is over we learn that the one like a son of man both suffers and will be exalted before God, the Ancient of Days, and this son of man will rule over the kingdom.

Now to the connection between Jesus and the title "Son of Man": *Jesus chose "Son of Man" to interpret himself because this term ties together both suffering and vindication to his vocation to rule.* The character of the king shapes the character of the kingdom. So, by becoming part of the kingdom of this Son-of-Man-Jesus, we are connected to the one who suffers and is exalted.

What title did others give to Jesus?

Jesus as Son of God: Others' Interpretation

Many think of the *deity* of Christ when "Son of God" is used. But we first must ask what "Son of God" would have meant in the world of Jesus, where that term was used for Israel's king and, to cast our vision beyond the land of Israel, for the emperor of Rome.[7] What is striking in the Synoptic Gospels is that "Son of God" is not so much the language of Jesus as it is far more often the language of Jesus' opponents.[8] As compared to how Jesus talks about himself (as Son of Man), others often call him Son of God; here is a listing of those who call Jesus Son of God:

- the devil (Matt. 4:3, 6)
- the demonized (8:29)
- the high priest (26:63)
- opponents at the cross (27:43)
- Jewish leaders (John 19:7)
- Mark's Gospel (Mark 1:1)
- the disciples (Matt. 14:33)
- the centurion (27:54)
- Gabriel (Luke 1:35)
- Nathanael (John 1:49)
- Martha (11:27)
- John's Gospel (20:31)

We surely can't know all that each of these various opponents and friends had in mind when they called Jesus Son of God, but there is a bottom to this water that can be seen, and it can be sketched in two basic points. The *opponents* call him Son of God when they encounter a claim by Jesus that transcends what they think he ought to be claiming for himself, but the *friends* of Jesus call him Son of God because they think he is "Messiah," the King of Israel. To call Jesus Son of God, then, was to say he was the Messianic King.

This latter use is just what a normal Jewish reader of the Bible would think. "Son of God" in the Old Testament is a title used for the king of Israel. It begins when God calls David his son (2 Sam. 7:8–16), but my favorite expression is found in Psalm 2:7: "You are my son; today I have become your father." On top of this, the whole Roman Empire referred to Caesar Augustus as the son of God.[9] We can boil this down to an astounding conclusion: when people called Jesus Son of God they were unquestionably claiming he was the King. Once again, kings shape their kingdom in their own image, and that means the mission of the king will be shaped by the king and his kingdom—but more on that below.

Jesus as Messiah: Disciples' Interpretation

Our concern is not whether Jesus thought he was the Messiah[10] but whether his followers did; and if they did, what they meant by it; and what Jesus thought of what they thought! The evangelists, who have to be seen as über-disciples of Jesus, call Jesus "Messiah" on a regular basis, none more forcefully than Mark and Matthew in their opening lines. Mark 1:1: "The beginning of the good news about Jesus the Messiah, the Son of God," and Matthew 1:1: "This is the genealogy of Jesus the Messiah the son of David, the son of Abraham." John closes off his Gospel by revealing his intent: "But these are written that you may believe that Jesus is the Messiah, the Son of God, and that by believing you may have life in his name" (20:31). The evangelists write "Messiah" into their Gospels as a way of interpreting Jesus for their readers. Luke, too: "Today in the town of David a Savior has been born to you; he is the Messiah, the Lord" (Luke 2:11). Peter's confession of Jesus as Messiah led to the great revelation: Yes, Jesus is Messiah, but he will die on a cross. Peter's confession also

132

leads to the first powerful discipleship lesson by Jesus, a lesson repeated three or four times, that if he is Messiah and if he is to die on the cross before the resurrection, then discipleship is cruciform (Mark 8:27–30, then 8:31–33, then 8:34–9:1). In other words, the character of the king shapes the character of the kingdom and life for its citizens.

The evidence in the Gospels leads to these observations: anticipation of the Messiah was in the air; Jesus' ministry provoked questions about whether or not he was that Messiah; some said yes and some said no. Clearly, his followers all thought he was the Messiah, which leads to what Jews at the time of Jesus thought "Messiah" meant.[11]

The word "messiah" comes from the Hebrew word for "smear" or "anoint" (usually with oil), and they "smeared with oil" the kings of Israel and Judah (1 Sam. 9:16; 10:1; 16:1, 12–13; 1 Kings 1:34, 39). Prophets could be "oiled" too (1 Kings 19:15–16). In the story of Israel it was the prophets who over and over announced a future kingdom and, by inference, a Davidic king, who would rescue the nation from its enemies, restore Israel to observance of the Torah, revive the kingdom, and rule the kingdom in peace and justice. But the specific expectation of a Messiah in the sense of a Davidic king began to flourish only in the two or three centuries leading up to the time of Jesus.[12] Jesus' words to Peter, then, either swerve around the standard Jewish expectation or, better yet, deconstruct that expectation with a tragic twist: the Messiah will die on a cross (and then be raised to new life to rule).

We sketched the Gospel texts above, so I want to narrow our discussion now to the singular contribution of Jesus to the idea of Messiah. When Peter calls Jesus Messiah (Mark 8:29), and Jesus responds by revealing that he will suffer and rise again (8:31) and by rebuking Peter's perceptions (8:32), we enter into the unique interpretation of "Messiah" by Jesus and the church: *the Messiah will rule, but only after dying the death of others and by rising and being exalted far above all rule.* Jesus is that Messiah, but his kind of Messiah bewilders his contemporaries, including his closest followers. He cannot be embraced as Messiah until his story is embraced; that story is the life, death, burial, and resurrection of Jesus, and it is that life story that shapes what "Messiah" means. Jesus is the gospel-shaped King. There is no other messianic story like the one Jesus told and lived.

Summary

Three titles, three interpretations of Jesus, but each title *tells the same basic story in different ways.* They are, to use musical terms, variations on a theme. That old A-B-A' story is told in each title but with a radical shift because in Jesus *the story is cruciform*: God now rules through a king who died and was raised in order to rule. Now we must recall that a kingdom gains its profile from its king, and that means the cruciform King Jesus creates a cruciform kingdom. The Son of Man suffered and was vindicated; the royal Son of God is confessed at the cross; and the Messiah cannot be comprehended until he is seen as the one who will die and then be exalted to the throne of God. This discussion about Jesus Christ leads to three implications for kingdom mission.

Kingdom Mission Is Determined by Who Jesus Is

We need to reclaim a more robust Christology and let it work its way through us into mission. We must begin, then, with Jesus and not with our social visions or our grandest ideas. Let the words of Karl Barth set the tone for what follows:

> We must emphasize the "he" [Jesus Christ]—not, then, an it, however lofty or profound;
>> not a transcendent world of light;
>> not an original and finally binding moral law;
>> not a self-resting and self-moved ground of being as the origin and goal of all being;
>> not a new philosophy, pedagogy, or politics asserting itself as better or the best;
>> not a quintessence of personal human life either exemplary in love, purity, humility, and so forth, or fascinating in its originality;
>> and, finally, not a Christian dogmatics triumphantly proclaiming the triumph of grace,
>> not a doctrine about him,
>> not a Christology,
>> not a doctrine of the kingdom of God.[13]

134

Simply and solely *he himself*: accomplishing and completing God's work for the salvation of the world, that is, its reconciliation to God; speaking without reservation or subtraction God's word to all people without exception; *he*, this man in the history of his life and word and work and passion and death. Whoever knew and loved and proclaimed him knew and loved and proclaimed the imminent kingdom of God. Speaking about God's kingdom could only mean telling his story.

One need say no more, though the force of the genre of this book demands that more be said. But it must be reiterated that no more than what Barth has said need be said. Kingdom mission begins and ends with Jesus, the cruciform King.

Kingdom Mission Must Embrace the Full Story of King Jesus

My contention is that the three titles we explored—Son of Man, Son of God, and Messiah—are not only the three central titles for Jesus in the Gospels, but they are each a variation on the same theme in the kingdom story. Each tells the story of Jesus as one who is sent by God to bring fulfillment to Israel's story by reclaiming the rule of God in this world. Each tells the story of Jesus' full life: he was born of a virgin, lived a very Jewish life, declared the kingdom with himself at the center, formed a group of followers, died both as a victim of injustice and as an act of God to end injustice by dying the death of others, and was raised to the right hand of the Father to rule. Nothing less will do. More important, until we get the fullness of this story on the table, kingdom mission will be sold short. When we do, we learn that mission is actually not the first word, but Christ is; we gain a new understanding of evangelism; we discover that genuine kingdom mission is cruciform, shaped by and toward the cross; and we also are reformed into the hope of the kingdom. All these flow directly from seeing the first word as Jesus.

"Mission" Is Not the First Word

Although "mission" is not the first word, sometimes people approach it as if it were. That is, for some, one's mission determines one's Christology, and Christ is then *used* for an agenda. For example, as can be found in appendix 2 under the theme of liberation, liberation theologians have a mission: the economic and social liberation of the marginalized. A Christ designed for that liberation is often a king who speaks prophetically and leads the charge into liberation for the poor, while other elements of the Christology are discarded as useless for the mission.[14] But this approach gets things backward: Christology ought to shape mission, rather than mission shaping Christology. I find this backward approach in Elisabeth Moltmann-Wendel,[15] who rejected the "traditional German Pauline Christ, crucified and risen, who is at the centre of theological statements," in order to embrace "the Jesus of Luke 4 who proclaims freedom to the prisoners." This leads her ultimately, then, to reframe justification by faith as "I am good. I am whole. I am beautiful." Without undoing the fundamental importance of Luke 4, let us not deny Romans 3, or we will have a Christology that no longer fits the New Testament.

Evangelism Transformed

Evangelism is transformed when the full story of Jesus becomes the center of the Christian message. Instead of telling a story of Jesus as (only the) Savior or, even more narrowly, of the need for humans to escape the torments of hell and Jesus as the escape route, kingdom mission evangelism declares Jesus as King and calls people to answer the central question of evangelism: "Who is Jesus?" What they say determines how they live.

Kingdom Mission Is Cruciform

Kingdom mission shaped by the titles for Jesus calls for a *cruciform message*. This message confesses that Jesus died

with us,
instead of us,
and for us.

Jesus' death was first the death of a human, and it was an unjust death, as the apostle Peter states in Acts 10:39–40: "They killed him," he says of the Jewish leaders who were propped up by Roman law and power, "but God raised him from the dead." Jesus experienced the death we all die, and in so dying he died *with* us. We find in him the solidarity of God in our pain. Not only did he die with us, but he died *instead* of us. We deserve death because we are sinners, and death is the consequence of sin. He does not deserve death because he is sinless, but "God made him who had no sin to be sin for us" (2 Cor. 5:21). He died because he shouldered our sin. Therefore, he died our death. We call this *vicarious* or *substitutionary atonement*. Peter himself teaches substitutionary atonement explicitly at 1 Peter 2:24: "'He himself bore our sins' in his body on the cross." Paul says this with clarity on two occasions.

> Christ redeemed us from the curse of the law by becoming a curse for us, for it is written: "Cursed is everyone who is hung on a pole." (Gal. 3:13)

> God made him who had no sin to be sin for us, so that in him we might become the righteousness of God. (2 Cor. 5:21)

In addition to Jesus dying *instead* of us, he also died *for* us. His death procures benefits for us—namely, the elimination of guilt before God, the forgiveness of sins, and the reestablishment of a peaceful relationship with God (Rom. 5:1–2).

Kingdom Mission Establishes Hope

Kingdom Christology challenges Western cynicism's cold shoulder to hope and its surrender to cultures of death with the message of hope. Kingdom Christology knows that Jesus indeed died *but came out of the other side of death with new creation life*. The last word for kingdom mission, then, is not death, expressed in cynical despair and flippant apathy and fearful living. The last word is the resurrected life of Jesus who embraces us and carries us into that same new creation life. This hope is not the blind hope of positive thinking served up on the pragmatic dish that "at least optimism makes us happier." This hope is solely grounded in the conquering of death by the crucified Messiah. This resurrection gives the noble courage to tear down injustices, to welcome to the table those who are unlike us, and to live a life that draws its strength from the conviction that the kingdom now will someday be the kingdom then.

Kingdom Mission Is Incarnational

Kingdom mission is grounded in kingdom Christology, and the heart of Christology is the incarnation, God-become-human. Some early great theologians framed incarnation and its impact this way: he became what we are so we could become what he is. Athanasius said the same in a much more provocative way: "For he was made man that we might be made God."[16] I'd rather not try to unravel those words of Alexandria's famous theologian but instead draw his words into our discussion: Kingdom Christology is incarnational, and, since Christology shapes kingdom, kingdom mission is incarnational. We are to learn to avoid using the word "incarnation" cheaply. God alone is incarnate in Jesus Christ. God becomes what we are. We cannot become what others are *in the way God did*. God *ontologically* enters into our condition so that he is *completely identified* with us. We mimic the incarnation when we enter into the conditions of others in order to mediate redemption so that they can enter into the conditions of the kingdom. Our "incarnation" is the human attempt to go where God went, so that we can mediate where God wants people to go.

But there is more to it than "becoming what we are," because the "what we are" was dead and sinful. So the "becoming" is a becoming-sin and an entering-death. If we want to be accurate about "incarnation," we have to define it as becoming death in order to bring life. In a shorter formula, incarnation means dying in order to bring someone else life.

In the general and more defined sense, then, kingdom mission *must be incarnational*. We, too, must leave in order to lead others to find God; we, too, must become what others are in order to help them to become what God wants for them; and we, too, are to morph in order to guide others into kingdom transformation. We must die so that others may live.

For me the apostle Paul's words, italicized for emphasis, in 1 Corinthians 9:19–23 are the prime example of incarnational mission.

Though I am free and belong to no one, *I have made myself a slave to everyone*, to win as many as possible. To the Jews *I became like a Jew*, to win the Jews. To those under the law *I became like one under the law* (though I myself am not under the law), so as to win those under the law. To those not having the law *I became like one not having the law* (though I am not free from God's law but am under Christ's law), so as to win those not having the law. To the weak *I became weak*, to win the weak. *I have become all things to all people* so that by all possible means I might save some. I do all this for the sake of the gospel, that I may share in its blessings.

Four Themes of One Incarnational Kingdom Mission

What does a kingdom mission that focuses on incarnation look like today? Tim Dickau, in a ministry in Vancouver, has sketched four themes at work in a postmodern incarnational ministry that represent the move from our world toward the healing word of incarnational redemption. In the following quotation from his book, I have italicized the four specific kinds of incarnational missional practices at work in this missional church community:

I have described these [missional and incarnational] practices as four trajectories, which call upon the church to participate in the mission of God by moving:

1. from isolation to community towards *radical hospitality*;
2. from homogeneity to diversity towards *shared life among cultures*;
3. from charity to friendship towards *seeking justice for the least*;
4. from the confrontation of idolatries to repentance towards *new life in Christ*.[17]

We are today tempted into or already dwelling in isolation, homogeneity, charity (or benevolence), and idolatries. These are what we die to in order to bring about hospitality, shared life in diversity, justice for the least, and new life in Christ. Again, this is an example of theoretical reflections on what incarnational dying-to-bring-life looks like.

The Core Pattern of Incarnation: Dying to Bring Life

The pattern of God's incarnation in Christ is our pattern: it is the pattern of dying and rising, the pattern of dying to self—who we are, what we have, where we are, what we like, what we want—in order to live unto God. The incarnational kingdom mission, then, means that we die to self *so others can live*. "Coach" (Wayne Gordon) has died a million deaths since he graduated from Wheaton College to become a football coach in the Lawndale neighborhood of Chicago.[18] He died the death of time when he formed a Bible study for young players who needed spiritual and social wisdom; he died the death of success as a coach when he became the founding pastor of Lawndale Community Church; he died the death of safety when he got married and then nurtured a family in a crime-stricken neighborhood of Chicago; he died the death of financial security when he threw himself onto the wheel of church ministries that demanded even more than he could give and took what he had until he learned to trust in God for all that he has; he died the death of controlling his schedule when he devoted himself to other people to teach and train them into a life of holiness and love; he died the death of power when he chose to become co-pastor and serve his associate; he died the death of sleep when he committed himself to spill Lawndale Community Church's energies into restoring the neighborhood.

On the other side of an incarnational kingdom mission is the new life of the resurrection. Thousands worship God because of that death; thousands have been discipled because of that death; dozens have been called into ministry because of that death; families have been redeemed, criminals have been set free, pushers have repented, prostitutes have been rescued—all by that death; buildings have been restored to new creation life, while other buildings have been raised from nothing but rubble and faith to provide a place for holistic care for the neighborhood.

The Incarnation as Kingdom Community

In the United States, where the church is suffering at the hands of bad practices, abusive priests and pastors, and diminishing credibility, there are two features of evangelism that need special focus: the church itself as a witness to the gospel and individuals dwelling in loving, credible ways with their neighbors. The text cited in the previous section from Acts 2:42–47 notably ends with these words: "[The church was] enjoying the favor of all the people. And the Lord added to their number daily those who were being saved." Credible living makes for credible witness to the truth of the gospel. Furthermore, when Christians love their neighbors, they offer to others the most credible element of the gospel: love spreads the very essence of God's mission, which is to dwell with us in love and for us to dwell with God and one another in love. To love is to spread who God is. I recently read the conversion story of Kirsten Powers, a well-known news reporter, and what jumped off the page were the two features I mentioned: a credible church and a loving friend.

When I went away to college, whatever little faith I had, I lost. I ended up graduating from college. I worked in the Clinton administration. All my friends were secular liberals. At this point, I really got even more deeply into an incredibly secular world because now, all my friends were basically atheists, or if they had any kind of spirituality, they were very hostile towards religion, Christianity in particular. So, I really didn't have any interest in it.

I started dating someone who went to Tim Keller's church, Redeemer Presbyterian in New York City. Out of curiosity, I went with him. But I told him upfront that I would never become a Christian; that it's never going to happen. After about six or seven months, I began to think that the weight of history is more on the side of what [I was hearing at this church] than not. Tim Keller had made such a strong case, that I began to think it's not even smart to reject this. It just doesn't seem like a good intellectual decision.

Really, it was like God sort of invaded my life. It was very unwelcome. I didn't like it. Obviously, I started having a lot of different experiences where I felt God was doing a lot of things in my life. It's kind of hard to describe, but I did have this moment where the scales just fell off of my eyes, where I was saying, "this is just totally true, I don't even have any doubt." . . . I don't really feel like I had any courage when I became a Christian, I just gave in. I wasn't courageous; I didn't have any choice. I kept trying to not believe but I just couldn't avoid [accepting Christ]. If I could have avoided it, I would have. There is nothing convenient about it in my life or in the world I live in. It's not like living in the South where everybody is a Christian. I live in a world where nobody is a believer. But God pursued me.[19]

I said "two features" influenced Kirsten Powers's conversion—the church and loving relationships—but I hasten to add a third: the gospel about Jesus Christ. The New Testament's understanding of the gospel comes to clear expression in three sets of passages in the New Testament: in 1 Corinthians

15:3–8, in the gospel sermons in Acts (chaps. 2, 3, 10–11, 13, 14), and in the Gospels themselves (which are called "the gospel" because they are the gospel!). These passages make one thing abundantly clear: the gospel is the story *about* Jesus, not just the story about you and me and what we get out of it. The aim of gospeling is to get others to surrender themselves to Jesus or to come to terms with who Jesus is. Carl Henry, in his splendid memoir called *Confessions of a Theologian*, recounts that he was converted and wanted to offer a credible witness to his family members. His own telling of his conversion story involved a quiet, lengthy struggle with God alone on a beach. Leaving the beach, he headed home in his car to be greeted by a furious thunder and lightning storm. As he waited on the storm so that he could open the barn door and park the car, "a fiery bolt of lightning, like a giant flaming arrow, seemed to pin me to the driver's seat, and a mighty roll of thunder unnerved me. When the fire fell, I knew instinctively that the Great Archer had nailed me to my own footsteps." How Henry describes things reveals that for him the gospel is *about God ruling in King Jesus*. Notice these words. A few days later he gave in with this realization: "I now knew God to be King of my life." The first opportunity to tell his mother came next, and this is how Henry describes it: "Mom, I gave my life to Jesus today."[20] It is about *God* as *King* and giving himself to *Jesus*.

Kingdom mission is church mission is gospeling about Jesus in the context of a church witness and a loving life. Anyone who calls what they are doing "kingdom work" but who does not present Jesus to others or summon others to surrender themselves to King Jesus as Lord and Savior is simply not doing kingdom mission or kingdom work. They are probably doing good work and doing social justice, but until Jesus is made known, it is not kingdom mission.

9

KINGDOM REDEMPTION
UNLEASHED

All kingdom thinking touches on what experts today often call "utopia" thinking. When the kingdom comes there will be justice, there will be peace, there will be wisdom, there will be holiness, there will be righteousness, there will be love, there will be no enemies, there will be no tension between animals and humans, there will be no famine, no death, no war, no pain, no suffering, no sickness, no disease, no bad marriages, no disobedient children . . . and on and on it goes, all depending on who is sketching the utopia. Kingdom only comes by way of total redemption. The sick have to be healed, the poor have to be enriched, the oppressed have to be empowered, the dead have to be raised, the enemies have to be vanquished, the oppressors have to be disempowered, the rich have to be divested, the crops have to bud and flourish . . . and so on.

Kingdom theology, then, must be redemptive, or it is not kingdom theology. When kingdom is divorced from redemption, it ceases being kingdom and becomes social progressivism, social conservatism, progressive politics, and the betterment of world and culture. But kingdom is a redemption-based reality, as one can see, for instance, in the parallel between Luke 21:28 and 31: "When these things begin to take place, stand up and lift up your heads, because your *redemption* is drawing near. . . . Even so, when you see these things happening, you know that the *kingdom of God* is near."

In John's Gospel this redemption is profoundly personal as well, and there are two important enter-the-kingdom sayings that reveal redemption as necessary before we can even begin to talk about kingdom, kingdom work, and kingdom mission.[1] Here they are:

> Jesus replied, "Very truly I tell you, no one can see the kingdom of God unless they are born again." (John 3:3)

> Jesus answered, "Very truly I tell you, no one can enter the kingdom of God unless they are born of water and the Spirit." (3:5)

Kingdom realities are redemptive realities. So what I want to lay out in this chapter is the next element of the kingdom: the kingdom people is a redeemed, liberated, saved people.

Here is where both Skinny Jeans and Pleated Pants theories make golden contributions, even if each has a tendency to ignore the other. The former emphasizes the social dimensions of justice and peace, while the latter emphasizes the spiritual dimensions of reconciliation with God. But kingdom redemption is holistic. To push off from the dock in the right direction, I quote Richard Bauckham's summary list of Jesus' holistic kingdom-redemptive actions, which I italicize.[2]

> In relation to demonic oppression, *conquest*;
> in relation to misrepresentation of God's rule, *sharp rebuke*;
> in relation to selfish complacency, *warning*;
> in relation to sin and failure, *forgiveness and assurance of love*;
> in relation to sickness, *healing*;
> in relation to material need, *provision of daily bread*;
> in relation to exclusion, *welcoming inclusion*;
> in relation to desire for power, *an example of humble and loving service*;
> in relation to death, *life*;

144

in relation to false peace, *painful division*,
but in relation to enmity, *reconciliation.*

These are the marks of kingdom redemption, but even these must be explored once again by pointing our noses toward Scripture.

Four Major Kingdom Redemption Texts

When the kingdom is unleashed, redemption is unleashed. In fact, it makes no sense to talk kingdom and ignore the redemptive power of God at work. Four texts will now be the focus as we examine the redemptive nature of the kingdom: Matthew 12:28; 11:2–6; 8:14–17; and that eye-opening event where Jesus turned water into wine at Cana in John 2.

Matthew 12:28

Jesus exorcised a demonized man whose symptoms were that he couldn't see or speak, and the crowds wondered if Jesus might be the "Son of David."[3] Their label for Jesus suggests that some expected the Davidic Messiah to have curative powers, and Jewish expectations about the kingdom included holistic redemption. Matthew[4] quotes Isaiah often, and these are texts that deserve our reading:

Nevertheless, there will be no more gloom for those who were in distress. In the past he humbled the land of Zebulun and the land of Naphtali, but in the future he will honor Galilee of the nations, by the Way of the Sea, beyond the Jordan—

The people walking in darkness
have seen a great light;
on those living in the land of deep darkness
a light has dawned. (Isa. 9:1–2)

In that day the deaf will hear the words of the scroll,
and out of gloom and darkness
the eyes of the blind will see.
Once more the humble will rejoice in the LORD;
the needy will rejoice in the Holy One of Israel. (29:18–19)

145

Then will the eyes of the blind be opened
    and the ears of the deaf unstopped.
Then will the lame leap like a deer,
    and the mute tongue shout for joy.
Water will gush forth in the wilderness
    and streams in the desert. (35:5–6)

"Here is my servant, whom I uphold,
    my chosen one in whom I delight;
I will put my Spirit on him,
    and he will bring justice to the nations.
He will not shout or cry out,
    or raise his voice in the streets.
A bruised reed he will not break,
    and a smoldering wick he will not snuff out.
In faithfulness he will bring forth justice;
    he will not falter or be discouraged
till he establishes justice on earth.
    In his teaching the islands will put their hope." (42:1–4)

Surely he took up our pain
    and bore our suffering,
yet we considered him punished by God,
    stricken by him, and afflicted. (53:4)

The Spirit of the Sovereign LORD is on me,
    because the LORD has anointed me
    to proclaim good news to the poor.
He has sent me to bind up the brokenhearted,
    to proclaim freedom for the captives
    and release from darkness for the prisoners. (61:1)

This string of texts from Isaiah is the resource on which Jesus drew for his kingdom theology of holistic redemption.

So when Jesus heals or exorcizes, he makes the connection to kingdom through Isaiah's visions of the kingdom. For example, when he heals the demonized man, the Pharisees pitch a fit. How? By contending that Jesus exorcizes in allegiance with the prince of demons, Beelzebul. Jesus counters with logic: kingdoms stand only if they are unified; if Satan permits his allies to exorcize, Satan would be undoing his own dark kingdom. He then makes an astounding claim in a verse that has a notable difference from its parallel in Luke, so I quote them both, with the difference in italic:

> "But if it is *by the Spirit of God* that I drive out demons, then the kingdom of God has come upon you." (Matt. 12:28)

> "But if I drive out demons *by the finger of God*, then the kingdom of God has come upon you." (Luke 11:20)[5]

When Jesus says this is the kingdom of God now at work, he is tying his miracles into the A-B-A′ story: the long-awaited kingdom is unleashed by the power of God—whether it is called "finger" or "Spirit of God."

Matthew 11:2–6

In the squalor, the manacles, and the absence of light and rights in a first-century Herodian prison,[6] John the Baptist is pondering what Jesus meant at his inaugural sermon when he said his mission was "to proclaim freedom for the prisoners" (Luke 4:18). John must be muttering, "Jesus, you promised release of prisoners. I'm a prisoner; where's the release? What part of this picture have I got wrong?" So John sends two of his own disciples to Jesus with a question: "Are you the one who is to come, or should we expect someone else?" (Matt. 11:3). Jesus tells John's disciples that they ought to go back to John and read to him in his prison cell the words of Isaiah 29:18–19, then roll the scroll to 35:5–6, and then finish off with 61:1 (each cited above). Jesus is the biblical figure laid out in the visions of Isaiah. There John can find the mission of Jesus, and what he will find in Isaiah is the very thing Jesus has been doing (with quite a noticeable shift from the days of that inaugural sermon, because this time nothing is said about setting prisoners free!).[7]

What John will learn is that the kingdom of God has begun to invade the land, and holistic redemptive powers are unleashed. So now we return to the words Jesus gave to the disciples of John, who gave them to John back in prison.

The blind receive sight.
The lame walk.
Those who have leprosy are cleansed.
The deaf hear.
The dead are raised.
The good news is proclaimed to the poor. (Matt. 11:5–6, reformatted and shortened)

Kingdom redemption is holistic, restoring eyes and legs and skin and ears and bodies to new creation life. In addition, it restores the formerly excluded—the poor—to the table of fellowship. But there is a (christological) hook in Jesus' kingdom redemption: "Blessed is anyone who does not stumble on account of me" (Matt. 11:6). The hook is about to gain in significance.

Matthew 8:14–17

The following words do not come from Jesus but from Matthew's summary of a day and evening of kingdom redemption in Capernaum:

When Jesus came into Peter's house, he saw Peter's mother-in-law lying in bed with a fever. He touched her hand and the fever left her, and she got up and began to wait on him.

When evening came, many who were demon-possessed were brought to him, and he drove out the spirits with a word and healed all the sick. This was to fulfill what was spoken through the prophet Isaiah [53:4]:

"He took up our infirmities
and bore our diseases."

Matthew cites one of the most important texts in the Old Testament for how Christians came to understand the death of Jesus as atoning, that famous passage about the suffering servant in Isaiah 52–53. The words Matthew chooses to fasten onto are the ones about the servant suffering for others, but even more than that, suffering *on behalf of* and *instead of* others. So in the passage cited above, Matthew claims kingdom redemption of Jesus *happens because Jesus, in the role of the servant of Isaiah, has entered into such solidarity with the suffering of others that he can reverse the suffering.* Even more, the language is substitutionary: the Servant "took up" *our* infirmities and "bore" *our* diseases. Jesus, at the cross, absorbed the deep cause of our own pain and suffering—namely, the consequences of *our* sin. *Jesus heals, the kingdom-redemptive powers are unleashed, because at the cross sins are remedied and the powers of new life are unlocked.*[8]

John 2:1–11; 10:10

At a wedding in Cana—a small village near Jesus' hometown of Nazareth—Mary, Jesus' mother, informs Jesus that the wedding guests have consumed all the wine. For some reason, Jesus brushes her aside with "Woman [or mother], why do you involve me?" (John 2:4). That is, he wonders why she thinks he can do something about the wine supply. Jesus informs her that he'll do God's work at God's time. He proceeds to wait a minute or two, but then does what Mary was hoping he would do. Well, not quite.

Jesus didn't just do what his mother asked. He did so much more, and it is this "more" that makes this story a kingdom story (though the word is not used). Jesus reveals what is involved when he speaks of kingdom redemption. Here are the important words we find in the opening paragraphs of John's Gospel, the second chapter: "six stone jars," each holding "thirty gallons." Jesus told the servants to fill the jars with water, and then he transformed the water into wine. There's a secret to understanding this wedding event.

One hundred eighty gallons of wine . . . That's 907 bottles of wine. That's a lot of wine!

With the six stone jars holding a total of about 180 gallons (perhaps a little less), and with each gallon being the equivalent of just a shade over five ordinary (modern) bottles of wine, that means Jesus just served up to the wedding party the modern equivalent of about *907 bottles of wine.* Jesus could have just filled up each person's wineskins or mugs or pitchers, but instead he chose to do something incredibly and beautifully extravagant. He took ordinary stone jars of water that were used to purify and made them vessels of abundant joy. There's no indication that the wedding was for royalty with thousands of guests or for lots of Pharisees who would be most concerned about purification. Every indication is that this was an ordinary wedding for ordinary Galileans in an ordinary community. Nine hundred and seven bottles is an abundance of wine. The response of the guests at this wedding party surely was to rock back and just laugh out loud about the extravagance that Jesus created. Kingdom redemption is sheer abundance.

But kingdom life is also a battle for Jesus. Jesus is in a battle, and he knows his opponent: the thief wants to "steal and kill and destroy." Here are the words from John 10:10: "The thief comes only to steal and kill and destroy; I have come that they may have life, and have it to the full."

Jesus saw something sinister at work among his friends. The thief was at work to steal dreams, to kill hopes, and to destroy lives. The thief wanted them to miss out on real love and to kill their careers and never come to terms with the person God made them to be. He wanted them to grab all they could get and forget about justice. He wanted to divide humans against one another to provoke wars. He wanted them to forget life now and bunker down for the afterlife. But Jesus came to turn dreams into living reality, and all they had to do was drink the wine he offered. His abundant wine was the expression of his abundant life.

We have now gained insight from four paradigm-creating texts about kingdom redemption, and this is what they reveal:

- The long-awaited kingdom has been unleashed.
- The kingdom brings kingdom redemption in Jesus.
- The center of Jesus' kingdom redemption is the cross and resurrection where sin is dealt with and new life created.
- The new-wine life of kingdom redemption abounds and flourishes beyond anyone's dreams and expectations.

Kingdom redemption, then, is the work of God, through Jesus, and by virtue of his sin-solving cross and new-life-creating resurrection, unleashed to those who are needy because of their sins. Any kind of "redemptive" activity that does not deal with sin, that does not find its strength in the cross, that does not see the primary agent as Jesus, and that does not see it all as God's new creation life unleashed is not kingdom redemption, even if it is liberating and good and for the common good.

Kingdom Redemption Is Spiritual-Cosmic: Jesus the Exorcist

Present in the various sketches of Jesus' kingdom-redemptive ministries, as is found for instance in Matthew 8–9, are instances of liberating people from spiritual forces and evil powers, called demons (8:16–17, 28–34; 9:32–34), leading us to see that kingdom redemption is *cosmic*. There are in fact five more instances of Jesus exorcising in the Gospels (Mark 1:23–28; 7:24–30; 9:14–29; Matt. 12:22–23; Luke 8:2). We live in a world that by and large finds exorcism to be a piece of hocus pocus, even when social scientists are doing their part to say, "Hold on, folks. Modernity teaches us to use evidence, and there's not a little evidence for human beings experiencing spiritual warfare." C. S. Lewis's famous line is worth repeating: "There are two equal and opposite errors into which our race can fall about the devils. One is to disbelieve in their existence. The other is to believe, and to feel an excessive and unhealthy interest in them. They [the devils] themselves are equally pleased by both errors and hail a materialist or a magician with the same delight."[9] Jesus experienced and conquered deep and dark cosmic forces.

Satan-shaped actions lead to death, always, as the writer of Hebrews says (2:14), as also does Peter (1 Pet. 5:8). This story is deep in Israel's story, for in Eden Park the punishment threat of God was death, and it was precisely what the serpent of Eden wanted—for Adam and Eve to die. In God's grace (and our good fortune) God let them off the hook for decades. But due to this sin, this world in some sense has been given over to the dark forces of the devil: Satan offers the world to Jesus as if he has it to give (Luke 4:6). When Jesus enters into the world to bring abundant, flourishing life, it is time to judge the world and drive out death by his own death (John 12:31). The "prince of this world," Jesus says, wants Jesus (14:30), but the prince stands condemned through Jesus' death-ending condemnation (16:11). In the meantime the devil impacts people physically, morally, and institutionally, the latter of which are often called "principalities and powers" and can be coagulated into one being called Antichrist, who works the "abomination of desolation" (Mark 13:14; 2 Thess. 2:8; Rev. 11:7; 13:1–4).

It is in that context that Jesus breaks in with kingdom redemption, liberating people physically, morally, and institutionally. Jesus redeems cosmically by virtue of the Spirit of God: "If it is by the Spirit of God that I drive out demons, then the kingdom of God has come upon you" (Matt. 12:28). Graham Twelftree, the world's expert on exorcisms in the ancient world, puts it all into a dense sentence: "For Jesus his ministry of exorcism was not preparatory to the kingdom, nor a sign of the kingdom nor an indication that the kingdom had arrived, nor even an illustration of the kingdom, but actually the kingdom of God itself in operation."[10] Cosmic redemption, including systemic dismantling of evil, then, is what Spirit-shaped redemption creates.

What, Then, Is Kingdom Redemption?

Kingdom redemption is the work of God, in a world of cosmic forces that ink the sign of doomed-to-death on everything, in which God through Jesus in the power of the Spirit liberates people by forgiving their sins from any kind of death-aimed captivity, whether that captivity is physical, spiritual, institutional, or systemic. The power of kingdom redemption is centered in Jesus, his life, his death-absorbing death, and his resurrection. This resurrected Jesus unleashes kingdom redemption in the here and now through the Spirit.

So often today, kingdom gets boiled down to ethics; for those who make that move, the kingdom is little more than justice. Others reduce kingdom redemption to personal salvation. Both sides deny holistic redemption, and I now want to explore what this sketch of kingdom redemption means for kingdom mission.

Since the kingdom is the unleashing of God's redemptive powers through Jesus' redemptive death and resurrection, as well as the unleashing of the empowering Spirit, all kingdom mission must be about redemption. From what? Kingdom mission redeems us from all that binds and shackles us to death. Thus, *kingdom redemption is holistic redemption.*

Christian activism tends toward the ends of a spectrum. Some commit themselves to personal evangelism and to the salvation of souls, which means they focus on the kind of evangelism that speaks of sin and the need for personal salvation. For this crowd, kingdom redemption is about personal salvation, and kingdom mission becomes evangelism (only). Others focus on social justice and on the redemption of the body or the psyche or one's community as a whole. For them, kingdom redemption is about disestablishing injustice and establishing justice, and kingdom mission becomes activism for justice and peace. There are then two poles to the spectrum: evangelism and justice, or the spiritual and the social dimensions of the mission. In contrast to these two perspectives, I would like to offer a third perspective on what kingdom mission is by identifying three main characteristics.

First, *kingdom mission admits the primacy of evangelism but sees the locus of the social dimension to be first and foremost in the church as a witness to the world.* Christians have been fighting this one out for a century or more. Chris Wright, in *The Mission of God's People*, a follow-up book to his colossal *The Mission of God*, asks the question of primacy: Which has primacy, the spiritual or the social?[11] I quote from a most important framing of the whole issue by Wright, who is himself quoting John R. W. Stott:

> This brings us to the question whether the partnership between evangelism and social responsibility is equal or unequal, that is, whether they are of identical importance or whether one takes precedence over the other. *The Lausanne Covenant* affirms that "in the church's mission of sacrificial service evangelism is primary" (Paragraph 6). Although some of us have felt uncomfortable about this phrase, lest by it we should be breaking the partnership, yet we are able to endorse and explain it in two ways, in addition to the particular situations and callings already mentioned.
>
> First, evangelism has a certain priority. We are not referring to an invariable temporal priority, because in some situations a social ministry will take precedence, but to a logical one. . . . If social activity is a consequence and aim of evangelism (as we have asserted), then evangelism must precede it. In addition, social progress is being hindered in some countries by the prevailing religious culture; only evangelism can change this.
>
> Secondly, evangelism relates to people's eternal destiny, and in bringing them Good News of salvation, Christians are doing what nobody else can do. Seldom if ever should we have to choose between satisfying physical hunger and spiritual hunger, or between healing bodies and saving souls, since an authentic love for our neighbour will lead us to serve him or her as a whole person. Nevertheless, if we must choose, then we have to say that the supreme and ultimate need of all humankind is the saving grace

of Jesus Christ, and that therefore a person's eternal, spiritual salvation is of greater importance than his or her temporal and material well-being (cf. 2 Cor. 4:16–18). As the Thailand Statement expressed it, "of all the tragic needs of human beings none is greater than their alienation from their Creator and the terrible reality of eternal death for those who refuse to repent and believe." Yet this fact must not make us indifferent to the degradations of human poverty and oppression. The choice, we believe, is largely conceptual. In practice, as in the public ministry of Jesus, *the two are inseparable*, at least in open societies. *Rather than competing with each other, they mutually support and strengthen each other in an upward spiral of increased concern for both.*[12]

This statement comes to the heart of current thinking when it says, "the two are inseparable." Chris Wright wonders aloud of the silliness of posing two other important actions and wondering which is primary: prayer or Bible reading? So he calls us to see both as God's missional concerns and for "integral mission" as his stance, while agreeing on the logical primacy of personal redemption.[13]

I am troubled by the polarity of this debate. That is, we pose spiritual redemption over against social redemption and wonder if one has primacy. But the problem is that "social redemption," again, is about doing good in the public sector for the common good and probably should not even be called "social redemption." In fact, often in this approach the church becomes something spiritual, and society becomes something unspiritual and social. In contrast, holistic redemption creates both a spiritual and a social redemption in the locus of the church, and the church's people spill over in love and holiness and justice and peace into the community. The polarity, then, stems from the assumption that the church is *only* a spiritual fellowship, when it is designed by Jesus to be the embodiment of the kingdom in the here and now. In other words, the "social" dimension of holistic redemption is *first and foremost* found in the social reality called the church. That the follower of Jesus should be concerned with society, with what I described earlier as "good works," is a nonstarter for me. If he or she isn't interested in good works, then he or she has failed as a follower of Jesus. But that we should call our social actions, our good works, "social redemption" once again turns the word "redemption" into a secular equivalent, and we compromise the glory of what redemption means, which is what I now need to explain.

Second, *kingdom mission focuses on a multidimensional redemption among kingdom citizens.* Salvation, then, is from *sin*, or from what Paul calls our Adamic condition (Rom. 5:12–21; 1 Cor. 15:20–23). The gospel statement of 1 Corinthians 15:3–8 makes this clear: "Christ died *for our sins* according to the Scriptures." One of the tensions in the "story" of the Christian faith is that the characters of God's Story have rebelled against God and decided they'd rather *be gods and goddesses* than be *like God.* With a variety of words—rebellion, infidelity, disloyalty, ingratitude, getting dirty, wandering, trespassing, transgressing, and failing—the Bible describes humans as sinners, and sinners need redemption. This redemption likewise can be described with a variety of words—if we are dirty, we need to be cleansed; if we rebel, we need to be subdued and brought into order; if we wander, we need to be found and returned to the path.[14] The most succinct statement of this in the entire Bible is probably Romans 5:12: "Sin entered the world through one man [Adam/Eve], and death through sin, and in this way death came to all people, *because all sinned.*" Sin, then, creates tension in the story: the King of the kingdom redeems, saves, and forgives people from their sin by shouldering the burden of sin and carrying it away and by taking upon himself and removing the debt and guilt due to others. Kingdom mission unleashes this cross- and resurrection-shaped redemption from sin.

Salvation also rescues us from the *dominion of the evil one.* The Bible's "cosmology" scares some away and leads yet others to demythologize it, but both fidelity to Scripture and alertness to the social sciences reveal that there are cosmic and diabolical forces at work in this world.[15] Jesus' first assault was from the prince of demons in the temptation narrative, where he was offered food, credibility, and rule of the world (Matt. 4:1–11). The battle rages in the pages of the Gospels and into the apostolic writings, where we encounter the forces of darkness distorting life and seeking death as the hostile enemy of God and God's people (2 Cor. 4:4; 1 Pet. 5:8–9).[16] The New Testament evidence is so pervasive and clear that we are led to two options: either we embrace a cosmology in which there are diabolical spirits at work, or we don't. Kingdom mission, I contend, embraces that cosmology. Therefore, kingdom mission seeks liberation and redemption from Satan and his minions. Kingdom mission is unafraid to name some forms of evil as deriving from Satan. It is also unafraid, then, to describe salvation as divine rescue from the clutches of Satan and to name that kind of salvation as ransom and liberation.[17] Kingdom mission enters into what it knows is enemy territory—namely, the world—and it enters into the power of the cross, armed with the power of the Spirit, seeking liberation for victims captured by the enemy.

Salvation also rescues from *systemic evil*. I agree with those who see systemic evil in the "principalities and powers" in the New Testament, and I agree that these powers have been defeated in the cross and resurrection (Col. 2:13–15).[18] One of the more noteworthy features of earliest Christianity was insight into the true enemy: the enemies of Israel were empires like Rome and Egypt and Greece and Babylon, and those earthly foes lurked on the edges of all Jewish thinking. But by the time of Jesus and the apostles, those earthly foes were connected to deeper forces, the "principalities and powers." The enemy becomes Satan and the impact of Satan on the powers of this age.[19] In the diabolical and unjust systems of Rome, Paul saw Satan at work, and in the cross and resurrection Paul saw those powers—indeed, saw Rome itself—defeated. Hence, Paul can state his thesis this way: "For our struggle is not against flesh and blood, but against the rulers, against the authorities, against the powers of this dark world and against the spiritual forces of evil in the heavenly realms" (Eph. 6:12). And he can then follow it up with spiritual practices of resisting the powers of this age this way:

> Therefore put on the full armor of God, so that when the day of evil comes, you may be able to stand your ground, and after you have done everything, to stand. Stand firm then, with the belt of truth buckled around your waist, with the breastplate of righteousness in place, and with your feet fitted with the readiness that comes from the gospel of peace. In addition to all this, take up the shield of faith, with which you can extinguish all the flaming arrows of the evil one. Take the helmet of salvation and the sword of the Spirit, which is the word of God. (6:13–17)

Kingdom mission—or, by way of reminder, church mission—seeks to unleash the redemptive powers of God in this world to defeat these powers

(1 Cor. 15:24). How? By declaring God as King in Jesus and by offering redemption in King Jesus and—to bring this once more back into the picture—through the people called the church. This redemption is manifold and holistic: people are offered redemption from burden and guilt of sin, from the victimizing forces of Satan, and from the oppressive features of systemic evil *to establish the kingdom community in the here and now.*

Once again, the temptation of many who embrace cosmic kingdom redemption today is to work against unjust systems in governments, and no one but a fool would deny such efforts as anything but good. Yet, if kingdom mission is church mission, we are to see these redemptive powers unleashed in the church for kingdom citizens. Put differently, *opposing the principalities and powers manifests itself first and foremost in a local church unaffected and uninfected by the evil systems of this world.* Kingdom mission seeks to embody the kingdom of God in the kind of fellowship established in local churches. To be sure, as citizens of this world, kingdom citizens will oppose injustices like racism and economic injustices and legal oppressions and seek to establish what is best for the common good. But the temptation to think it is kingdom work must be resisted because kingdom is about the people of God living the will of God, and kingdom mission is first and foremost about a redemptive reality of living under King Jesus as a fellowship.

Third, *kingdom mission, once again, is only partial redemption in the here and now.* We all recognize the problem: Why is the church so messy and inept and divided and pock-marked by the infections of the powers and principalities? Why is the church so battered by incomplete redemption and in fact belittling itself by thinking redemption is only spiritual? How can we call our local church the kingdom of God or even associate kingdom with it? I suggest once more we look to eschatology, and in particular at the tension we observed already: that the kingdom has been inaugurated but not yet fully consummated, that the kingdom is partly here and partly in the future, that the church is the holy bride of Christ but will only be spotless and pure in the final kingdom. In the New Testament, salvation is found in all three tenses because the kingdom has only been inaugurated. That is, we have been redeemed (past), we are being redeemed (present), and we will be redeemed (future).[20]

For in this hope *we were saved.* (Rom. 8:24)

Therefore, my dear friends, . . . *continue to work out your salvation* with fear and trembling. (Phil. 2:12)

The hour has already come for you to wake up from your slumber, because *our salvation is nearer now* than when we first believed. (Rom. 13:11)

This threefold sense of salvation pertains to the holistic sense of salvation, to kingdom redemption: in the past our salvation is achieved in the death and resurrection of Christ; in the present that salvation is manifesting itself in a variety of ways, is growing, and is not yet complete in any sense; but in the future that holistic salvation—our whole selves, our whole body, our whole fellowship—will be completed and perfected.

Kingdom mission offers holistic salvation in the context of the church of the redeemed, those who are being redeemed and those who will be redeemed. Kingdom mission forms communities of the redeemed. Any kingdom mission that does not offer this kind of redemption is not kingdom mission.

10

Kingdom Is
a Moral Fellowship

For a first-century Galilean Jew to use the term "kingdom" implied several elements: a king; a citizenship; a land or place, which often included some sacred space like a temple; a redemptive reality; and a law that governed the behavior of the citizens. At the core of Israel's vision of its own kingdom is the Torah of Moses. Israelites are defined by their conformity to the Torah; "others" are defined as outside of Israel by their nonconformity. If Jesus announces the arrival of God's kingdom, will there be a new, kingdom Torah? In this chapter I want to sketch what "kingdom law" looks like for King Jesus who rules over his kingdom citizens in the land, a land that expands somewhat in Jesus' time but most notably under the apostles, who took the gospel to the ends of the earth. Those kingdom citizens, even those who are to come into the kingdom circle from the gentile world, are to be marked by specific behaviors and core orientations. But first they need to "enter" the kingdom or become kingdom citizens; that is, they need to enter into what Hauerwas and Willimon call the "Christian colony."[1]

159

Entering into the Kingdom's Moral Fellowship

The kingdom is the redeemed people governed by King Jesus who live according to his way of life and teachings. But to live under Jesus, one must come under Jesus or "enter" the kingdom, which means there is either a moment when that happens or a series of moments when conversion begins.[2] Now the challenging part for all of us is this: Jesus conditions entry into the kingdom of God on morality. There are seven "entrance" sayings in the Gospels, and each of them deserves to be read slowly to find an echo of what Jesus sounded like on the hills and in the homes of Galilee.[3] Here they are, with the conditions italicized:

> "For I tell you that *unless your righteousness surpasses that of the Pharisees and the teachers of the law*, you will certainly not enter the kingdom of heaven." (Matt. 5:20)

> "Not everyone who says to me, 'Lord, Lord,' will enter the kingdom of heaven, but *only the one who does the will of my Father who is in heaven*." (7:21)

> And he said: "Truly I tell you, *unless you change and become like little children*, you will never enter the kingdom of heaven." (18:3)

> "*If your hand or your foot causes you to stumble, cut it off and throw it away*. It is better for you to enter life maimed or crippled than to have two hands or two feet and be thrown into eternal fire. *And if your eye causes you to stumble, gouge it out and throw it away. It is better for you to enter life with one eye than to have two eyes and be thrown into the fire of hell*." (18:8–9)

> "Why do you ask me about what is good?" Jesus replied. "There is only One who is good. If you want to enter life, *keep the commandments*." (19:17)

> Then Jesus said to his disciples, "Truly I tell you, *it is hard for someone who is rich to enter the kingdom of heaven*. Again I tell you, it is easier for a camel to go through the eye of a needle *than for someone who is rich* to enter the kingdom of God." (19:23–24)

"Woe to you, teachers of the law and Pharisees, you hypocrites! *You shut the door of the kingdom of heaven in people's faces.* You yourselves do not enter, nor will you let those enter who are trying to." (23:13)

The direct impact of slowly reading such verses does more good than analytical discussion. Why? Because it is the force of this pattern in his thinking that stuns us into thinking of what he wants from us. What Jesus says is that *in order to enter the kingdom*, one must have surpassing righteousness,[4] or do the will of God, or become like a child in humility and trust, or remove all sorts of obstacles, or keep the Torah commands, or abandon riches, or abandon the Torah teachings of the Pharisees and scribes. I emphasize "or" since Jesus does not give this list to any one audience but instead, in particular situations, brings to expression the core commitment required for kingdom entrance. In summary, *to enter the kingdom one must surrender to Jesus as King and live under King Jesus.* Entrance here is so unlike much of what occurs in church settings today, where if one is baptized as an infant or if one has walked the aisle or if one has been baptized as an adult or if one has made the decision, one is in. Not so for Jesus: to enter the kingdom means a person surrenders to live under King Jesus. Jesus is not talking here about sinlessness—the failure of the disciples, Jesus' rebuke, his forgiveness, and their resumption of discipleship proves that. He's talking about the core commitment of one's life. The only ones who enter the kingdom are those who give themselves to Jesus.

What does that "core commitment" look like? What is kingdom morality? What is the character of the moral fellowship of the followers of Jesus? No one word will do, so we will explore these questions under several headings, beginning with the cross and the cruciform life. One by one they all help us define what Jesus wants from us.

Cross

The most telling moral statement of Jesus, one that reveals the king's character, which shapes his kingdom's character, finds itself at Mark 8:34: "Whoever wants to be my disciple must deny themselves and take up their cross and follow me." Jesus pokes around in the fears of many with this word "cross." Many in the Roman Empire feared Roman power to crucify, and Jesus himself knew the power of Rome because John the Baptist had been decapitated by a Roman-sponsored ruler. He knew a similar fate could be on his own horizon. He knew his fate was the cross.[5] Crucifixion rose from the Roman Empire's attempt to overpower any rebellion. The Roman authorities stripped and tortured the victim, watched as animals picked at the flesh, and deprived the family of the decency of burial—all justified as a deterrent to rebellion. That's what "cross" meant to Jesus and his followers.

To follow Jesus as the community of Jesus meant embracing the cross as the way of life: that meant the way of suffering, of death, of humiliation, and through that death into resurrected life. What the world said—and by "world" I mean both Rome's and Israel's leaders—came face-to-face with what Jesus said: where they said preservation, he said cross; where they said life, he said death; where they said victory, he said defeat. His death, paradoxically, is the way of life, and his defeat is the way of victory. What Jesus advocated, then, was a cruciform existence for his followers. The moral fellowship of the kingdom, then, is a fellowship in the cross. Think briefly over the pages of the New Testament where cross becomes the norm for discipleship (and not just the atoning sacrifice). Jesus maps the Christian life along the coordinates of the cross (Luke 9:23), Paul sees the cross as pattern of his own ministry (2 Cor. 4:10; Phil. 3:10–11), and the pattern of Christ's own self-sacrifice becomes the solution to the local church's struggle for a loving fellowship (Phil. 2:5–11). Most potent perhaps is what Jesus told his disciples when they were courting notions of power.

> Jesus called them together and said, "You know that those who are regarded as rulers of the Gentiles lord it over them, and their high officials exercise authority over them. Not so with you. Instead, whoever wants to become great among you must be your servant, and whoever wants to be first must be slave of all. For even the Son of Man did not come to be served, but to serve, and to give his life as a ransom for many." (Mark 10:42–45)

Jesus' life is the paradigm of Christian living, and his life is the life of cross and resurrection.

Holed up in an underground seminary under the shadows of Hitler's gaze, Dietrich Bonhoeffer lectured on discipleship to his students. His words bring to fresh expression—nearly seventy years after those students heard them—what Jesus meant when he said, "Take up your cross."

> Those who enter into discipleship enter into Jesus' death. They turn their living into dying; such has been the case from the very beginning. The cross is not the terrible end of a pious, happy life. Instead, it stands at the beginning of community with Jesus Christ. Whenever Christ calls us, his call leads us to death. Whether we, like the first disciples, must leave house and vocation to follow him, or whether, with Luther, we leave the monastery for a secular vocation, in both cases the same death awaits us, namely, death in Jesus Christ, the death of our old self caused by the call of Jesus.[6]

The first word in the moral fellowship under King Jesus is the word "cross." The cross creates us, the cross shapes us, the cross guides us, and the cross reminds us.

Righteousness

A second word that speaks to the character of the moral fellowship of the followers of Jesus stands out in the Sermon on the Mount, the word "righteousness." Jesus blesses those who "hunger and thirst for righteousness" (Matt. 5:6), and he blesses those who are "persecuted because of righteousness" (5:10). As we saw above in the entrance sayings of Jesus, he calls kingdom citizens to a righteousness that "surpasses that of the Pharisees and teachers of the law" (5:20), and he calls his followers to "practice [their] righteousness" privately (6:1). To get to the heart of the Sermon, Jesus says, "Seek first his kingdom and his righteousness" (6:33). This word "righteousness" had a very clear meaning in the world of Jesus: it described the faithful Israelite, the Israelite who observed the Torah. In slightly different terms, it describes the person who does the will of God. The Sermon ends in 7:15–28 with a parable calling those who listen to these words to do the will of God. From this sermon's beginning to its end, the kingdom fellowship is a moral fellowship marked by *righteousness*. A brief sketch of four themes in the Sermon opens the hand of righteousness for all of us to see.[7]

RIGHTEOUSNESS MEANS A LIFE OF GOOD DEEDS

Kingdom citizens have a mission to the world. Jesus informs kingdom citizens that they have a twofold mission: they are the "salt of the *land*" and they are the "light of the *world*." While many think that "land" and "world" are the same, and that "salt" symbolizes social influence while "light" refers to evangelism, I suspect different meanings were at work when Jesus said these words. The disciples have a mission to the Jews in the land and a mission to the gentiles in the world. This mission is profoundly moral. What is it? "Let your light shine before others, that they may see your good deeds and glorify your Father in heaven" (Matt. 5:16). Both "salt" and "light" are "good deeds" in this world. The fundamental mission of kingdom citizens is to glorify God by living a life of "good deeds." God is most glorified when kingdom citizens live under King Jesus as a faithful community.

RIGHTEOUSNESS REQUIRES LISTENING TO JESUS

The next section is in many ways the core of the Sermon on the Mount's ethical vision (5:17–48). King Jesus gives to kingdom citizens nothing less than *a kingdom Torah.* The essence is found in 5:17–20, a text so important it must be quoted and put to memory.

> Do not think that I have come to abolish the Law or the Prophets; I have not come to abolish them but to fulfill them. For truly I tell you, until heaven and earth disappear, not the smallest letter, not the least stroke of a pen, will by any means disappear from the Law until everything is accomplished. Therefore anyone who sets aside one of the least of these commands and teaches others accordingly will be called least in the kingdom of heaven, but whoever practices and teaches these commands will be called great in the kingdom of heaven. For I tell you that unless your righteousness surpasses that of the Pharisees and the teachers of the law, you will certainly not enter the kingdom of heaven.

A few observations: First, kingdom Torah is revealed in and by Jesus, the kingdom's King. Jesus says he has come to "fulfill" both the law and the prophets. He's claiming that the Torah and the prophets of Israel come to completion in his own teachings. Second, he is not destroying

Torah for his followers; he's not dismissing Torah. He's sustaining Torah by bringing Torah to its fullest expression. Third, entrance into the kingdom is determined by practicing Jesus' kingdom Torah. Most important, Jesus' kingdom Torah *transcends* the Torah teaching and practice of the Pharisees and teachers of the law, not because Jesus teaches internal righteousness while they, muckety-mucks that they are, reduce it to external conformity. No, the Pharisaic teaching of the Torah was fine until Jesus came along to reveal that the core of the Torah was loving God and loving others as oneself. Jesus saw through the rulings of the Pharisees to the core of God's will, and anyone who follows the core of the will of God—again, loving God and loving others—will do all the rules, more and better and deeper.

This is what Jesus illustrates in Matthew 5:21–48. Murder transcends the external act of putting someone down; Jesus wants reconciled relations, even with one's enemies. Adultery is more than having sex with another man's wife or another woman's husband. Adultery begins in the heart with lust. Divorce, too, catches the piercing eye of Jesus: divorce is wrong; marriage is a lifelong covenant commitment. There is an exception, of course, for sexual infidelity, but the focus of Jesus is on the inviolability of the marital covenant and not the grounds for divorce. Jesus keeps pressing his case for a transcendent or surpassing righteousness. Tell the truth, Jesus says, and you will not need oaths to prop up your claims. The law commanded justice and retaliation but limited retaliation. Jesus, however, calls his followers to a new kind of grace: "Do not resist an evil person" and "turn to them the other cheek" and "hand over your coat as well" and "go with them two miles" and "give to the one who asks" and "do not turn away from the one who wants to borrow from you." Somewhere, and it is not entirely clear where, someone believed the Jews of Jesus' day were to love their neighbors (fellow Jews, fellow observant Jews) and hate their enemies (Romans). Jesus says this is completely wrong for one simple reason: God created all; God sustains everyone; everyone is a neighbor; there are no enemies; therefore kingdom citizens are to love their enemies and pray for their persecutors. When they love as God does they will be "perfect," a term that does not mean "sinless" but rather loving God and loving others with all of one's heart, soul, mind, and strength.

To be sure, Matthew 5 is not pragmatics, and we are left dangling, like worms on a hook, wondering what's in store for us, but this chapter reveals kingdom Torah. It is what life looks like in the kingdom and *therefore it is what life is to look like in the moral fellowship of the kingdom citizens who live under King Jesus.* Whether it works well in Washington, DC, is not the point; what is the point is that *this is how kingdom citizens are to live with one another* in a world of people who don't live this way.

RIGHTEOUSNESS MEANS DOING PIETY BEFORE GOD

Judaism at the time of Jesus had charged specific practices with particular weight, as every religion and culture does. Jimmy Dunn has in many contexts called these "boundary markers," while a Finnish scholar calls these "covenant path markers."[8] Piety is marked by behaviors, and those behaviors mark people as pious; those who do them are pious, and those who don't aren't. Three typical markers of piety at the time of Jesus were almsgiving, sacred prayers at set times, and fasting (Matt. 6:1–18). Jesus reshaped each of those markers of piety with a *kingdom piety*. The essence of Jesus' kingdom piety is to practice each of those disciplines to please God and not to gain the approval of others. Jesus does not prohibit public acts of piety, for how else do we explain his teaching the Lord's Prayer as a public prayer, which is what he does in Luke 11:1–4 (see Matt. 6:7–15), or his praise of the widow's mite in Mark 12:41–44? Kingdom righteousness focuses on God and not on the approval of others.

RIGHTEOUSNESS MEANS GOD FIRST

From the very beginning of Israel's story to the factions of various groups in Judaism, one theme is consistent: Israel is to obey God regardless of the consequences. Whether we look at Abram in Ur of the Chaldees and his leaving his land to find the land God promised, to Moses in Egypt and his giving of the Torah to the wilderness generation, to the days of Joshua and Judges, to the bitter story of divorce and recommitment under Ezra and Nehemiah, to the heroic story of the Maccabees and the radicalism of the Essenes harboring themselves alongside the Dead Sea at Qumran, Israelites knew that God wanted their all. So too with Jesus, and it is all brought into a tight bundle at Matthew 6:19–34: treasures are those that

166

are for heaven (kingdom of God); healthy eyes are morally sound eyes and bodies; there is but one master; and then we get Jesus calling his disciples to seek the kingdom of God and God's righteousness first and foremost. Everything else is in second place, and God will take care of those who give themselves to him.

From the beginning to the end of the Sermon, which Jesus finishes with a robust summons to practice what he teaches, the theme of righteousness keeps our attention focused. The moral fellowship of the kingdom is marked by righteousness, a life marked by following the teachings of Jesus. If the first word in the moral fellowship under King Jesus is "cross" and the second word "righteousness," the third word is "love."

Love

Two passages reveal the centrality of love for the kingdom's moral fellowship: Mark 12:28–32 (and Luke 10:25–29) and John 13:34–35.

THE CENTRALITY OF LOVE

There are apparently two different settings for Jesus' reduction of Torah to love, one found in Mark (followed by Matthew) and the other in Luke. In the last week of Jesus' life an expert in the Torah asks Jesus to weigh in on a crucial debated question of the day: how best to read the Torah. The scribe's question to Jesus is, "Of all the commandments, which is the most important?" (Mark 12:28). In Luke, seemingly out of nowhere, a scribe asks Jesus, "Teacher, what must I do to inherit eternal life?" (Luke 10:25). That is, what does one have to do to enter the kingdom? The questions lead to the same answer: God's will is centrally found in loving God and in loving others. I call this focus on loving God and loving others the Jesus Creed. Jesus didn't make this up. Love of God and others flows straight out of the Torah: Deuteronomy 6:4–9, commonly called the *Shema*, and Leviticus 19:18, where we find the command to love one's neighbor as one's self. The single most significant illustration of the importance of loving one's neighbor is when Jesus called his followers to love their enemies (Matt. 5:43–48). In effect, he turned their "enemies" into their "neighbors."

From a slightly different angle, and with a few new themes, this emphasis on love appears in the Gospel of John at 13:34–35: "A new command

I give you: Love one another. As I have loved you, so you must love one another. By this everyone will know that you are my disciples, if you love one another." Jesus says that the love command is "new," and this new kind of love reveals their relationship to the watching world. If we add John 15:12, which says "Love each other as I have loved you," to 13:34–35, we learn that Jesus is the model of that love. What is most distinctive in John's Gospel, though, is the prejudicial focus of this love on those in the church. In John 13:34–35 and 15:12 the focus is on loving fellow kingdom citizens, something John will emphasize in his own letter (1 John 3:11, 16, 23; 4:11). Any act of love, the apostle Paul was to say more than a decade after Jesus' death, fulfills the entire Torah (Gal. 5:14; Rom. 12:19; 13:9). James, the brother of Jesus, was to say the same (James 2:8–11). Love is the heart of the moral fellowship for kingdom citizens.

Love, then, is not one of the virtues; love is the one and only virtue that creates space for all the other virtues. We can agree that Jesus made love central to the kingdom, to the church. We can agree that the Jesus Creed expresses the heart of Jesus' teachings for his followers. The apostles followed in his steps, and we risk the moral vision of Jesus when we wander from this past.

THE MEANING OF LOVE

We cannot enter into the kingdom mission of love until we answer this question: What is love?[9] This question has perplexed the best of Christian thinkers for two millennia, so we need to look at two representative examples of how love has been defined. One contemporary philosopher-theologian is Tom Oord, who defines love in the following terms: "To love is to act intentionally, in sympathetic response to others (including God), to promote overall well-being."[10] From a former generation is the towering American theologian H. Richard Niebuhr, who offered this definition: "By love we mean at least these attitudes and actions: rejoicing in the presence of the beloved, gratitude, reverence and loyalty toward him [or her]."[11] While each of these definitions gets us closer to defining love, I offer an alternative. The Christian view of love begins with the belief that in order to define love, we first have to describe what God's love is and how God shows that love. I see these four elements in divine love:

1. God's love is a rugged covenant commitment.
2. God's commitment is to be present, or to be "with."
3. God's commitment is to be an advocate, or to be "for."
4. God's commitment has direction: God's love is "unto" kingdom realities.

I will now offer a sketch of each element. The fundamental relationship of God with humans, most notably with Israel and the church, is as a covenant or a rugged commitment to them. From Genesis 12 onward, covenant forms the core of God's relationship with humans. That covenant is formed first as divine presence: God is "with" his people in entering vulnerably into the covenant with Abraham in Genesis 15, in the tabernacle, in the temple, in the dwelling of the glory (*kavod*) in that temple, and then radically in the incarnation where God is Immanuel in the flesh (Matt. 1:23; John 1:14). This principle of divine presence is the utter completion of God's loving covenant when he comes to dwell with his people in the new heavens and the new earth (Rev. 21:3). God's covenant is to be "for" his people, which is precisely what "I will be your God and you will be my people" means as a covenant formula in the Bible (e.g., Gen. 17:7–8; Exod. 6:2–8; Lev. 26:12; Rev. 21:7).[12] "With" and "for" lead to the direction of divine love, what I call the "unto": God forms a covenant with Israel to make it a people for his own possession, God liberates Israel from the clutches of Pharaoh to lead them to the Torah for life in the land, and God saves Israel and the church in order to make his people holy and loving and pure. God doesn't just dwell with and God is not just for his people; God's love transforms "unto" kingdom realities.

The three words we have just explored—"cross," "righteousness," and "love"—mark the moral fellowship of the kingdom, and these three words then define kingdom mission. Therefore, kingdom mission is to establish communities, local churches, that are marked by the cross, by righteousness, and by love.

Kingdom Mission and the Moral Fellowship

Jesus' Torah is designed for kingdom citizens who live in this world in light of the next world, which leads us to the following theses about kingdom mission in the sections that follow.

Living under King Jesus

Kingdom mission summons humans to live under King Jesus in the church as kingdom citizens. A number of themes in this book now come together: the kingdom has been inaugurated but not consummated, which means kingdom citizens are to live in the now in light of the not yet. But they know the now is only a shadow of the future kingdom. That A-B-A′ story comes to fulfillment in Jesus and his kingdom people, Israel Expanded, or the church. Kingdom citizens live under King Jesus, and that means they are to be formed by the cross, righteousness, and love. Kingdom citizens are a redeemed people—people who have been saved by Jesus. But their salvation is holistic, so kingdom citizens live in a new fellowship, the moral fellowship of the kingdom.

These three terms—"cross," "righteousness," and "love"—describe the kingdom, and since the kingdom people is the church people, these three terms are for church people. Churches are to be shaped by a life marked by the cross, by righteousness, and by love. The kingdom ethic is an ethic designed for a community. That means those who are part of that community are to be marked by the cross, by righteousness, and by love.

Seeking Peace

Kingdom mission, because it is marked by listening to Jesus, who calls us to the cross, to righteousness, and to love, is also marked by peace. But we once again encounter a problem we have seen before. Like justice, peace has been politicized. Here's what is happening. It is rather clear that God wants *shalom*. It runs right through the Bible, and so just a few lines from Jesus are all we need.

"Blessed are the peacemakers." (Matt. 5:9)

"When you enter a house, first say, 'Peace to this house.'" (Luke 10:5)

"If you, even you, had only known on this day what would bring you peace." (Luke 19:42)

"Peace I leave with you; my peace I give you." (John 14:27)

"I have told you these things so that in me you may have peace. In this world you will have trouble. But take heart! I have overcome the world." (John 16:33)

"Peace" is one of those great biblical words that captures the entire intent of God for his people: God wants his people to dwell in peace. This of course means not only the absence of strife but the joy of reconciliation with God and with one another. It means that kingdom citizens are to seek peace and not division or war. (Though it is clear from Jesus' own words that his mission will sometimes be divisive, as he says in Matt. 10:34.) The peace Jesus is talking about is redemptive peace: it comes in Christ. As Jesus said it above, "In me you may have peace." This means the peace he's talking about is *ecclesial* peace. But I don't mean by this that our primary field of action is actually the "world"; I am not saying we believe in peace, and so we work peace into the world. Of course we will seek the peace of the city, and of course we will want peace in the world, and of course we will strive for peace in the world. But the primary way we influence the world is by summoning the world out of its worldliness into the church, where true peace can be found.[13]

The problem, which I just mentioned, is that we have secularized the peace work of the kingdom, which means, ironically, that we are succumbing yet again to the Constantinian Temptation (see appendix 1) to coerce our nation into our beliefs by recourse to the political process.[14] Those who talk most about peace are talking about peace in the world, and almost never about peace in the local church. The peace of the kingdom, I am contending, is first and foremost a *shalom* that marks the kingdom as it is present now—that is, in your local church as it is now. First we are to seek peace in our local fellowship, to end strife and to seek reconciliation with God and with one another, and *out of this peace-shaped, kingdom-shaped church we spill over peace into the world*. But our tendency today is to politicize peace, to make it about global relations and ethnic strivings, both of which are instinctual desires for anyone who follows Jesus. But I assign these to the expression "good works," while I assign the peace Jesus talks about to be fundamentally about how members of a local church, or the church universal, live with one another under the King of Peace.

I have gone on record that I am a pacifist,[15] and I am more confident today that pacifism is the most consistent application of Jesus' kingdom vision for Christians in the world today. But pacifism is a kingdom ethic that begins in the local church fellowship. That is, when we politicize peace into the pacifist program for denuclearizing our world or ending wars, we too often decenter the church as the kingdom's true embodiment and turn it into a world ethic for people who largely ignore King Jesus. So I will bang this gong one more time: *first the local church, then the world*. When the local church is marked by peace, the world may listen. When the local church is not marked by peace, but by strife and divisions and bickerings, why should the world care what the church believes about peace?

Listening to a Higher Voice

Kingdom mission knows that Jesus' kingdom Torah is not the "law of the land" in any country and that therefore kingdom citizens are listening to a higher voice. The most common complaint against Jesus' kingdom moral vision is that it is impractical or utopian or unrealistic or only a vision that cannot be fully achieved in the here and now. Perhaps the biggest bee sting is that too many Christians think of Jesus' ethics as a public ethic, so they try to force, or translate, his vision into the framework of Western liberalism's focus on rights and liberty and justice and equality. This renders unto Caesar what is God's and needs to be named for what it is: Constantinianism.

We can go back to the Constantinian compromises or lay blame on Luther, who sundered the realm of the kingdom from the realm of the state, or we can look more closely at the many Americans who equate the vision of Jesus with their political party's platforms. Democrats see Jesus as for the poor, and being for the poor for them means voting Democrat (compassion, aid, equality). Republicans see Jesus as for the poor, and being for the poor means voting Republican (enterprise, free market, capitalism). We could dig in there or here, but I'll move to the more important place to poke the land with this shovel.

Jesus' moral vision is not designed for America or Ireland or Korea or China or South Africa or Peru or New Zealand or India. The moral vision of Jesus is for kingdom people, for church people. Jesus summons the church to listen to his words and do them. He is not offering constitutional

172

amendments or wisdom for America's founders. He's revealing the will of God for God's people. Yes, since it is God's will and God is King over all, God's will is for all people. But the way to inscribe the will of God on the hearts of people in this world is not by way of law or vote but by way of redemption through Jesus. Jesus' kingdom vision is for his redeemed people and for them alone. We are, of course, called to be salt and light in this world, but the best way to be salt and light is not to coerce the rest of the nation through political power but to witness to an alternative reality by living out the kingdom vision of Jesus in our local church.

Surrendering Money and Possessions

Kingdom mission must touch upon one of the most important issues of life for Westerners: money and possessions. The moral fellowship of the kingdom has a new view of money and possessions. So, when it comes to money and possessions, kingdom mission requires that we seek to live the cross, live righteously, and love God and others.

What happens to our possessions and our money if we live in light of the cross, if we want to be righteous, and if we love God and others with them?

RIGHTEOUSNESS

I begin with the second. Righteousness means we are committed first and foremost to the kingdom, to Jesus as our King, to what he teaches us, and to whom we belong in the fellowship. Our first commitment is not to the "law of the land" but to Jesus. So, kingdom mission means that I, that you, that we—together—seek to practice what Jesus teaches. It means we don't compromise what Jesus teaches by appealing to the law of the land, that we follow Jesus at work and in the community just as we do at home and at church. Step one, then, is the commitment to do what Jesus teaches when it comes to possessions and money in every phase of our life because, as Lord, Jesus rules over our possessions and money. The "surpassing righteousness" of Jesus means his will shapes our possessions.

CROSS AND LOVE

The cross not only atones but also models a way of life. The cross forgives our sin, and it offers us a way of living before God and the world.

We focus here on the second. The cross-shaped kingdom mission means *a life of self-denial in sacrifice to others*. In the cross, then, we see God's love and a model for our love. A cross-love revolutionizes our attitude and practices of possessions and money. Jesus did not so much have a theory of economics as a theory of love that found its way into economics. Long ago, a proponent of the social gospel made an observation about Jesus and economics that probably was as off-putting to fellow social gospelers then as it is today to both conservatives and progressives. His name was Shailer Mathews, and this is what he said:

> [Jesus] is neither a champion nor an opponent of *laissez faire*; he neither forbids trade unions, strikes, and lockouts, nor advises them; he was neither socialist nor individualist. Jesus was friend neither of the working nor [of] the rich man as such. He dealt with persons, not economic classes. The question he would put to a man is not "Are you rich?" "Are you poor?" but "Have you done the will of my Father *and loved all men*?"[16]

Mathews knew Jesus reoriented everything through his commitment to love others. What is noticeable about the teachings and the praxis of Jesus is how much he said about money, possessions, and therefore in some ways about economics.[17] The question he forced upon kingdom citizens was not "How does the world work?" or "How can we make more money?" or "Which policy is 'best'?" but "How are kingdom citizens to live under King Jesus?" Or put more directly, what happens when the cross and love of neighbor invade the world of possessions?

We dare not forget that there was already a ready-made answer at work in the Jewish world of Jesus, and it is strangely in accordance with the law of the land in Western democracies today: the law of blessings and curses, found in Deuteronomy 28 and woven deeply into the conscience of observant Jews of Jesus' day, taught that wealth was a sign of God's blessing for obedience while poverty was a sign of God's judgment for disobedience. Westerners may not see wealth so much as a blessing of God, but they do see it as the reward of labor; they tend also to see poverty as the just reward for laziness. To be sure, the more liberal see a systemic problem in free enterprise itself, but the *system* is one in which reward, or possession, correlates with labor. The impact of this is that what we earn is ours, and what others earn is not ours. In other words, self-centeredness rules much of what we believe about possessions and ownership in Western economy. Self-centeredness makes us blind to injustices.

Already in the pages of the Bible the simple correlation theory of obedience leading to material blessings, or the law of correlation between work and money, was being challenged. I mention a few. Solomon proved that blessings and not obedience but sin could go hand in hand (1 Kings 4:20–26; 10:14–29; 11:1–13). Sometimes poverty itself is the result of oppression and injustice, not disobedience (Prov. 13:23; Mic. 2:1–2). In fact, so much was the law of correlation challenged that God ends up on the side of the poor throughout the Bible. How so? God is the God of the poor (Prov. 19:17; Ps. 140:12), so there are laws written into the fabric of Torah that reveal God's care for the poor—laws about the Jubilee (Deut. 15:1–11), laws about the sabbatical year (Exod. 23:10–11), and most especially laws about tithing for the poor (Deut. 14:28–29) and gleaning—those instances where Israelites were to leave portions of their harvest for those in need (Lev. 19:9–10). Put in the simplest of terms, *Israel's God and therefore Israelites were to take care of the poor by becoming a people marked by generosity*. But the biggest challenge of the law of correlation is the warning, which begins in Deuteronomy (8:11–14, 17) but finds full expression in Jesus and Paul (Mark 10:23; 1 Tim. 6:9–10), that wealth *in and of itself carries the temptation to self-satisfaction and a lack of generosity*. When James writes the word "wealthy," it is code for "oppressor" (James 5:1–6).

This is where cross and love of others enter into the picture. Under King Jesus the question becomes, "Do you use your possessions for the good of others or for your own consumption?" So Jesus forced people to decide, and the rich young man illustrates his approach.

> A certain ruler asked him, "Good teacher, what must I do to inherit eternal life?"
>
> "Why do you call me good?" Jesus answered. "No one is good—except God alone. You know the commandments: 'You shall not commit adultery, you shall not murder, you shall not steal, you shall not give false testimony, honor your father and mother.'"
>
> "All these I have kept since I was a boy," he said.

When Jesus heard this, he said to him, "You still lack one thing. Sell everything you have and give to the poor, and you will have treasure in heaven. Then come, follow me." (Luke 18:18–22)

To follow Jesus was to surrender one's possessions to Jesus and to repent and turn from "mammonolatry," the worship of possessions. The rich ruler wanted no part of the cross or of surrendering what was most dear to him, and Jesus found his idolatry and put it to the test. Instead of loving others with his money, the rich ruler loved himself alone. King Jesus is Lord, and he wants our all, including what we possess.

Kingdom citizens, then, are challenged by Jesus to surrender their mammon to King Jesus as part of kingdom mission. Perhaps the classic expression of this is Zacchaeus (Luke 19:1–10). He is described as a "chief tax collector" and "wealthy," but he wanted to see Jesus. Unlike the rich ruler who opts not to surrender his wealth, Zacchaeus does. Consequently, Zacchaeus experiences "salvation." As the wine was provided in abundance out of the generosity of the King of the kingdom (John 2:1–11), so Zacchaeus outdoes himself in paying "four times the amount" he had pinched from those he overtaxed (Luke 19:8). Jesus unleashes kingdom realities, and that means he unleashes love for all, including those from whom Zacchaeus had stolen—one can say that his enemies became his neighbors. Zacchaeus' conversion shows that genuine conversion, as John the Baptist himself taught (Luke 3:7–9), erupts into a life of love for others that includes economic care for others. The cross of self-denial leads to loving others.

Acts 2:42–47 (or 4:32–36) is often cited as an example, for good reason, of what kingdom redemption creates in a kingdom moral fellowship: a church marked by economic sharing. For the one who gives, there is the cross of self-denial; for the one receiving, there is a taste of resurrection and new creation. There is the sensibility of righteousness where folks perceive that they are living under King Jesus, and there is the undoubted experience of loving and being loved. What we see embodied in Acts is also taught by the apostle Paul in what is one of the most radical statements in all of the New Testament about possessions. In urging the Corinthians to generosity for the poor saints of Jerusalem, Paul clarifies what is going on.

Our desire is not that others might be relieved while you are hard pressed, but that there might be *equality*. At the present time your plenty will supply what they need, so that in turn their plenty will supply what you need. The goal is *equality*, as it is written: "The one who gathered much did not have too much, and the one who gathered little did not have too little." (2 Cor. 8:13–15, emphasis added)

The distinguishing word here brings the moral fellowship of the kingdom into view: "equality." The word does not mean that everyone has the same possessions or that income is distributed equally, but that each person has their "fair share" or what they need. Perhaps the most exacting translation is "reciprocity." The word assumes the mutual fellowship of the church, the mutual loving care each has for others, and the mutual sharing of what one has with those who are in need. The principal ideas are responsiveness to the needs of others, the availability of each to the other, and the requisite self-denying love for the good of the other and the body. The opposite of cruciform generosity is greediness and selfishness and hoarding.

Many of us know that the theme of cruciform love reshaping our possessions into a radical generosity is all over the New Testament. We tend also to say we like those words, but then ignore them. Our pretense reminds me of something Flannery O'Connor once wrote in a letter: "Everybody here shakes my hand but nobody reads my stories."[18] We, too, glad-hand the sayings of Jesus. My fellow blogger "RJS" asks, then, if we know this, what becomes of our belief in the Bible as Word of God? She sharpens the edge of this issue with these words:

This is a command that seems rather ignored at times in the Church today. And this is a conundrum. We talk about being Bible believing Christians, about inerrancy and authority at great length. After all, women in ministry is an issue because of only two key passages (1 Cor. 14:34–35 and 1 Tim. 2:11–13). These lay down an absolute law to which we must submit, at least according to the interpretation of many. Sorry ma'am, we are told, I didn't make the rules, God did. I just follow them.

But there are far more than two passages calling for generosity, condemning greed, and in favor of the poor, and they are pretty clear. Far more clear than 1 Corinthians 14 and 1 Timothy 2.[19]

The apostle John, in fact, illustrates my very point, that cross and generosity are tied into one set of lines: "This is how we know what love is: Jesus Christ laid down his life for us. And we ought to lay down our lives for our brothers and sisters. If anyone has material possessions and sees a brother or sister in need but has no pity on them, how can the love of God be in that person? Dear children, let us not love with words or speech but with actions and in truth" (1 John 3:16–18). Here we see John saying that love is cross-shaped, and cross-shaped love becomes generosity.

John Wesley, the founder of the Methodist Church, preached over and over on a saying of Jesus about money: Luke 16:9, which reads, "Use worldly wealth to gain friends for yourself."[20] The editors of an anthology of Wesley's sermons, when introducing Wesley's radical words about money, say, "On no other single point . . . is Wesley more insistent, consistent, and out of step with the bourgeois spirit of the age." What did Wesley teach?

Gain all you can.
Save all you can.
Give all you can.

To be sure, Wesley's context was not Jesus', nor is Wesley's ours, but what Wesley says here is in my opinion the kingdom view of possessions: kingdom citizens are marked by industry, by intention, by simplicity, by wisdom, and most especially by generosity. Earning and saving and giving are designed to provide, as Wesley put it, for ourselves, for our families, for the household of faith, and for fellow humans. What strikes me about Wesley is not the virtues of industry and wisdom but the orientation of both toward *generosity*. Kingdom mission requires that the cross, righteousness, and love reshape what we do with our possessions and money.

11

KINGDOM IS HOPE

Kingdom begins with a story, and a good story has characters and a plot that creates a problem or some tension, and the plot seeks resolution for that tension. Kingdom story has a resolution. Someday the inaugurated kingdom will be a consummated kingdom. Someday the education will lead to the vocation. The future is the magnet pulling the past and the present toward it. As Christian Wiman said it, "Remove futurity from experience and you leach meaning from it just as surely as if you cut out a man's past." Just a glimpse of that future, which is the subject of this chapter, is, to use Wiman's words again, "that spirit-cleansing whiff of the ultimate."[1] As a man with a death-dealing cancer, Wiman knows that whiff.

When many Christians hear the word "kingdom" they think of "heaven," and that means where they go when they die. Most seem to think life in heaven will be a spirit-kind of existence rather than a body-kind of existence.[2] We'll be able to flit around like angels and pass through walls. This kingdom-heaven equation leads to further hopes and expectations like being with our loved ones and meeting people like Abraham and David and Isaiah and, for me at least, Hosea. Then we add into that mixture Peter and Paul and Mary and John and Priscilla and Junia, for whom I have a couple questions. There's more: we have to add those early Christian saints like Perpetua and Irenaeus and Athanasius, and we can march right through church history, ignoring the multitudes we don't know and mentioning our favorites like Anselm and Luther and John Wesley and Rebecca Protten and William Wilberforce and Mary Bethune Cookman and John Stott. You get the idea. Heaven is a glorious and glorified reunion of spiritual, disembodied saints.

But what does Jesus say about the future kingdom? The kingdom is both now and not yet, so we ask, what is the "not yet" like? There are at least four themes at work in the New Testament's vision of the future kingdom of God, themes that can animate our hope and redirect our mission. The future kingdom

- will be a flourishing fellowship or society,
- will begin with a climactic judgment,
- will be a perfected community, and
- will be uninhibited joy and happiness.

All we can do is sketch each one.

Flourishing Fellowship

The first thing that should come to mind when we think of the kingdom is not later Christian ideas about heaven but—get this—Jerusalem, the city in the Holy Land. Tan hills surrounding the city, cool evening breezes, dusty, hot desert to the east and south, the hills of Galilee to the north, and the great Mediterranean Sea to the west. The New Testament image of the kingdom is Jerusalem reshaped, reformed, revised, remade, and reworked, but it is still Jerusalem. The gates are there, but no one needs to tend the gates at night since it is entirely safe; the people are carrying on business and family life (we'll get to that below) and worship and teaching and praise. The first image of kingdom, then, is that it will be *an earthly, flourishing fellowship of God's kingdom people, the church,* which as I said earlier is Israel Expanded (not Israel Replaced). I emphasize this because many of us discover—when we begin to think about it—that our idea of heaven is an eternal Sunday morning worship service, but this time God gets to do the preaching . . . and we hope, among other things, there'll be more comfortable seating.

To appreciate this I want to revisit the list Jimmy Dunn provides of what Jews at the time of Jesus were expecting when the kingdom arrived. Here is that list again (see p. 46 above):

- Return from exile
- Hope for prosperity, healing, or paradise
- A Messiah
- The renewal of the covenant
- Building a new temple
- Return of YHWH to Zion
- Triumph over, destruction of, and sometimes inclusion of gentiles
- Inheriting and expanding the land
- A climactic period of tribulation
- Cosmic disturbances leading to a new creation
- Defeat of Satan
- Final judgment
- Resurrection
- Sheol/Hades morphing into a place of final retribution

What do we see here? The Jewish expectation for the kingdom of God, the very language Jesus chose to capture his entire vision, was earthly if not earthy. The kingdom in Jewish expectation was Jerusalem functioning the way God meant Jerusalem to function. The Jews will return to Zion, they will prosper and be healed, they will have a Messiah on the throne ruling, they will have a new temple, the covenant will be so deeply interwoven that all Jews will be observant of the Torah, God will himself return to the temple as God was present during the days of Solomon, the gentile oppressors will be sent home, the land will be the location of the kingdom, and all of this will be set in the context of a cosmic judgment, the disestablishment and radical elimination of evil, and the resurrection to eternal life. This, not the history of Christian speculation about disembodied angel-like flitting around, is the context for Jesus' and the apostles' teaching of the future kingdom. This saying of Jesus establishes our point: "I say to you that many will come from the east and the west, and will take their places at the feast with Abraham, Isaac and Jacob in the kingdom of heaven. But the subjects of the kingdom will be thrown outside [into Gehenna, the valley south of Jerusalem], into the darkness, where there will be weeping and gnashing of teeth" (Matt. 8:11–12).

Here Jesus depicts the kingdom as the inclusion of gentiles, or (perhaps only) the regathering of the tribes of Israel to Zion, to participate in a flourishing fellowship with the patriarchs of Israel. At his last supper with the disciples, Jesus revealed to them that he would not eat with them again until the kingdom of God, which he described as a banquet; here are his words: "Truly I tell you, I will not drink again from the fruit of the vine until that day when I drink it new in the kingdom of God" (Mark 14:25). This means he thought of the future kingdom as a holiday feast with family and friends.

Jesus often peered into the future kingdom through parables, but the stories he told often shocked listeners. One such parable is called the parable of the wedding banquet, where the wrinkles in the wedding celebration reveal hidden truths about that final flourishing fellowship.

The kingdom of heaven is like a king who prepared a wedding banquet for his son. He sent his servants to those who had been invited to the banquet to tell them to come, but they refused to come.

Then he sent some more servants and said, "Tell those who have been invited that I have prepared my dinner: My oxen and fattened cattle have been butchered, and everything is ready. Come to the wedding banquet."

But they paid no attention and went off—one to his field, another to his business. The rest seized his servants, mistreated them and killed them. The king was enraged. He sent his army and destroyed those murderers and burned their city.

Then he said to his servants, "The wedding banquet is ready, but those I invited did not deserve to come. So go to the street corners and invite to the banquet anyone you find." So the servants went out into the streets and gathered all the people they could find, the bad as well as the good, and the wedding hall was filled with guests.

But when the king came in to see the guests, he noticed a man there who was not wearing wedding clothes. He asked, "How did you get in here without wedding clothes, friend?" The man was speechless.

Then the king told the attendants, "Tie him hand and foot, and throw him outside, into the darkness, where there will be weeping and gnashing of teeth."

For many are invited, but few are chosen. (Matt. 22:2–14)

We see two major themes in this parable: first, those invited to the wedding refuse to come and instead kill the servants who were sent out with the invitations; second, the king destroys the city and invites everyone, "the bad and the good," and the wedding hall fills up (Matt. 22:8–10).[3] A similar parable in Luke describes those invited as "the poor, the crippled, the blind and the lame" (Luke 14:21). In fact, in that parable there's still room left for more, so they go out to the "roads and country lanes" in order to fill the banquet hall (14:23). What this parable teaches is that the future kingdom will be a colossal fellowship of revelers, the sort of revelers one finds at weddings. The original guests may refuse their invitations, but the king is gracious and will fill his kingdom banquet with celebrants.

The operative word in this section is "fellowship." For Jesus and his contemporaries, *banquet* became the metaphor for kingdom realities because the essence of the kingdom is a celebratory fellowship with one another in peace and love and joy and abundance and safety. The focal metaphor for Jesus, then, is not my personal, absorbing, and glorious union with God but is *God dwelling with the people of God and the people of God dwelling with one another in a celebratory fellowship.* There is much here for understanding kingdom mission, but we have other themes to sketch before we get there.

Judgment

Judgment is far too often restricted to "Who is in?" and "Who is not?" But judgment in Israel's story is about *God stepping in to end what is wrong and to establish what is right in the world.* When Jesus steps onto the pages of history, he brings these central themes into new shape, and I see a number of themes we need to keep in mind when it comes to what it means to follow Jesus into kingdom mission.

The Jewish Context Is Earthly

If one reads the Old Testament as a narrative from beginning to end, the reader is struck by the constant need for God to step into history to judge and to reward. The themes in the cycles of the book of Judges illustrate what divine judgment means: obedience and blessings, unfaithfulness and discipline, God judges through a "judge," and Israel is restored to obedience and blessings (Judg. 2:6–3:6). Judgment in Israel's story is about the land, about the temple, and about the king and Israelites either dwelling in the land under God's blessing or being exiled from the land to experience the judging discipline of God. Punishment involves foreign armies invading and the tribes of Israel or Judah being transported against their will to foreign countries (Jer. 1:14–15; 4:6; 6:1, 22; 10:22). Reward means dwelling in the land with God's faithful people, where they will experience big fat grapes and wonderful wheat crops and big families and no foreign oppressors and the glorious presence of God in the temple. This very earthly understanding of judgment forms the context for which Jesus spoke of judgment.

Jesus Is the Judge

Judgment is prominent in the teachings of Jesus, beginning with a notable feature: Jesus will be the judge. In one of the most well-known parables of Jesus we read this opening line: "When the Son of Man comes in his glory, and all the angels with him, he will sit on his glorious throne" (Matt. 25:31). In the parable of the weeds and wheat Jesus says, "The Son of Man will send out his angels, and they will weed out of his kingdom everything that causes sin and all who do evil" (Matt. 13:41), and the rewarded ones will "shine like the sun in the kingdom of their Father" (13:43). The mother of John and James asks Jesus, "Grant that one of these two sons of mine may sit at your right and the other at your left in the kingdom" (Matt. 20:21). The thief on the cross asks Jesus to remember him "when you come into your kingdom" (Luke 23:42) because Jesus has made it very clear

184

that entrance into the kingdom is through him: "Whoever acknowledges me before others, I will also acknowledge before my Father in heaven. But whoever disowns me before others, I will disown before my Father in heaven" (Matt. 10:32–33).

Jesus is the gate to the kingdom, even if in the end the kingdom is ruled by the Father (Matt. 13:43; 1 Cor. 15:24–28).

The Judgment Is Earthly and Important to Jesus

At the last supper Jesus says this to his disciples—and if you read it carefully you notice significant connections between Israel, the disciples, the land, and the kingdom: "You are those who have stood by me in my trials. And I confer on you a kingdom, just as my Father conferred one on me, so that you may eat and drink at my table in my kingdom and sit on thrones, judging the twelve tribes of Israel" (Luke 22:28–30). Kingdom, judgment, the Twelve—this all sounds very earthly in orientation. Along the same line, then, what stands out above all other Gospel texts about judgment is Jesus' predictions of the fall of Jerusalem. These are found in Mark 13, Matthew 24, and Luke 21. Jesus was talking about the destruction of Jerusalem at the hands of Rome in the Great War of AD 66–73 and, if I may offer an exhortation, we need to read Josephus alongside Mark 13 to see just how lucid Jesus' images and prophecies were.[4] These seemingly historical judgments are intensified as Matthew 24 continues into the next chapter's parables of the final judgment, where we are to understand God's judgment in history—like that against Jerusalem in AD 70—as foreshadowings of the final judgment itself.

Briefly, any reading of the Gospels—or of any one of the Gospels—leads one to see how frequently Jesus brings up judgment. Yes, his sense of judgment is earthly, and the gravity of the language used can at times be breathtaking.

> "If your right eye causes you to stumble, gouge it out and throw it away. It is better for you to lose one part of your body than for your whole body to be thrown into hell. And if your right hand causes you to stumble, cut it off and throw it away. It is better for you to lose one part of your body than for your whole body to go into hell." (Matt. 5:29–30)

"Do not be afraid of those who kill the body but cannot kill the soul. Rather, be afraid of the One who can destroy both soul and body in hell." (Matt. 10:28)

Judgment is everywhere in the teachings of Jesus; one scholar estimates that about 25 percent of Jesus' words involve judgment.[5]

The Judgment Involves Punishment

In postmodern culture, to say that the judgment theme of the Bible is about establishing justice and undoing injustice is a good thing, but to say God's judgment is about punishment draws down boos and hisses. But there's a full sleeve of punishment sayings tattooed on the arm of Jesus when it comes to the future kingdom. Think of the parable of the wheat and weeds in Matthew 13:24–30, 36–43. The "enemy" (the devil) sows "weeds" (people of the devil) in the wheat field. The farmer's servants want to rip out the weeds, but the farmer tells them to wait because they'll ruin some of the wheat. The Son of Man, at "the harvest" (an image of judgment) at "the end of the age" (prior to the kingdom), will send angels to cut it all up and divide the weeds from the wheat. They will "throw them into the blazing furnace where there will be weeping and gnashing of teeth." Here there is punishment—retribution at some level—on the people of the devil.

But what is this punishment? Over and over the image of punishment for Jesus is destruction. The broad and roomy path leads to destruction (Matt. 7:13), and the one who hears Jesus' words and does not practice them will be destroyed (Luke 6:49). The betrayer is the "son of destruction" (John 17:12). God, then, is "the One who can destroy both soul and body in hell" (Matt. 10:28), even if "the thief comes only to steal and kill and destroy" (John 10:10). The idea, then, is that the punishing judgment of God will ruin the life of some and create eternal life for others.

The Judgment Involves Reward

Protestants naturally chafe at Jesus' routine use of "reward" as language for what good people get at the hand of God for their proper way of life. Because it is hard for many to accept this "economy of heaven," it is important to list a few texts that use the word "reward" as the eternal consequences of moral living.

> "Rejoice and be glad, because great is your reward in heaven, for in the same way they persecuted the prophets who were before you." (Matt. 5:12)

> "Be careful not to practice your righteousness in front of others to be seen by them. If you do, you will have no reward from your Father in heaven." (Matt. 6:1)

> "Whoever welcomes a prophet as a prophet will receive a prophet's reward, and whoever welcomes a righteous person as a righteous person will receive a righteous person's reward. And if anyone gives even a cup of cold water to one of these little ones who is my disciple, truly I tell you, that person will certainly not lose their reward." (Matt. 10:41–42)

Clearly, for Jesus, entrance into the kingdom corresponds to how one has lived one's life; the good enter the kingdom, while the evil are banished from the kingdom and destroyed. One of the clearer statements along this line can be found in Mark 10:28–30.

> Then Peter spoke up, "We have left everything to follow you!"
> "Truly I tell you," Jesus replied, "no one who has left home or brothers or sisters or mother or father or children or fields for me and the gospel will fail to receive a hundred times as much in this present age: homes, brothers, sisters, mothers, children and fields—along with persecutions—and in the age to come eternal life."

Both now and in the kingdom one receives the reward for following the will of God: in the now one receives a new family among kingdom citizens, and in the age to come one receives "eternal life," the abounding life of God forever and ever in the fellowship of God's people.

We do not have space here to develop this theme, so I offer a sketch of the line of thinking at work in this sense of reward. For Jesus, our life is a probation and God is the judge. Entering into eternity cannot be taken for granted because those who enter the kingdom must meet certain conditions. Jesus is the Bread of Life; he is the Gate; he is the Way, the Truth, and the Life. Those who want to enter the kingdom must listen to him and do what he says. The reward for responding to Jesus is fellowship in the kingdom community now and eternal fellowship in that same community in the kingdom of God.

The themes so frequent in what Jesus says about judgment also have a vital role to play in kingdom mission, but we must postpone that discussion until we have discussed one more theme in what Jesus says about the future kingdom.

Perfected Community

An important element in kingdom as hope is *utopia*.[6] Driving every kingdom vision in Jewish contexts is utopia, but this term itself requires definition. Let us distinguish two dimensions of all hopes for utopia:

- First, *u*-topia is the imagined future reality.
- Second, *eu*-topia is the attempt to put *u*-topia into place in the here and now.

Before we take another step toward Jesus, we notice that Jesus' idea of his future kingdom is *u*-topia while the present inauguration is *eu*-topia. This clever nuance aside, there remains one highly important observation: Jesus' kingdom vision needs to be seen in the context of utopian ideas. And he was not alone.

We are grateful to Mary Ann Beavis for her summary sketches of utopian vision in the Greek and Roman worlds, as well as those from the Jewish world.[7] The *Greco-Roman* utopian ideas spanned from the mythological and fantastic to political utopias. Plato sketches the *ideal* city-state that serves as a model, while other political thinkers develop *realistic* programs for the city-state that can more or less be put into practice (Plato's *Laws*, Aristotle's *Politics* 7–8, Cicero's *On the Republic*). But Jesus is much less connected to the Greco-Roman utopias than to the Jewish ones. The best example of a utopian society made real can be found at Qumran among the Essenes. So we are on firmer turf if we turn to Jewish utopian visions, and Beavis finds three streams in the Jewish utopian visions. First is the mythological utopia of Eden. Second are land-based utopias that focus on such things as a land flowing with milk and honey, golden-era visions of the temple and Jerusalem, ideal epochs as with Moses or David or the return from the exile under Ezra and Nehemiah, and legal utopias in which the Torah of Moses is not just the ideal law but is lived out by Israel. Her third stream is the dynamic-theocratic vision in which God is in control and any king is simply serving God as King (our A-B-A' story).

This all at once clarifies Jesus' kingdom vision in historical context: Jesus does not much draw on the Eden traditions. Instead he draws upon particular periods or events—Moses and the exodus, as well as the exile—and in particular Jesus declares the rule of God. *Jesus' utopian vision is theocratic in a messianic key.* God rules, and he, Jesus, rules on God's behalf. This utopia of Jesus, then, is not apolitical but simultaneously antipolitical (against the rulers of this age like Herod and Pilate and Caesar) and hyperpolitical. I call it *hyper*political because a theocracy transcends earthly political rule.[8]

What will the future kingdom—*u*-topia—look like according to Jesus? I see two major themes: magnificence and the utopian society.

Magnificence

Nothing makes a kingdom vision more utopian than the theme of magnificence and glory. To begin with, over and over Jesus speaks of such things as the "end" or the "consummation" of the ages (Matt. 13:39, 49). The term "consummation" translates *synteleia*, which refers to the age in the unfolding drama of God in this world in which all previous ages come to their completion. So when Peter announces that he has given up so dad-gum much to follow Jesus, Jesus responds by speaking of the magnificence of the age to come (and I will quote this text again for reminder).

> Then Peter spoke up, "We have left everything to follow you!"
>
> "Truly I tell you," Jesus replied, "no one who has left home or brothers or sisters or mother or father or children or fields for me and the gospel will fail to receive a hundred times as much in this present age: homes, brothers, sisters, mothers, children and fields—along with persecutions—and in the age to come eternal life." (Mark 10:28–30)

In this life (the *eu*-topia) Peter gets "a hundred times as much in the present age," but in the age to come (*u*-topia) he will get so much more, which Jesus calls "eternal life."

We ought to pause briefly to observe the *continuity* between this age and the age to come. Jesus tells Peter that what he gets now will be given in abundance in the kingdom. We do not start all over again; instead what we have now will become what it was meant to be. Chris Wright takes up this theme with a crystal-clear set of observations.

> "The world to come," as it is sometimes called, will not be a blank sheet, with all that humanity has accomplished in fulfillment of the creation mandate simply crumpled up and tossed in a cosmic incinerator. Rather it will take that accomplishment, purged and disinfected of all the poison and corruption of our fallenness, as the starting point of an unimaginable future—an eternity of new creation and new creativity, totally glorifying to God and satisfying to us, to be enjoyed forever by both in intimate and unspoiled communion.[9]

Jesus' favorite term for the age to come is "banquet," as seen already, but another term that touches on the theme of magnificence is "glory." Notice these statements by Jesus:

> Jesus said to them, "Truly I tell you, at the renewal of all things, when the Son of Man sits on his glorious throne, you who have followed me will also sit on twelve thrones, judging the twelve tribes of Israel." (Matt. 19:28)

> "Then will appear the sign of the Son of Man in heaven. And then all the peoples of the earth will mourn when they see the Son of Man coming on the clouds of heaven, with power and great glory." (24:30)

> "When the Son of Man comes in his glory, and all the angels with him, he will sit on his glorious throne." (25:31)

The future kingdom is a time of magnificence; in particular, it will be an eternal banquet in the presence of God where the crucified Son forms the central story that exudes the very glory of the glorious God of Israel.

190

Utopian Community

Every utopian vision of the future imagines a society marked by nothing but good and the elimination of evil. Hence, the future kingdom of Jesus, touching as it does upon Israel's theocratic utopian tradition, entails, first, rule by God and God alone. Second, it entails a society marked by justice, peace, and love. Nothing expresses this better than the songs of Mary and Zechariah in Luke 1. If we give them the leading songs in the musical, we also observe that Jesus himself very much sings the same songs, sometimes as *u*-topia and sometimes as *eu*-topia. Here are the songs of Mary and Zechariah. I will highlight the major terms and then draw our attention to them briefly.

And Mary said:

> "My soul glorifies the Lord
>   and my spirit rejoices in God my Savior,
> for he has been mindful
>   of the *humble state* of his servant.
> From now on all generations will call me blessed,
>   for the Mighty One has done great things for me—
>   holy is his name.
> His mercy extends to those who fear him,
>   from generation to generation.
> He has performed mighty deeds with his arm;
>   *he has scattered those who are proud in their inmost thoughts.*
> *He has brought down rulers from their thrones*
>   *but has lifted up the humble.*
> *He has filled the hungry with good things*
>   *but has sent the rich away empty.*
> He has helped his servant Israel,
>   remembering to be merciful
> to Abraham and his descendants forever,
>   just as he promised our ancestors." (Luke 1:46–55)

[John the Baptist's] father Zechariah was filled with the Holy Spirit and prophesied:

> "Praise be to the Lord, the God of Israel,
>   because he has come to his people and *redeemed* them.

He has raised up *a horn of salvation for us*
    in the house of his servant David
(as he said through his holy prophets of long ago),
salvation from our enemies
    and from the hand of all who hate us—
to show mercy to our ancestors
    and to remember his holy covenant,
    the oath he swore to our father Abraham:
to rescue us from the hand of our enemies,
    and to enable us to serve him without fear
    in holiness and righteousness before him all our days.

And you, my child, will be called a prophet of the Most High;
    for you will go on before the Lord to prepare the way for him,
to give his people the knowledge of salvation
    through the forgiveness of their sins,
because of the tender mercy of our God,
    by which the rising sun will come to us from heaven
to shine on those living in darkness
    and in the shadow of death,
to guide our feet into the path of peace." (Luke 1:67–79)

What are the themes of the arrival of the messianic kingdom, of the *u*-topia of Jesus? Justice and the end of injustice, provision for the poor and the end of impoverishment as well as rich exploitation, the end of foreign rule and the establishment of divine home rule, forgiveness of sins and a people marked by holiness and worship of the one true God. And peace.

But a theme often ignored in these songs must be brought to the fore: there is a powerful and relentless christocentricity here. Jesus is the Messiah, Jesus is the King, and it is through Jesus that God will rule and establish his kingdom. Jesus, too, emphasizes the same themes in his inaugural sermon at Nazareth (Luke 4:16–30) and in his Beatitudes (Luke 6:20–26). For Jesus, the kingdom will be marked by the end of oppressive injustices against the poor, the mourning, and the righteous; and the establishment of a Torah-observant people from the inside out, people who do God's will as taught by Jesus, which means they are holy, reverent, loving, and wise.

It is a small step from Mary and Zechariah to Jesus, and it is no more of a step to see in Revelation 21–22 the same utopian vision of a society at peace, a society full of justice and love and wisdom, and God's people dwelling with God and worshiping God eternally. The *u*-topian visions of the New Testament, while each bearing nuances, support the same grand theme: the kingdom of God is the perfected community of God's people (Israel, kingdom citizens, church). But what perhaps needs to be said now by way of reminder is that the overarching theme of Jesus' utopian vision is that it is a fellowship, a community, a society, and not simply the eternal life of an individual in the presence of God. Notice in each of these visions just sketched, and many more could be added, how *social* the vision is.

Blessing

One word summarizes the hope of the future kingdom: "blessed." Numerous passages in the Gospels use this term to describe the person who is ultimately approved, beginning with the Beatitudes (Luke 6:20–26) and moving on to "Blessed is anyone who does not stumble on account of me" (Matt. 11:6), or one of my favorites, "Blessed are your eyes because they see, and your ears because they hear" (Matt. 13:16). Not to be forgotten are Jesus' words to Peter upon his confessing Jesus as King: "Blessed are you, Simon son of Jonah, for this was not revealed to you by flesh and blood, but by my Father in heaven" (Matt. 16:17).

The word "blessed" is a blessed problem.[10] Translations have done their best to find the perfect English word to translate the underlying Greek word (*makarios*) or sometimes the hypothetical Hebrew or Aramaic word Jesus actually used (perhaps *ashre*, as in Psalm 1:1 and 32:1, or *baruka*, as in Gen. 14:19 and Deut. 28:3). Furthermore, the entire history of the philosophy of the "good life" and the late-modern theory of "happiness" are at work when one says, "Blessed are . . ." Thus, this swarm of connections leads us to consider Aristotle's great Greek term *eudaimonia*, which means something like happiness or human flourishing, but it also prompts us to consider modern studies of what makes people happy.[11] All of this gets bundled into the decision of which English word best translates the Greek word *makarios* now in the Beatitudes. An adventurous journey across the terrains of possible English words would be fun if this term were found in a subordinate clause in an otherwise insignificant verse in the Bible. But on this one word the entire passage stands and from this one word the whole list hangs. Get this word right, the rest falls into place; get it wrong, and the whole thing falls apart. We need to drill down to get it right.

The secret is to see this term in light of the Bible's story about who is blessed and who is not. Once we get that story's perspective, we are given parameters and content for understanding the term in this context, and once that happens, we can examine the history of the quest for the good life and happiness. There are at least five major themes at work in this word "blessed."

First, the one who is "blessed" is blessed *by the God of Israel*. The entire biblical story is in some sense shaped by God's watching over God's elect people, Israel, evaluating their covenant observance, and either approving or disapproving of them in tangible ways. This theme has two primary points of origin: Leviticus 26–27 and Deuteronomy 28 as well as the Wisdom tradition, where it refers to a tangible, flourishing life rooted in common sense, hard work, and listening to one's elders (Prov. 3:13; 8:32; 20:7; 28:20; Ps. 1; 32:1–2). The theme of God's blessing on the obedient shapes the historical books like Judges and 1–2 Samuel, 1–2 Kings, 1–2 Chronicles, Ezra, and Nehemiah; it clearly reverberates throughout the prophets and in many ways gave rise to the sectarian movements at the time of Jesus, like the Pharisees and Essenes, who were seeking God's blessing.

Second, there is a clear *eschatological* and *utopian* focus in the word "blessed." If a focus of the Old Testament was on present-life blessings for Torah observance, there is another dimension that deconstructs injustice and sets the tone for Israel's hope: the future blessing of God in the kingdom when all things will be put to rights, and no text in the Old Testament fits more than Isaiah 61. As Dale Allison correctly points out, "We have here [in the Beatitudes] not commonsense wisdom born of experience but eschatological promise which foresees the unprecedented: the evils of the present will be undone and the righteous will be confirmed with reward."[12] This blessing, while its focus is future, begins now (Matt. 11:6; 13:16).

A third theme at work is *conditionality*: those blessed are marked by specific attributes or characteristics, and those who are implicitly not blessed (the Bible's word is "cursed"; see Luke 6:20–26; Deut. 28) are marked by the absence of those characteristics and by the presence of the opposite characteristics. There is, then, an element of conditionality to the blessing: one must believe, trust, obey, persevere, or walk in faithfulness under King Jesus to enter into the kingdom. This—and one can immediately see hands rising—does not mean one "earns" one's way into the kingdom. What it does mean is that those who enter the kingdom are marked by the patterns of faith, without which patterns a person will not enter the kingdom.

A fourth element of this list concerns the person's *relational disposition*. It is easy to think of the "blessed" as those who are in proper relation to God alone. But what stands out in the Beatitudes is one's relation to God as well as to self and others. When Matthew adds "in spirit" to "poor," we find what we also find in the third blessing ("meek"): an inner disposition that relates to God and others because of a proper estimation of one's self. Furthermore, some blessings are for those who relate to others in a loving disposition: "mourn" and "merciful" and "peacemakers." Others are concerned more directly with one's relation to God: "hunger and thirst for righteousness" and "pure in heart" and probably those who are persecuted. But the blessed people are noted by godly, loving relations with God, self, and others.

A final theme is *reversal or contrast*. Here I beg the reader's patience in appealing to the way Luke records the Beatitudes. Luke lists not only those who are blessed but also those who are cursed (Luke 6:20–22, 23–26). Anytime someone blesses a group, as Jesus does here, one is non-blessing others. Luke's curse list is implicit in Matthew, but this contention gains support from the very oddity of those who are blessed: it is unconventional to bless those who are persecuted or those who are meek. It gains even more strength from the radical presence of Jesus' unconventional ways of relating to "all the wrong people" (e.g., Matt. 9:9–13) and for the sorts of people he included among the apostles (Matt. 4:18–22; 10:1–4). What Jesus blesses is countercultural and revolutionary and so turns culture inside out and society upside down. This can be seen simply by comparing Matthew 5:3–12 with a conventional list in Sirach.

> Happy is the person who meditates on wisdom
>   and reasons intelligently,

who reflects in his heart on her ways
and ponders her secrets,
pursuing her like a hunter,
and lying in wait on her paths;
who peers through her windows
and listens at her doors;
who camps near her house
and fastens his tent peg to her walls;
who pitches his tent near her,
and so occupies an excellent lodging place;
who places his children under her shelter,
and lodges under her boughs;
who is sheltered by her from the heat,
and dwells in the midst of her glory. (Sir. 14:20–27 NRSV)

I can think of nine whom I would call blessed,
and a tenth my tongue proclaims:
a man who can rejoice in his children;
a man who lives to see the downfall of his foes.
Happy the man who lives with a sensible wife,
and the one who does not plow with ox and ass together.
Happy is the one who does not sin with the tongue,
and the one who has not served an inferior.
Happy is the one who finds a friend,
and the one who speaks to attentive listeners.
How great is the one who finds wisdom!
But none is superior to the one who fears the Lord.
Fear of the Lord surpasses everything;
to whom can we compare the one who has it? (25:7–11 NRSV)

Clearly, Jesus goes against the grain. Instead of blessing the one who pursues wisdom and reason and develops a reputation as a sage, and instead of blessing the one who has a good family or who observes the whole Torah or the one who has all the right friends and develops a reputation as righteous or as a leader, Jesus blesses those no one else blessed. The genius of the Beatitudes emerges from this contrastive stance: they are a countercultural revelation of the people of the kingdom.

If we add all this together, we get something like this: a "blessed" person is someone who because of a heart for God is promised and enjoys God's favor regardless of that person's status or countercultural condition. To be blessed, then, is to enjoy the favor of God. But what I want to draw attention to here is the *utopian* element of this. In the future kingdom this blessedness is eternal and boundless and unconditional and deepening and widening and lengthening and heightening. It is the pure pleasure of God for the people of God.

Kingdom Mission and Hope

It is time now to move from exposition of what Jesus says about hope to the significance of hope for kingdom mission.

Anchored in Hope

Kingdom mission is anchored in hope for the kingdom. I am constitutionally optimistic, extroverted, hopeful, and a dreamer. You will not be shocked if I say I get annoyed with pessimists, introverts, cynics, and the dreary. They, no doubt, are annoyed by the likes of me. What the Bible means by hope, however, depends not on our constitution but on our faith. Over time our faith may dig into our constitution to make us more hopeful, but we need to learn to disconnect what the Bible means by hope from our psychological proclivities. What is this hope? Let me quote a marvel among New Testament thinkers from the previous generation, C. F. D. Moule, who at the end of his incisive study about hope concluded with these words:

> For Christian hope is emphatically more than a doubtful wishing—more even than expectation of good:
>> it is trust in God and love in his family;
>> it is securely anchored in the triumph of Christ's resurrection;
>> it is exhibited in the community in which the Holy Spirit lives and acts. . . .
> The Christian hope cannot be itself without being evangelistic, and it cannot be evangelistic without concerning itself with the *whole* of life. . . .
> Does not Christian hope stultify itself unless it is as wide as all mankind, as wide as the universe, as wide as the love of God in Jesus Christ himself?[13]

Kingdom mission offers hope because what the kingdom will be generates such hope. Until we grasp what it will be, we will not develop a biblical sense of hope. I want to draw our attention to three themes of kingdom mission's hope.

TABLE FELLOWSHIP ANTICIPATING THE FINAL KINGDOM

Kingdom mission finds its daily life in an inclusive table fellowship that anticipates the future kingdom. Jesus embodied the kingdom in how he acted, and the one notable act of Jesus was table fellowship with his followers. This fellowship, however, was not tightly controlled; Jesus held the invitation open for others, including notorious sinners, to come to the table with Jesus. The byword for Jesus was that he was a "friend of tax collectors and sinners" (Matt. 11:19), and one of the more provocative acts of Jesus was when he was dining at the home of a well-known Pharisee, Simon by name, and a prostitute entered the room and washed Jesus' feet with her grateful tears (Luke 7:36–50). His praxis of table fellowship is not simply symbolic of the future kingdom but brings the future kingdom into the reality of now.

Kingdom mission hope is found when we sit at table and eat with one another. I am not, however, talking about small-group friendships that are formed by likeness. What I have in mind is the final banquet's amazing width, breadth, depth, and height. We see a glimpse of it in Revelation 5:11–14.

> Then I looked and heard the voice of many angels, numbering thousands upon thousands, and ten thousand times ten thousand. They encircled the throne and the living creatures and the elders. In a loud voice they were saying:
> "Worthy is the Lamb, who was slain,
> to receive power and wealth and wisdom and strength
> and honor and glory and praise!"
> Then I heard every creature in heaven and on earth and under the earth and on the sea, and all that is in them, saying:
> "To him who sits on the throne and to the Lamb
> be praise and honor and glory and power,
> for ever and ever!"
> The four living creatures said, "Amen," and the elders fell down and worshiped.

What do eating together and table fellowship look like if this is the final banquet, if this is the kingdom? *U*-topia becoming *eu*-topia means our tables are to look more and more like that table, which means *focused, intentional inclusiveness.* All who want to focus their praise on the Lamb are welcome, and that means *all are welcome*, and that means striving for all to be invited and welcomed. In the final banquet angels and humans and all created beings will sing praise to the Lamb who redeemed people for the kingdom through his suffering and atoning work and through his victory over death. The forgiven and ransomed and reclaimed and healed are the ones who sing praises to the Lamb. In the kingdom, a denomination's petty theological tests will be burned up in the glorious fire of the Lamb's rule. The test is focused worship and surrender to the Lamb on the throne. This is why the Eucharist table is the purest symbol and embodiment of kingdom realities: we find food that sustains, alongside others who find the same sustaining food.

Do our tables spring out of this focused inclusiveness or out of a focused exclusiveness? I can think of many Christian groups who are intent on excluding some and are abundantly welcoming of those who remain, but their welcome is sectarian and their table is a tribe of the like-minded. The final kingdom includes Jews and gentiles, slaves and free, and males and females. Does our fellowship include ethnic diversity? Economic diversity? Sexual diversity? Or is our fellowship tribal?

So, gather friends, gather together as a fellowship. Instead of permitting each family or person to pick her or his table, draw names from a hat and randomly fellowship with one another. Gather friends, not in the name of likeness but in the name of focused inclusiveness. Gather friends, not in the name of theological agreement but in the name of focused inclusiveness. This focused inclusiveness of the final banquet is *u*-topia with a challenge to be *eu*-topia in your church this morning, at noon, at dinnertime, and whenever the fellowship gathers. Kingdom mission is about generating the hope of the final kingdom by the way we live now in focused inclusiveness.

ACHING FOR THE JUDGMENT

Kingdom mission means aching for judgment. Kingdom mission hope is found when we ache for God's judgment. Once again we bring into play the notion of utopia. The future kingdom is a utopian vision of justice, peace, the end of suffering, joy in safety and health, the reconciliation of fractured relationships, a society marked by love and wisdom and joy . . . I could go on. Many today long for those days, but for those days to come, the injustices, broken relationships, betrayals, pain, suffering, and tragedies of this world have to be named for what they are—sinfulness, systemic evils, satanic manifestations—and done away with through judgment.

Kingdom mission promises, then, a hope constituted by judgment of sin and establishment of a kingdom order. I recently read a manuscript by Leslie Fields (with Jill Hubbard) called *Forgiving Our Fathers and Mothers*, and it is exactly a story that lives up to that title. It takes courage to tell such a story of parental disasters and learning to live without a history of experiencing love in the one and only time we get: when our parents nurture us into this world through loving, wise, and just ways. Instead, Leslie learns that her sister was routinely sexually abused by her father. She "reconciles" with her father, but lurking through the whole story is the irretrievable past, the impact of power and abuse on the health and vitality and hope of Leslie and her siblings, the crushing realities of the now, the conviction that God is judge and someday will judge, the occasional hope of repentance and restoration and reconciliation and the pain that will entail, and the reality that reconciliation often falls through the fingers like sand, even blowing that sand into one's eyes and hopes.

What does kingdom mission hope look like here? I want to suggest it means that the many evil-deed doers are named for what they are and for what they did; that hope for repentance continues; that someday God will judge that evil and put it away forever and ever. I will tell you something else I believe about a kingdom utopian hope: that abused children will not only watch that evil be named and be done away with but that they will suddenly find their lives remade all over again, that they will know the love they should have known, that they will know the father's love and the mother's love that they deserved, and that their fellowship in the kingdom will be so glorious and good that memory of the past will be swallowed up into the kingdom's redemptive powers.

Can this *u*-topia become *eu*-topia now? In part, yes. In light of the judgment to come, when God brings to light the hidden acts of all and establishes order, we begin to lean into that order now through the processes of forgiveness and, when possible, reconciliation.[14] God alone makes forgiveness possible, and God makes it possible in the atoning death of King Jesus. Any act of bringing the aftermath of judgment into our world reenacts and reexpresses the forgiveness God provides. Since that judgment will name the sins, our forgiveness cannot occur until we attempt to name what God names. God's judgment on sin entails admission and confession on the part of the perpetrator, which also means our judgment on the sins against us requires admission and confession before reconciliation can be inaugurated. Yes, I draw distinctions between forgiveness and reconciliation, with the former describing what the victim enacts and the latter what possibly happens between the victim and perpetrator if the person repents from the sin.

Because kingdom citizens know the *u*-topia where God makes all things right, and because they know that the kingdom is filled with pure, godly love, kingdom citizens commit themselves to forgiveness and reconciliation so far as is possible in the *eu*-topia. As Jesus forgave those who sinned against him at the cross in light of the *u*-topia or paradise (Luke 23:34), so his followers are to forgive those who sin against them (Matt. 6:12, 14–15).

Kingdom Fellowship Now

Kingdom mission creates fellowship with one another. Kingdom mission hope is found when we learn to live in fellowship with one another. At times pastors ask me for advice on church conflicts and struggles to enhance fellowship. My wisdom flows directly from kingdom realities: *if* the final kingdom centers on a fellowship of God with the people of God, of the people of God with God, and of the people of God with one another, *then* fellowship in the here and now *anticipates* the final kingdom. So, once again, churches need to create and develop more "social" gatherings of God's people.

Here's how "church" works for most of us, and pastors are every bit as much to blame as the congregation. We "go to church" on Sunday morning. We arrive early enough to talk to plenty of folks or late enough to talk to few. We then sit in our pews and stand for songs and prayers and then sit for the sermon and then walk forward or keep sitting for the Eucharist and then stand again for a closing song. We then bump into some folks on our way out, we get in our cars and go to lunch or go home, and church is done for the week. Pastors, as I said, participate in such a culture and at times establish that kind of church culture. This barely brushes up against the meaning of fellowship.

Two stories from pastors. One, the pastor of a megachurch, confessed to me over a round of golf that he could do away with Sunday morning services because small groups did everything he believed a church should be. Of course I asked, "How so?" To which he replied, "Because church is about fellowship, and I'm not sure that happens on Sunday mornings." Another pastor, convinced that churches ought to be marked by fellowship, created the practice of the church gathering for a church-sponsored, cheap meal on Thursday evenings. For a long time the only ones who gathered were the pastor and his wife and the youth pastor and his wife, with an occasional straggler. It took years for the congregation to embrace the idea. Over lunch at an Italian restaurant he said these two things: "Our people are too busy for fellowship," and "One person asked me what fellowship had to do with church!"

If a flourishing fellowship is the essence of the kingdom, we need to shape church life into kingdom gatherings by enhancing opportunities for fellowship. How can we do this? Small groups that don't overdo the Bible study or theology study dimensions but include generous times for sharing life. Potlucks or social events for the whole congregation. I grew up in a potluck church, and not that long ago I was invited to speak at a church in the heartland of America—Pekin, Illinois—and it began with a potluck. Kris and I loved the weekend, and for us the highlight was the potluck! Sure, it brought back old memories, but it also created space for us to talk with the folks to whom I'd be preaching and teaching the next two days. Some churches develop dinner fellowships where folks mix with those they don't know just to get to know one another better.

Before we go too far I must say a word for the introverts among us. Churches tend to magnify what appeals to extroverts and ignore what appeals to introverts, and surely the very proposal of more social events can scare what remains of a social desire out of the introvert. So some may prefer the quiet evening instead of the potluck, or the smaller group with someone more trusted than the random gathering of Christians. Maybe the final kingdom will calm down the extrovert and excite the introvert into social fellowship. With this sensitivity in place, let us remind ourselves again that the future kingdom is a fellowship of God and God's people. If that is the *u*-topia, then our attempts to bring that into existence now mean learning to fellowship with one another more and more.

Kingdom Mission Aims at the Blessed Life

To be blessed is to be ushered into an endless life of flourishing in the best senses of happiness.[15] Five observations: First, we all want to be happy. Saint Augustine once laid down this observation: "It is the decided opinion of all who use their brains that all men desire to be happy." Second, we all associate happiness with the experience of pleasure and the nonexperience of pain. As Stewart Goetz summarizes it, "Perfect happiness consists of nothing but conscious psychological states of . . . pleasure." Third, these good pleasures we experience now are the *eu*-topia of the final pleasures in *u*-topia. As C. S. Lewis once said, "I [would] say that every pleasure (even the lowest) is a likeness to, even, in its restricted mode, a foretaste of the end for [which] we exist, the fruition [enjoyment] of God." Fourth, God made us for this purpose. Again C. S. Lewis: "God not only understands but *shares* . . . the desire for complete and ecstatic happiness. He made me for no other purpose than to enjoy it." Finally, and once again from Lewis, "If I find in myself a desire which no experience in this world can satisfy, the most probable explanation is that I was made for another world."

To be blessed by God is not just to experience justice finally, nor is it simply to have the smile of God upon us. God's blessing transcends words and ushers us into a new reality of unstoppable, ever-intensifying, and glorious joy, pleasure, and happiness. But I want to add a sixth observation that seeks to take this line of brilliant thinking to a new level: this endless kingdom blessedness is love—beautiful and glorious and intense relations with God and with others. Final blessedness forms an eternal and developing intimate, flourishing union with God and with others in the endless interaction of the kingdom of God.

Now kingdom mission. Genuine kingdom mission points people toward kingdom blessedness and offers to people in the here and now a foretaste of that blessedness in two ways: first, it offers union with God through Jesus Christ—the gospel—and, second, it offers union with others through the fellowship of the kingdom, the church. That neither of these can be experienced now in their fullness should no longer cause us to be discouraged by the messiness of church life now since we live in the *eu*-topia as we await the *u*-topia. But we gain glimpses of this blessedness when we hear the words of approval and forgiveness in the Eucharist, in moments of prayer, in the approving words of those who love us. And we gain glimpses of this in the loving relationship we have with others, the kind of love that makes that rugged commitment to presence and to advocacy and to kingdom direction in all of life.

Kingdom mission, in a word, is love: God's love for us, our love for God, and God's love dispersed into us through the Spirit so that we love others and embrace them in God's love. We offer in kingdom mission, then, the glories of joy.

12

KINGDOM THESES

I conclude *Kingdom Conspiracy* with a listing of the various theses presented in the pages above.

1. The word "kingdom" in Judaism (the Old Testament, Josephus, etc.) has a natural synonym in the words "nation" and "Israel," not the words "redemption" or "salvation." Thus, kingdom is front and center about a people and cannot be limited either to a social ethic or a redemptive moment.

2. Kingdom is—almost always, with varying degrees of emphasis—a complex of king, rule, people, land, and law. Church is also a complex: a king (Christ), a rule (Christ rules over the body of Christ), a people (the church), a land (expanding Israel into the diaspora), and a law (the law of Christ, life in the Spirit).

3. Kingdom is "eschatological": both present and future. The kingdom's future entails a flourishing fellowship of people following final judgment and the establishment of righteousness, and that kingdom sets the tone for kingdom living now. Church is also eschatological: both present and future. The church's future is also one of a flourishing fellowship forever according to the plan of God in history.

4. When comparing kingdom to church, most people make fundamental logical errors. The most common is to compare future kingdom and present church. Kingdom is a both-and, a now and a not yet. The church also is a both-and, a now and not yet. The church, then, is an eschatological reality. To compare kingdom to church, one must compare now-kingdom with now-church and not-yet-kingdom with not-yet-church. When we compare present kingdom and present church, or future kingdom and future church, we come out with near-identical identities. This means it is reasonable to say that *the kingdom is the church, and the church is the kingdom*—that they are the *same* even if they are not identical. They are the same in that it is the same people under the same King Jesus even if each term—kingdom, church—gives off slightly different suggestions. In particular, "kingdom" emphasizes royalty while "church" emphasizes fellowship. Slight differences aside, the evidence I have presented in this book leads me to the conclusion that *we should see the terms as synonyms*.

5. The church's historical temptation is to make "kingdom" public by aligning itself with the state or the powers of culture, often called the Constantinian Temptation. In the United States, both the Moral Majority (or the Christian Coalition) and the Christian progressives have succumbed to Constantine; that is, they are tempted to use the state's force (even if of the majority) to legalize the Bible's teachings and its arena to carry out their battles.

I see three modes in the Constantinian Temptation:

- Ethicize: we ethicize the kingdom into justice and then turn justice into "social" justice. We do the same with peace.
- Secularize: we secularize our deeply grounded ethic of love when it becomes tolerance; we secularize the cross when it becomes service; we do the same with resurrection when it slides into generalized hope.
- Politicize: we politicize the kingdom when we enter the political process in order to bring about the desired kingdom realities of Jesus and the Bible.

6. The historical context of much of Christian activism today is rooted in the social gospel, which turned Christians into public advocates for the poor and powerless, and this was often propped up by political or social

progressivism's theory of political action. The social gospel then morphed in the middle of the twentieth century into liberation theology, which turned the Christian toward economic systems at work in the world. In particular, Marxism (or neo-Marxism, or softer forms) shaped much of liberation theology. Then liberation expanded into a message liberating all who are oppressed (women, African Americans, etc.). Most notably, building somewhat on the social gospel, liberation theology *decentered the church* and made the church *an arm of the government's progressivist aims.* It is not unfair to see conservative Christian politics as a conservative liberation theology rather than its opposite. Either way, each side of the culture war has succumbed to Constantine and operates with the mistaken belief that the most important arena of God's mission in the world is the political sector.

7. Christ came to build the church/kingdom, not to make the world a better place and not for the "common good."

8. The character of a king determines the character of the kingdom. The "character" of Jesus can be seen in the titles used for him—Son of Man, Son of God, and Messiah—titles that evoke the story of one exalted to be King following suffering and death. Thus, the kingdom becomes cruciform by virtue of the character of King Jesus.

9. Kingdom citizens are Jesus-redeemed humans, people who have been saved from sin, liberated from cosmic powers, and who are conquering systemic evil through the power of the Spirit. Unredeemed persons are not kingdom citizens, and so only the redeemed can do kingdom work.

10. Kingdom and church don't resolve their relationship until one forms a biblical understanding of the "world." The New Testament use of this is almost entirely negative. It is what Yoder calls "structured unbelief." Since Niebuhr, especially, "world" has become "culture," and in the Reformed wing, then, "culture making" is a Christian activity of preeminent concern. The use of the term "culture" too often puts a mask over the summons of God to redeem people from the world into the kingdom/church, rather than to improve the world for its own sake.

11. Since kingdom theology believes in a final reckoning and knows the future judgment is God's, and because kingdom citizens know the reality of injustices, kingdom citizens ache for God's judgment, the judgment that both ends sin and establishes the kingdom of God.

12. Kingdom citizens are a moral fellowship marked by a cruciform life of righteousness and love, and this life permeates every dimension of life, including peace and possessions.

13. Connecting kingdom to church does not "disengage" the Christian. It *redefines engagement* toward

- an alternative community in the local church;
- a loving community of good deeds, seen in Matthew 5:13–16 but especially in the "good works" in 1 Peter (public benevolence) *out of love.* Christian public actions are, then, the "spillover" of the church's inner workings. A Christian not engaged in the world in "good works" has failed to live according to the kingdom vision.

14. Kingdom mission, then, is local church mission.

- Evangelism
- Worship
- Catechesis: wisdom
- Fellowship: love
- Edification: advocacy
- Discipleship: nurture
- Gifts: Spirit unleashed

15. The only place kingdom work is and can be done is in and through the local church when disciples (kingdom citizens, church people) are doing kingdom mission.

Appendix 1

THE CONSTANTINIAN TEMPTATION

Kingdom theology today faces a constant temptation, which I call the Constantinian Temptation: the temptation to get the state to combine its powers with the church's powers to accomplish, institutionalize, and legalize what is perceived to be divine purposes. In this appendix, I want to sketch some basic elements in the Constantinian Temptation, but my approach will be to focus on how the church and state have related in American history.

The Bible Is for Everyone, Everywhere, Forever

If God is creator and ruler of the world, and God has made his will known through the Scriptures, then God's will is the will for all humans, Christians or not. The logic here is inescapable. If the Bible is God's will for humans, it is the will for all humans, including Americans and Canadians and Asians and Africans. This truth presents the temptation to think of the kingdom as God's universal rule in the world regardless of who and how many recognize God's will.

We Are Tempted to Use Political Power

Knowing God's will is grace, privilege, and responsibility. Because Christians know (or think they know) God's will in Scripture, their responsibility to make God's will known comes with a temptation toward conformity and coercion, or at least compelling persuasion. At the soft side is the Christian exercising public influence and transformation and liberation; at the other end of the spectrum is Constantine, the first Christian Roman emperor. He began the process that eventually led to what we call the Holy Roman Empire. That empire, often called Christendom or Constantinianism,[1] combined the church's beliefs with the state or the state with the church so much so that the state's power was used to legalize, enforce, and coerce those who threatened the state or the church with disagreement. I quote memorable words of John Howard Yoder that show the impact of connecting church to state:[2]

> Before Constantine, one knew as a fact of everyday experience that there was a believing Christian community but one had to "take it on faith" that God was governing history.
>
> After Constantine, one had to believe without seeing that there was a community of believers, within the larger nominally Christian mass, but one knew for a fact that God was in control of history.

We are also tempted to think of Constantinianism as what was back then, when Catholics ruled Europe, but we need to resist the temptation. For example, the Puritans were a godly Constantinian and Christendom movement. To be sure, they differed radically from the Holy Roman Empire, but their disagreement was not so much on political and social strategies as on their theology. Remember, the Puritans escaped England because of "Constantinianism" at work in King James and others, but what they left behind they recreated in the colonies. Conformity, coercion, and violence accompanied the Puritans. If you'd like to see it all played out in the Massachusetts Bay Company, read a biography of John Winthrop, the governor of the Massachusetts Bay Company, or a biography of Roger Williams, who was forced to run for his life because of his radical commitment to freedom, democracy, and certain theological beliefs.[3]

Not without reason many Leftists today worry about the Religious Right's blending of church and state, and not without reason the Right worries that the Religious Left does the very same thing with its version of a naked public square. Any and every attempt to get the government or state to legislate what Christians believe and therefore to enforce Christian beliefs through the law is to one degree or another Constantinian. Let's name names: both Jim Wallis and Ralph Reed operate on the basis of a Constantinian blending of church and state. Both want Washington, DC, to enact their brand of Christian virtue. Whenever church and state get connected, the word "kingdom" quickly takes on the sense that it is the sociopolitical and church government of a given city, state, or country.

Stanley Hauerwas tells the story of a conversation he once had with a Jewish philosopher who thumped Hauerwas in the chest with the contention that he (Hauerwas) was opposed to prayer in public schools only because he was against Jerry Falwell, which staggered Hauerwas momentarily. So he wrote up a splendid piece called "A Christian Critique of Christian America," where he drew this important conclusion: "What I have attempted to do is to show that the reason Falwell is such a challenge to the Christian mainstream is not because he is so different from them, *but because he has basically accepted their agenda*."[4] Exactly, forever and amen. The Christian Left and the Christian Right are doing the same thing—seeking to coerce the public or, more mildly, seeking to influence the public into their viewpoint through political agitation and majority rule. Hauerwas describes the ultimate goal of both sides: "their common goal of making American democracy as close as possible to a manifestation of God's Kingdom." I need not provide details in a history that has been told well by others.[5] But I will say that Hauerwas and I agree that American democracy can't be the kingdom of God until it submits, for one thing, to Jesus as the redemptive King.

We Are Often Tempted to Serve an Ideology

In the history of the church Christians have often enough gotten lost in ruling ideologies. David Koyzis has recently sketched what might be taken as the major ideologies at work when it comes to the Christian and the state, or a Christian politic, or the church and the state.[6] I repeat his simple summaries to get these ideas into the discussion: liberalism focuses on the sovereignty of the individual, conservatism on history's flow as the source of social norms, nationalism on the deification of a nation, democracy on belief in the people's voice as the voice of God, and socialism on commitment to common ownership as the way of salvation.

Each of these ideas, we might remind ourselves, can be seen as emerging from the Bible and the Christian tradition; each can be seen as a fundamental value or even worldview on the basis of which one can mark the future; and yet each of them carries the temptation to serve it at all costs. These themes throb throughout the discussions in the history of the church, hence our need to recognize their presence. Each beckons the person to engage in the political if that ideology is to become secure.

We Know Political Power Does Not Work and Freedom Must Be Protected

This is a bold, yet necessary, observation, and it requires a brief sketch of history. The sixteenth-century Protestant Reformation had three different surges. First, Martin Luther broke the Roman Catholic control of Germany and formed what we now call the Lutheran Church. Second, in Geneva John Calvin pushed in a slightly different direction to create what we now call the Reformed Church. These two Protestant movements involved courageous leadership and fearless application of Christian theology, but a third group believed neither Luther nor Calvin went far enough. The third group is called the Anabaptists, and they broke completely free of the Catholic Church as well as the Reformation movements. That is, the Anabaptists not only had to battle the Constantinian legacy in the Catholic Church, but they encountered a new kind of Constantinianism in the Lutherans and the Reformed. How so?

It is sometimes forgotten that Luther and Calvin formed a new kind of state-church relation. Although their movements were marked by a different theology, *neither broke entirely free of the Constantinian blending of church and state and the use of the state to enforce Christian beliefs.* But the Anabaptists broke completely free from the state church and created, without using such terms, a wall of separation between church and state fired by the principle of freedom of conscience. The finest summary statement that distinguishes the magisterial Reformation of Luther and Calvin from the radical Reformation of the Anabaptists is from John Howard Yoder: "In their debates with the official Reformation, the Anabaptists applied the principle of sola scriptura not only to the question of soteriology but also to the questions of ecclesiology and social ethics."[7] That is, the Anabaptists did not think Luther and Calvin were willing to go all the way with Scripture-formed and Scripture-limited understandings of the local church or of how the church should relate to the state. The Catholics, the Lutherans, and the Reformed put to death—by the power of the state—Anabaptists because of their Christian beliefs and practices.[8] Thus, the Anabaptists experienced Constantinian persecutions from Catholics as well as their "fellow Protestants."

Though many today do not know much about the Anabaptists, their story made America what it is today. In the seventeenth and eighteenth centuries, when the United States created a new kind of country, the opportunity arose for a new approach to church and state. Under the "Constantinian" rule of the Puritans in Massachusetts Bay Company, some, like Roger Williams, fought for genuine freedom of conscience. He wanted not only freedom of belief and conscience; he wanted that freedom to become law so that the state would not interfere with faith. What Williams created in the Providence Plantation (now Rhode Island) was a state that protected and valued individual freedom of conscience, something he called "soul liberty."[9] Roger Williams won and the Puritans lost, but not without a long battle (still with us in some ways). That is, yes, many early Americans acted as though the country was a Christian state, and as long as the vast majority supported that approach, little was said. But something powerful and pervasive happened with Williams. By the time we get to Thomas Jefferson, Benjamin Franklin, and other founding fathers of the American way—not to ignore John Locke's privatizing of religion behind them[10]—we have laws that separate state from church. *This approach, which is enshrined in every church and denomination in the United States as a protected freedom, is shaped by the Anabaptist vision of Roger Williams.* That is why I say all church-state relations in the United States benefit from the Anabaptist vision, even if some are being tempted to bring back a Constantinian blending.

When many Americans protest under the Affordable Care Act that churches and religious organizations cannot *in principle and by law* be told what healthcare services to provide for their employees, they are asserting what we learned from Roger Williams. This separation of state from church interference is the Anabaptist principle. This separation theory, though, conflicts with the belief of Christians that the Bible is the revealed will of God for all, as indicated in our first point in this appendix. That tension leads to a variety of strategies on the part of Christians to influence the wider culture and the law, strategies that were first worked out when the Western world began to be more and more secular. But those strategies, I am arguing, always contain the Constantinian Temptation.

There was no voice more respected in the twentieth century among conservative evangelicals than Carl Henry's, and perhaps no one gave more thought to the Christian and society than Henry, yet he observed that many were too aggressive and getting things backward. It is worth quoting him as a good reminder. He begins with the important observation that Christians have hope and have a vision. He says, "Christians have biblical reason for seeking a predominantly regenerate society." That aim, however, he says, doesn't mean what many think it might mean. He asks some piercing questions: "But do they . . . have reason also to legislate all scriptural principles upon public institutions including government and schools? Even if they should become the majority, would it be wise to do so?" He presses even further: "Will not Christians be disillusioned and in fact discredited if by political means they seek to achieve goals that the Church should ideally advance by preaching and evangelism?" Then he makes a jarring observation that ought to be stirred deeply into the soup of American Christianity: "Despite all the media tumult over [the] Moral Majority and the high public visibility of its leader, its extensive solicitation of funds during a six-year political crusade—claiming to speak for six million households—*has not achieved passage of a single major piece of legislation cherished by the conservative right*."[11]

This is precisely the point that James Davison Hunter would make nearly three decades later, when he observed that evangelicals do not have sufficient political power to achieve their aims and maybe ought to rethink their entire approach to what he calls "faithful witness."[12]

Randy Balmer, one of America's finest historians of evangelicalism, after years of studying the relationship of evangelicals and politics, concludes on a similar note in his *God in the White House*: "My reading of American religious history is that religion always functions best from the margins of society and not in the councils of power. Once you identify the faith with a particular candidate or party or with the quest for political influence, *ultimately it is the faith that suffers.*" He concludes with a subtle, but searing, reminder: "Compromise may work in politics. It's less appropriate to the realm of faith and belief."[13]

Amen, and again I say Amen.

We Have Sought to Change Society through *Adaptation* and *Influence*

The rise of secular thinking in the modern world meant that church and state were less connected, Constantinianism declined, individual citizens had the freedom to believe or not to believe, and the church became less powerful. To negotiate how to live as Christians, how to influence culture and state in all directions, theologians and pastors began to probe new ways of understanding "Christ and culture." In essence, the church adapted to modernity by becoming modern. No better example in the history of the church can be found than Adolf Harnack's *What Is Christianity?*, in which Harnack reduced it all to his view of the kingdom of God, the fatherhood of God, the infinite value of the human soul, a higher righteousness, and the commandment to love. What we got was the transformation of the gospel into German culture and into morality and into the private life. As an illustration, Harnack, on the meaning of kingdom, says: "It is the rule of the holy God in the hearts of individuals. . . . It is not a question of angels and devils, thrones and principalities, but of God and the soul, the soul and its God."[14] The modern world drove the church out of the state and into the soul.

Influence happened in the other direction and can be heard in the voice of the Dutch theologian-politician Abraham Kuyper, who shaped public policies through his idea of common grace.[15] For Kuyper, the Christian's calling can no longer be control, so the objective is to *influence* the state and shape culture in the direction of God's will as revealed in the Bible. When the majority of the citizens are Christian, as they were more or less in Europe and North America until later in the twentieth century, the culture takes on Christian themes naturally, and Christians are able to influence culture. But when Christianity became less and less the majority, Christians began to raise their voices in protest and—here is the element we must observe—they sought *through political means* to influence culture and state. A good, if largely ignored, example can be found in the strong Christian advocacy for political progressivism of William Jennings Bryan.[16]

The keynote here is Christian agitation in the public forum for implementing a more Christian vision of society. That is, Christians muster their forces to influence through voting and policy a more Christian society. This is soft Constantinianism and, though many times what is accomplished is a huge relief for many Christians, it remains a push for the state to enforce Christian beliefs. This isn't just about the Religious Right or the Religious Left. It's about Christians taking their views into the public forum and through activism making their views public policy or law. To take an example not from the current issues at work, so as to avoid immediate excitement, I refer to *The Chicago Declaration of Evangelical Social Concern* in 1973,[17] signed by evangelical activists across the spectrum, including Samuel Escobar, Sharon Gallagher, Vernon Grounds, Nancy Hardesty, Carl F. H. Henry and his politician son Paul Henry, Stephen Mott, Richard Mouw, John Perkins, Ronald J. Sider, Jim Wallis, and John Howard Yoder. The themes are these: the Lordship of Christ includes the United States and the public life; love requires care for those suffering social abuses; God requires justice for the poor and oppressed, for all races; the need for America to repent from its systemic injustices; materialism and maldistribution of goods is sinful; citizens need to do their part to resist the temptations to empire and idolatry of nation; male chauvinism needs to be changed; the gospel liberates. No matter how good the vision or how little influence such gatherings muster, this is soft Constantinianism.

As mentioned above, and even if they are from opposite sides of the political spectrum, the prophetic protests of Jim Wallis about the state's lack of concern with the poor and marginalized and the prophetic protests of the Christian Right about abortion and euthanasia and economic liberty join together in a single strategy: use political means to influence American culture and the state in the direction of Christian beliefs. To be sure, often enough the case is argued on the basis of the US Constitution or on the basis of common consensus or moral logic. What we all know, however, is that Christians are advocating for Christian views on the basis of the Bible and Christian tradition and are making use of "secular" logic so it will appeal to the "common good." Regardless, the Christian influence theory is a kind of Constantinianism. Insider talk calls this "salt and light," but in the public sector it is called working for the common good, and sometimes it is called "kingdom work." Ironically, in calling social agitation for Christian values in the public sector "kingdom work," the Christian joins hands with Constantinianism itself, for it equates "kingdom" with "state." Winning in the Christian influence theory is getting the state to back up the Christian voice. Do we see what this means? *It means we give the final authority to the state.*

We Are Sometimes Tempted to Give Up on Society

The less influential Christianity becomes in a given country, as one sees at the turn of the twentieth century in many countries, the greater the temptation for Christianity to become a spiritual religion that has nothing or little to do with social realities. This clearly happened in the United States. Fundamentalism tossed fire and brimstone at culture and state, withdrew in some ways into sacred enclaves, and focused on personal holiness and going to heaven.[18] That's a simplification—perhaps too much so. At times fundamentalists longed for a return to earlier, even Puritan, days, but by the middle of the twentieth century fundamentalism had little to do with shaping American culture except in those pockets of America where Christians remained the majority voice, as was often the case in the South, less so in the Midwest, and much less so in the Northeast, the Pacific Northwest, and the West Coast. Their approach was to get people saved, and saved people would eventually make an impact on America. Kingdom for the fundamentalist crowd tended to mean "heaven," and any effort to work for the common good was perceived as tossing one's pearls before the swine or giving what is holy to the dogs. Fundamentalists had two favorite terms for their counterparts: they were "liberals" or "modernists."

We Are Tempted to See Social Progress as the Kingdom's Mission

Fundamentalism in some ways was a reaction to the social gospel. The leading light in America's social gospel was Walter Rauschenbusch, a New York City pastor and theologian. Rauschenbusch reacted to the evangelical and fundamentalist absence of concern with social issues and designed what many today call the "social gospel." In essence, the gospel saves people personally, economically, and socially, and can usher in the kingdom of peace and justice if enough folks enter into this kingdom vision. The social gospel expands the meaning of salvation and at times identifies social redemption as all that is needed. To save means to establish civil rights. For Rauschenbusch, a Christianity that did not transform society for the good was not what Jesus had in mind, so his passion was directed at finding solutions to the deep social problems. His solutions became part of the progressive agenda of American politics, or their agenda became part of his "kingdom" solutions.

Fundamentalism spurned Rauschenbusch, which created by the middle of the twentieth century a radical breach in America: on one side was the mainline social gospel orientation that both shaped American culture and was shaped by American culture, and on the other was the fundamentalist gospel orientation that wanted either to return to the former days of American Christendom or to turn from all things cultural. For the social gospel, kingdom became the moral vision of Jesus. In fact, many if not most in the social gospel approach abandoned the necessity and importance of personal redemption from sin and focused on social justice where "sin" was "systemic injustices." In so doing, the kingdom vision was modernized and secularized so that kingdom became modern liberalism, or it became the progressive quest for justice, peace, equality, economic security, and civil rights.[19] The social gospel is Leftist Constantinianism.

We Sometimes Have to Awaken from Our Lack of Engagement

In the middle of the twentieth century many fundamentalists had grown tired of the insulation of fundamentalists from culture and so began to argue for the older (Kuyperian) notion of a Christian presence that could influence culture and state in the direction of a Christian vision. I call attention to one major voice. Carl Henry, in 1947, sounded an alarm, calling American neo-evangelicals to a break with fundamentalism's separation from culture. He called Christians to engage culture, to participate in politics, and to become educated at the finest institutions. Henry's famous call, *The Uneasy Conscience of Modern Fundamentalism*, was in effect a revitalized attempt to *influence*. Henry's approach to kingdom is just like Kuyper's: kingdom is the rule of God in this world (common grace) as well as the personal reign of God in the heart and soul of individual Christians, and that kingdom will be fully manifested in the future, eternal kingdom.[20] On Henry's side was Billy Graham, but perhaps his biggest influence came through his vision for and editorial leading of the evangelical magazine *Christianity Today*. *Christianity Today* consciously and intentionally sought to counter the liberal, more social gospel orientation in the publication *Christian Century* by offering a Kuyperian evangelical vision for the second half of the twentieth century. The neo-evangelical revival of the Christian influence theory has come at a severe cost, in part because it is yet another manifestation of Constantinianism.

We Are Tempted to Form Coalitions That Create Civil Religion

I remember when it happened in the 1970s and 1980s. Active Christian leaders, like Francis Schaeffer and James Kennedy, joined hands with active Jewish leaders to form what some called a "Judeo-Christian ethic." This combined ethic created religious, moral, and political power behind a common political aim: to rid America of its secular slant, to curb federal intrusion in Christian churches and institutions, to block the claimed implications of the Equal Rights Amendment as well as the *Roe v. Wade* decision about abortion—and other items could be added. Alongside the rise of the Religious Right were more progressive Christians—the Religious

Left, whose efforts mirrored those of the Christian Right. They wanted social justice, peace, the end of nuclear proliferation, the end of war, and racial reconciliation and justice. People across a faith spectrum joined hands for these causes.

What this religious union—which also included traditional Roman Catholics and Mormons—created was a "civil religion."[21] While one might claim this is simply diversity organized on a common political front, the effect of such a union is the creation of a new religion. There is no such thing as an ethic that is both "Judeo" and "Christian," for one simple reason: the "Christian" part of the ethical equation adds Jesus as Messiah, the cross as the paradigm, the resurrection as the power, the Holy Spirit as the transforming agent, the necessity of the new birth, and the church as the place where God is at work. Hence, a "Judeo-Christian ethic" either strips the Christian elements or turns the "Judeo" part into a Christian ethic. What it usually does is secularize the ethic of all involved. Instead of letting each ethic stand in its own separable power, a common denominator is found, which both modifies each ethical system and creates a brand new one. Whether conservative or progressive, it is a political ethic with the veneer of a religious claim in order to create moral force and gather support from those with differing faiths. This, in other words, is a civil religion.

The attraction of a civil religion comes from two sides. First, politicians want votes. That means they want support from religious leaders, so the politicians enhance their "faith" connection to those leaders. Second, voters want to win, so they find candidates who will express their religious views in political offices. Civil religion is a toxic mix and can be called civil Constantinianism because we are back to the original Christian temptation: blending church and state, blending empire and faith, asking the state to enforce the faith. Allan Bevere has expressed this in memorable lines.

> Once the nation becomes the primary hermeneutical target of Scripture, the primary community of faith becomes the state. The church is eclipsed in this world and so is the kingdom of God.
>
> And once the state becomes the primary community of faith because the Scriptures are applied primarily to the state, civil religion is at hand. The church no longer plays the role of prophet to the nation; it becomes the puppet of the state.[22]

Civil religion works by denying everything unique and distinct to a religion and seeking the common ground of cooperation, *all to accomplish a political goal.* In the process, proponents and participants in this civil religion alienate the opposing political advocates and turn the Christian (or Jewish, or Mormon, or Catholic, or Baptist) set of beliefs into a political platform. Civil religion, then, surrenders faith to politics and turns the church into a tool of the state. Civil religion denies the cross, the resurrection, and the lordship of Christ over all, and therefore cannot be squared with the gospel. We are not talking here about the Moral Majority but also about the "moral minority,"[23] about the Right and the Left, because each forms a coalition that can achieve a platform only by denying central dimensions of the faith for the sake of the common good.

This "civil religion" emerges in American history in another way, the way of baptizing the nation by using biblical language for our civil hopes, civil unrest, and civil activism. There are a million examples, and I mention but one. In one of the most influential speeches in American political history, still studied for its rhetoric, is "The Cross of Gold" by William Jennings Bryan—yes, the same William Jennings Bryan who won the battle against evolution but lost the war and, in the process, brought civil religion to a new level.[24] "The Cross of Gold" was about whether the gold standard for commerce would be the only one and whether America could adopt "bimetallism" or also a "silver" standard. In advocating for the silver position at the National Democratic Convention in Chicago (July 9, 1896), William Jennings Bryan revealed not only his capacity for rhetorical flourishes but also his willingness to use biblical language in political battles. The issue is not what he believed or his activism; the issue is what happens to the biblical message when its language is used to sanction political positions.

Three instances will demonstrate my point. In one instance, Bryan said, "In this contest brother has been arrayed against brother, father against son," a clear swiping from the words of Jesus about the cost of discipleship. Has discipleship here not become "Which political party?" In a second instance, reflecting on the issue of tariffs and the money's standard, Bryan said, "If protection [tariff] has slain its thousands, the gold standard has slain its tens of thousands." Here the superiority of David over Saul has been captured into a battle over tariffs and the silver standard versus the gold standard. But nothing matches the conclusion to this memorable speech, where Bryan portrayed the plain working classes against the rich gold-standard folks of the Republican party in these words: "You shall not press down upon the brow this crown of thorns; you can not crucify mankind upon a cross of gold." Bryan's most recent biographer, Michael Kazin, adds a detail that simply cannot be omitted from the record: "As he spoke the final words, Bryan stunned the crowd with an inspired gesture of melodrama. He stepped back from the podium, pulled his hands away from his brow, and extended them straight out from his body—and held the Christlike [cross-like] pose for perhaps five seconds."[25]

At this point one can either salute civil religion or weep over the depth to which Christians will sometimes go by using Christian language or posture to make their political position compelling. Whether it is John Winthrop's "city on a hill" or William Jennings Bryan's "cross of gold," it remains Constantinianism softened into a kind of civil religion that spoils the Bible's goods for the sake of Caesar.

We Know Liberation from Injustice Is the Heart of God

The social gospel shaped on the more progressive side of the American political ledger was reformed by and reshaped into liberation theology at the hands of the Latin theologians, in particular, Gustavo Gutiérrez.[26] Gutiérrez had many friends with similar ideas and agendas, both in Latin America and in Europe, Jürgen Moltmann being one.[27] Liberation theology took the social and economic redemption of the social gospel to a new level by connecting it to Marxist thought. Redemption became economic progress in which the poor benefited from economic distribution, and the rich—corporations and proponents of free enterprise—were exorcised from the context. Salvation here becomes social revolution against free markets and the establishment of justice for the poor. What Gutiérrez spawned took on brand-new directions once his basic ideas pervaded especially the Americas and Europe. Liberation theology was both criticized and refreshed by marginal voices that were being ignored, like those of African Americans, women, and the gay rights movement of the twentieth and twenty-first centuries.

In essence, in the hands of many forms of liberation theology, salvation becomes social liberation from oppression and especially from poverty and social exclusion. A most remarkable turn of events accompanied liberation theology: the church was decentralized and the state was centralized. What began with common grace, and was pushed even further into the state by the social gospel, was slowly emerging in the Western world as a progressive belief in the capacity of the state to deliver redemption. Kingdom work became political work. Justice became social justice. Salvation became social and economic and racial and sexual liberation. In short, American liberal progressivism and kingdom were now wedded to one another. The kingdom is peace, justice, economic equality, and equal rights. Wherever one finds justice and peace and economic equality and equal rights, one finds the kingdom. Gandhi does kingdom work as much as Jesus because both worked for justice and peace.

We're done. This could go on and on, and there's a more detailed and slightly different approach in appendix 2. What we need to see is that the Skinny Jeans kingdom vision grows naturally on American soil and is now in full bloom as this new view of kingdom gains currency.

Kingdom Gets a New Meaning

In our culture today, then, kingdom can be defined in four short lines:

> Kingdom describes
> good deeds
> done by good people (Christian or not)
> in the public sector
> for the common good.

I'm going to ask you to begin paying attention to how "kingdom" is being used in the church and in literature today. I think you will see over and over these four lines. In Jonathan Merritt's recent column for *The Atlantic* we find a perfect example of what I am talking about.

Lisa Sharon Harper, director of mobilizing for Sojourners, a progressive Christian organization, says shifts are due to young people choosing to identify with Jesus and his teachings [kingdom] as opposed to a particular political party. Harper believes the GOP is being pulled to the far right by extremists on issues like abortion, thus forgetting and alienating those whom Jesus affirmed and advocated for: poor people, ethnic minorities, and women.

"I think the focus on the person of Jesus is birthing a younger generation inspired by [Jesus' Sermon on the Mount]," she says. "Their political agenda is shaped by Jesus' call to feed the hungry, make sure the thirsty have clean water, make sure all have access to healthcare, transform America into a welcoming place for immigrants, fix our inequitable penal system, and end abject poverty abroad and in the forgotten corners of our urban and rural communities."[28]

I call this Skinny Jeans kingdom not because I'm envious of young slender bodies nor to disparage the noble and admirable work of so many young Christians who want to make the world a better place. I call it this because it characterizes the current generation in its use of "kingdom." This vision of kingdom is essentially social gospel and liberation theology in an American context largely voiced by privileged whites. Its hallmark is *benevolence*, but benevolence is what the privileged and powerful and wealthy give as a donation to the poor and marginalized as a form of social redemption. One must ask if benevolence is not something more oriented to the privileged than to the actual transformation of society. Benevolence, then, is donation to the poor that promulgates the very injustices it seeks to ameliorate. One has to wonder if at times this kind of benevolence is not better called "reparations." This too, then, is yet another version of Constantinianism.

But there's one more simple observation that can be stated briefly: *the focus of energy in this theory of the kingdom is the political process.* Instead of seeing the church as the central place of kingdom expression, public activism for the common good, especially through acquiring votes and establishing public policies, becomes the place where kingdom work gets done best.

Appendix 2

KINGDOM TODAY

A friend once traded me his German volumes of Kittel,[1] a famous reference work on New Testament words, for my English translations. It was the worst trade of my life, though it does not rank with the Cubs trading Lou Brock to the St. Louis Cardinals for Ernie Broglio. Except in one regard. Although my edition of Kittel is in German and is unquotable and differently paginated, what I do have is the original German introductions to volumes 3 and 4, two volumes—now it gets serious—produced under the editorship of Gerhard Kittel, who was a member of the National Socialist Party and who was employed by the *Reichsinstitut* for the study of German history. It's rather obvious from the introductions that this massive project was funded by Hitler's Third Reich. One quotation, which I translate myself because the English editions did not translate the Third Reich introduction, will be enough to lead us to a discussion of how kingdom people are summoned to relate to the powers. The "In Memoriam" page lists four biblical scholars who died in defense of Germany—Albrecht Stumpff, Walter Gutbrod, Hermann Fritsch, and Hermann Hanse—and then the foreword speaks of their "sacrifice of blood" and how they were, like John the Baptist, "preparers of the way" (*Wegbereiter*). The entire production of volumes 3 and 4 of Kittel, the most widely used dictionary of

Appendix 2 can be read as a more academic introduction to *Kingdom Conspiracy*.

New Testament words, was in cooperation with the Third Reich, and Kittel himself was a National Socialist. In fact, he was scapegoated by many, most memorably with vitriol by a titan of American scholarship, William Foxwell Albright. After listing a number of prominent Germans and Austrians who came to Kittel's defense during the denazification and trial years, Robert Ericksen, in his book *Theologians under Hitler*,[2] comes to an inescapable and minimalist conclusion—namely, that Kittel's "Christianity was distorted to this unholy [Nazi] purpose." In 1933 the opportunist Gerhard Kittel tragically lost tolerance for Jews, and so this distinguished dictionary will forever be stained for anyone who cares to know by this "unholy purpose."

Kittel, to use the words of Ericksen, "swam in the Nazi stream, though he may have preferred a different stroke." Kittel was complicit in National Socialism. So, too, at a lesser level was Rudolf Bultmann, for no one could continue lecturing in German universities during the Third Reich without swearing allegiance to Hitler. The temptation in the 1930s in Germany was to become a "German Christian" (*Deutsche Christen*), a form of Lutheranism that was engulfed by race, nation, blood, and land. This story has been told by Abraham Joshua Heschel's daughter, Susannah Heschel, in her book *The Aryan Jesus*.[3] There are chilling tales about how German Christians, leaders in the church and professional exegetes and theologians, capitulated to Hitler, preserved their jobs, continued to teach, and then after the war were subjected to examination, most of whom somehow survived. That's another story.

Who did resist? The story of Bonhoeffer is probably known well enough to avoid rehearsing, and just how complicit Bonhoeffer was in the conspiracy to assassinate Hitler and therefore how much he compromised his pacifism is presently under intense investigation.[4] It appears that this research could overturn the traditional suggestions of complicity by Eberhard Bethge in his massive *Dietrich Bonhoeffer: A Biography*.[5] So, other than Bonhoeffer, who resisted? I'd like to draw your attention to Karl Barth,[6] probably the twentieth century's most significant theologian. Barth saw trouble looming on the horizon, as did the entire Bonhoeffer *Familie*, and quickly and loudly spoke up, out, and against the Third Reich. Barth serves to illustrate how a God-obsessed kingdom theology both perceives national idolatries and embodies a kingdom reality.

Barth began his career as a pastor at a small Swiss parish in Safenwil. He wrote a commentary on Romans, revised it, and then was propelled into the German theological world. He taught first at Göttingen, then at Münster, and then finally in Germany at Bonn, beginning in 1930. It was during his tenure at Bonn that Barth told a philosopher, Heinrich Scholz, that "academic theology was based on the resurrection of Jesus Christ from the dead." That claim typifies where Barth began all of his thinking, including his political thinking. Many pastors and theologians sat by, hoping the looming potential would not run its course, or trusting that things would alter their course, or simply joining in to one degree or another. Barth did not. As he said it, "I myself could not very well keep quiet, but had to undertake to issue the necessary warnings to the church about the danger it was in." He was behind the Barmen Declaration and the Confessing Church, but eventually Barth did not think either was radical enough, and so he was one to speak against Hitler himself. In essence, Barth saw National Socialism as a bold and diabolical renunciation of the first commandment. He saw all natural theology, from Schleiermacher to Brunner, as denial of that first commandment.[7]

So he refused to begin class with "*Heil Hitler!*," and on November 7, 1934, he refused to give the oath of loyalty . . . well, let Barth say it in his own terms: "I did not refuse to give the official oath, but I stipulated an addition to the effect that I could be loyal to the *Führer* only within my responsibilities as an Evangelical Christian." Knowing what may come, on November 26, Barth's class sang a hymn to God's good guidance, and the next day he was dismissed. No less than two hundred students protested his dismissal. On trial, Barth quoted from Plato's *Apology* that "I shall obey the god rather than you," and he announced they were "making Hitler a god incarnate and offending most seriously against the first commandment." The next spring, in a farewell to his students in a Bible study, Barth said, "And now the end has come. So listen to my last piece of advice: exegesis, exegesis and yet more exegesis!" On March 1, 1935, Barth was served with a total ban on speaking in public. Barth was offered soon thereafter a post in Basel, where he continued his prophetic critiques against National Socialism, Hitler, and the church's complicity in idolatry. The story goes on with a lifetime of theopolitics, some of it quite interesting in its own right, but none of it more important than the brilliant insight and immediate perception Barth had when Germany succumbed to the idolatry of nationalism.

This introduction serves only one purpose, to ask of ourselves, "What would I have done?" And we can also ask, "What does it take to have the perception of Barth or Bonhoeffer when other notable theologians, from Bultmann to Kittel, succumbed to one degree or another?"

No doubt at the heart of it is God, the exaltation of God in Barth's theology. Alongside that is a commitment to Scripture that runs so deep that one lets Scripture speak *against* culture *as the norm and not the exception of how Scripture speaks.* Barth's forthright resistance to National Socialism was more than the reflex of a contrarian. This is a man whose mind saw through idolatries. Which leads to yet another question: Where are the idolatries today? Where are we complicit? Where are we falling asleep on our watch?

I suggest that studying how we use the term "kingdom" opens up windows on the whole discussion.

Two Themes in Kingdom Theology: Transformation and Liberation

Specialists in the New Testament tend not to define kingdom with any concrete reality. Theologians, especially those who focus on ethics or political theology, are far less willing to leave kingdom alone. These folks tend to give kingdom living legs, and in my reading of the literature I see two major themes among those who want kingdom to be a living theology. Those two themes are, first, a culture-transformation kingdom vision and, second, a social and liberation kingdom vision. There is a long history here, one that I don't know well, but it includes especially Augustine, Aquinas, Luther,[8] and Calvin, and beyond them many, many variations. The first theme, transformation, contends that the church retains its place in a pluralistic world. It avoids taking complete control, but the Constantinian Temptation (see appendix 1) remains. In short, it seeks to influence and transform each of the various spheres of society and culture.[9] That is, a kingdom vision expands the Christian vision into a secular culture, but—and here is the major problem in this approach—often the transformationalist can be found reframing and reducing and reforming the kingdom vision of the Bible to make it fit culture. In the second theme of social liberation, the kingdom gets quickly connected to activism for justice and peace, and therefore it often gets tightly webbed into economic theories that need to be implemented at the political level in order to institutionalize what is perceived to be the "kingdom" vision. One final observation before we sketch each more completely: the transformational model more or less works *from within the system* while the liberation model works far more *against the system*. It should be obvious that minorities tend toward the liberation model, while majorities tend toward the transformational model.

Transformation

This conversation must begin with the transformation understanding of the kingdom because this view is the heritage of North American (and European) Christian thinking. It is true that the transformation view is being supplemented and corrected by the liberation understanding of the kingdom, and even at times totally replaced by liberation theology, but the American version of this story begins with the Calvinist, Reformed understanding of the kingdom of God. That is, we inherit the transformationalist approach to church and state from our Puritan heirs, who in various ways shaped both our culture and the founding fathers.[10]

Origins are one thing, and what the Puritans taught and thought is not what we now see and hear. So I move closer to our own times, smack-dab in the middle of the previous century, to H. Richard Niebuhr, who wrote *Christ and Culture*,[11] a book that established categories that have shaped how Christians think about the relationship of Christ and church to the world and culture, and therefore what is often called "kingdom" theology.[12] Niebuhr proposed thinking about this relationship in five different categories:

- Christ *against* culture: the Anabaptist tradition
- Christ *of* culture: natural law and cultural Protestantism
- Christ *above* culture: Aquinas and the Roman Catholic Church
- Christ and culture *in paradox*: Martin Luther and Reinhold Niebuhr
- Christ *transforming* culture: Calvin, Edwards, Barth

I speak from experience for the moment. The Christ-transforming-culture approach has ruled the American church on both the Right and the Left for its entire history. To anticipate where we are headed, this view has been *the view* in North America until the last twenty years or so where we are seeing a gradual shift toward the liberationist approach that falls outside any of Niebuhr's categories. If this trend continues, the American church, within two or three decades, could lose its "transforming" culture approach and become far more liberationist. But we need to look more closely at the transforming approach.

Whether we look to Puritan pilgrim founders John Winthrop and John Davenport or to the Princeton theologian Charles Hodge, or whether we skip into the twentieth century to activists like Francis Schaeffer, Jerry Falwell, Pat Robertson, James Kennedy, James Dobson, and Wayne Grudem, or to the much more moderating approaches we find in Tim Keller and James Davison Hunter, what we get is a "Christ-transforming-culture" approach to how the Christian relates to the world and to American culture. Yet it would be inaccurate to suggest that the only ones who advocate the transformation approach are those marked by Reformed theology or conservative politics. In fact, one can trace the progressive Christian posture as being every bit as much of a Christ-transforming-culture approach. I think, then, of the activism of John Wesley and the abolitionists of the nineteenth century, like Jonathan Blanchard or the even more influential Harriet Beecher Stowe (who wrote *Uncle Tom's Cabin*); or I think of Charles Finney, Phoebe Palmer, and Walter Rauschenbusch; or those in the second half of the twentieth century who were influenced by liberation theology, such as Tony Campolo and Jim Wallis—all of whom are just as representative of the transformationalist approach. The issue, then, is not simply substance; what determines where one stands here is general theory or approach. Each of these two sides of America's political spectrum seeks to influence in order to transform culture, and each does so from its own positions in theology, ethics, economics, and theories of justice and power and peace. Each side does this from within the system and so enters into the already existing public sector in order to shape the public sector on behalf of its own views.

There is in this thread of names a driving story, and that story is the kingdom. The Christ-transforming-culture approach has a kingdom theology at work shaping the whole. Each thinker named above follows his or her moral compass toward kingdom values, ethics, vision, and theology. We need to look at some of these names in what follows.

ABRAHAM KUYPER

One of the finest introductory sketches of this transformation approach can be found in the Dutch Calvinist Abraham Kuyper, whose thought is made easily accessible in Richard Mouw's *Abraham Kuyper: A Short and Personal Introduction.*[13] Kuyper doesn't represent the whole of the tradition, but what he says is a good portal into the whole of the tradition, and it is a tradition that goes back into the pre-Constantinian era but especially back into the days of Augustine when the church began to think about its influence on the powers of the Roman Empire. For the transformation tradition the church does not own or run society, the state, or culture. The church is but one facet of the whole; the church has the gospel, and the church's task is to Christianize and humanize (understood theologically in similar terms) culture so far as it can within the limits of the law and the terms of good Christian behavior and persuasion.

Abraham Kuyper, an encyclopedist, was born in 1837 in the Netherlands and had a noble career as a pastor, a newspaper editor, a university founder, a theologian, prime minister, and then minister of state (number-one leader). In 1898 Kuyper gave the Stone Lectures at Princeton, which became his celebrated and influential book *Lectures on Calvinism*, a book that sketched Calvinism's perception of religion, politics, science, and art.

Kuyper's major vision, and this is the vision of the culture-shaping approach, is expressed in this memorable challenge: "There is not a square inch in the whole domain of our human existence over which Christ, who is sovereign over all, does not cry 'Mine!'" This gives the Christian a cultural mandate to work against the impact of the fall and for the impact of the gospel in every sphere of life. Yet the Reformed vision knows the pluralism of our world and what Mouw calls the created order's "many-ness." Mouw himself has a memorable line: "What the Creator wants us to keep apart, let no human being try to squeeze together." This leads to Kuyper's highly influential spheres of sovereignty. For Kuyper and for the Christ-transforming approach, whether consciously or not, life in this world is segmented into "spheres," like education, church, state, family, business, art, education, and sports (I added the last one). Mouw says Kuyper is saying "that each of these is intended by God to do its own 'thing'; each has a different role or 'point' in God's design for his creation. Each sphere has its own rights and rules and orders. The state should not control the arts, nor should universities (or seminaries!) see themselves primarily as businesses." It is perhaps wise for us to see the big issue at work here: "Each cultural sphere has its own place in God's plan for the creation, and each is directly under the divine rule."

I want to press the pause button, because in this sentence a fundamental perception of kingdom has surfaced: the "kingdom of God" is perceived here as the all-encompassing rule of God over the whole created order, *and the church is but one element in God's universal kingdom.* As Mouw summarizes him: "Kuyper makes much of the fact that the Kingdom of Christ is much bigger than the institutional church. The Kingdom is that broad range of reality over which Christ rules." Even more: "Actually, Christ's Kingdom is the whole cosmos." Mouw nuances Kuyper a bit: "The Kingdom covers all of those areas of reality where Christ's rule is *acknowledged* by those who work to make that rule visible." To be sure, "The institutional church is certainly an important part of Christ's Kingdom," but "the church is only one part of the Kingdom." Mouw later says, "When I hear people equate 'church' and 'Kingdom' I inwardly (and sometimes visibly) cringe. You don't have to go into a church to do something related to the Kingdom." A little pushback against my friend Rich Mouw: when I hear people make kingdom the cosmic rule of God, I think Jesus cringes! And when I hear them make "church" something one goes "into," I cringe. Part of our problem here is that the word "church" has become a building or an institution and has lost its cosmic shape from the Bible (ever read Colossians and Ephesians?!), and "kingdom" has become everybody's favorite, neutral word that doesn't sound churchy. Kingdom, in other words, is not far from the Calvinist notion of common grace. We can do better.

Mouw keeps on nuancing his sketch: "The church, then, occupies a specific sphere, an area of cultural activity that exists alongside other spheres." "The Kingdom," in contrast, "encompasses the believing community in all of its complex life of participation in a variety of spheres. Wherever followers of Christ are attempting to glorify God in one or another sphere of cultural interaction, they are engaged in Kingdom activity . . . [arts, farmers, etc.]. It is all the Kingdom." One might call this a "worldly" view of the kingdom of God.[14]

The Christian's calling is to serve God and in so doing to influence each sphere toward the kingdom of God, efforts which will both strengthen each sphere and simultaneously prevent the government from extending its reach and control. Mouw's way of saying this is important: "Christians must form collective entities within each of the spheres in order to make our confession of God's sovereignty [rule, kingdom] concrete: art guilds, political parties, farmers' federations, laborers' associations." This is what Mouw meant in an earlier quote about seeing the kingdom as "where Christ's rule is acknowledged." When individual Christians work within the confines of a given sphere to make the rule of Christ visible, they are in the kingdom and doing kingdom work.

Mouw provides exceptionally helpful maps of three approaches. The medieval approach has God at the top, the church under God, and the church ruling on behalf of God over the state, art, economics, family, and science. This is the "Constantinian" approach. The secularist approach shoves God and church into its own column where the two can manage their own business in the private world, but in the public sector are politics, art, economics, family, and science. The Kuyperian view, or the Christ-transforming-culture approach to the kingdom of God, sees God over all with separable spheres each under God: state, art, economics, family, science, and the church.[15] This theory of the Christian involvement in culture and the state has its own set of problems, and I mention two.

The first problem for Kuyper is nothing less than its constant temptation—using the strongest set of terms—to a Constantinian model, and one Kuyperian confessed his own temptation to what he called "Kuyperian secularism," or Kuyper swallowed by the world's systems. James K. A. Smith, professor at Calvin College, says it this way:

> In strange, often unintended ways, the pursuit of "justice," *shalom*, and a "holistic" gospel can have its own secularizing effect. What begins as a Gospel-motivated concern for justice can turn into a naturalized fixation on justice in which God never appears. And when that happens, "justice"

233

becomes something else altogether—an idol, a way to effectively naturalize the gospel, flattening it to a social amelioration project in which the particularity of Jesus as the revelation of God becomes strangely absent. . . . If this feels like I'm pointing my finger at others, there are three more pointed back at me. In fact, consider this (another) letter to my younger self. As a former fundamentalist, it was heirs of Abraham Kuyper who taught me the biblical vision of a holistic Gospel. But I've come to realize that if we don't attend to the *whole* Kuyper, so to speak—if we pick and choose just parts of the Kuyperian project—we can end up with an odd sort of monstrosity: what we might call, paradoxically, a "Kuyperian secularism" that naturalizes *shalom*.[16]

Kuyperian secularism happens when the gospel is compromised, or even evacuated, in the name of social goods.

A second problem for Kuyper can be called overreaching. I appeal here to America's dean of religious history, Mark Noll, and his study of Christian influence in the political sector.[17] Noll concludes his admirable sketch of how Christians have been involved in politics by sketching four levels of involvement: (1) by advocating for principles and values derived from the Christian faith and moral vision, (2) through public mobilization to work on specific moral projects and to reform abuses, (3) by translating ideas and values that appear to be motivated by special interest groups into legislation and policy, and (4) in the creation of a Christian political party. Then Noll turns toward a potent reminder: "As a general rule, Christian politics has been most beneficial—in terms both of actual political influence and fidelity to the Christian faith—at the level of general conviction. It has done most poorly—again in terms of both politics and Christianity—in the effort to create complete political parties around an individual or a set of Christian convictions." These are good reminders of the seemingly inevitable course in history taken by the Kuyperian approach.

H. Richard Niebuhr

Abraham Kuyper provides one transformation approach from the Calvinist tradition; H. Richard Niebuhr provides yet another, and his approach has captured and continues to capture many today.[18] The transformation approach values God as creator, humans as created, and the importance of the created order. In addition, the fall of humans comes square into view to see creation as corrupted. This means that what humans do is "perverted good, not evil." Most important, Niebuhr taps into what many today might call the "mission of God." In Niebuhr's words, uttered more than a half century ago, the transformationist has "a view of history that holds that to God all things are possible in a history that is fundamentally not a course of merely human events but always a dramatic interaction between God and men." This means the unfolding of history becomes a field for hope in the power of God to transform. "This is what culture can be—a transformed human life in and to the glory of God." In other words, God's grace is at work through conversion to transform a person, and that person can then affect culture toward kingdom realities.

That Niebuhr prompts this approach by examining the Gospel of John and then Augustine sets him in good stead with the Kuyperian line of thinking, but Niebuhr's next example sets a new tone, for he finds a major English liberal, F. D. Maurice, much to his own liking. At the heart of Maurice's concept of sin is human selfishness, individualism, and pride—as if each person thinks he or she is the center of the universe. So for him it was all about conversion—transformation—from self-centeredness to Christ-centeredness and other-centeredness in the direction of the burgeoning attraction to Christian socialism. Liberal theology, it should be noted here, has within it a capacity both to shape and to be shaped by culture, and in its best forms it leads to nothing less than a "Christian" (better yet, Christianized) culture.[19] The reverse is its tragedy so that the transformational model sets in motion the possibility of the transformed-by-culture church.[20] Notably, in the words of Niebuhr, this universal conversion "was universal . . . since all were members of the kingdom of Christ by their creation in the Word." The kingdom of Christ is universal, redemption is universal, and the quest is to direct all humans toward that universal reign of Christ. In this we find a theme many have observed as characteristic of the Niebuhrian approach: the gospel and theology and ethics must be translated into cultural forms in such a way that they make sense to that culture and for that culture. This "secularization" approach has direct connections to the liberationist approach we will examine below. That is, in this approach the rule of Christ is in the spirits of humans even if it is not "of this world." But such progress cannot be explained simply as social improvement; no, it must be seen as the conversion of humans to God in a transformation of the whole of culture. In the words of Niebuhr, the "kingdom of God is transformed culture."

Niebuhr himself claimed he did not side with any of the five approaches, though his prose makes it abundantly clear that he sides with the transformation approach. But he takes this a step further into what may be called "theocentric relativism," an existentialist and pluralist posture, in his concluding chapter, and it seems to me many of his critics ignore what he said there.[21] In his words, "The problem of Christ and culture can and must come to an end only in a realm beyond all study in the free decisions of individual believers and responsible communities." All of our decisions are fragmentary and relative, and this means Niebuhr advocates existential freedom to the individual in the context of a community to render judgment on what to decide and what to do. This should not lead either to nihilism or to some certaintist approach. No, "they can accept their relativities with faith in the infinite Absolute to whom all their relative views, values and duties are subject." He deepens it with these words: "Every man [or woman] looking upon the same Jesus Christ in faith will make his statement of what Christ is to him; but he will not confound his relative statement with the absolute Christ." Our summons is to the loyalty found in Christ to his Father and the Father's loyalty to the Son. Stunning words, these next ones: "This faith has been introduced into our history, into our culture, our church, our human community, through this person and this event. Now that it has been called forth in us through him we see that it was always there, that without it we should never have lived at all, that faithfulness is the moral reason in all things." What Niebuhr means by faith, though, is neither faith in an inspired text nor faith in the orthodox church creeds; his idea is personal faith in God that pervades one's entire existence.[22]

He concludes this heroic book with these claims: "It is to make [our decisions] in view of the fact that Christ is risen from the dead, and is not only the head of the church but the redeemer of the world. It is to make them in view of the fact that the world of culture—man's achievement—exists within the world of grace—God's Kingdom." This is well beyond anything we find in Kuyper: kingdom has become the effects of God's common grace and human achievement; it has become the existential decisions and deeds of the Christian who enacts the universal revelation of the moral principle of faithfulness. But just like Kuyper, in Niebuhr the kingdom is nearly all assigned to the works of men and women in the public sector as they seek the common good.

There is debate within the transformation approach about *how best as Christians to influence the public sector through political means*—from the more strident to the more quietistic—but behind it all is a kingdom theology, and this kingdom is understood as the cosmic rule of God made manifest in society and culture through the efforts of Christian activists.

Something, however, changed in the middle of the twentieth century, and the largely unchallenged assumptions of the transformation approach were deeply challenged and at times abandoned by an even more radical approach: liberation theology.

Liberation

The more recent development of the twentieth century and into the twenty-first century when it comes to kingdom theology is liberation theology's reworking of this classic transformation model. The word "transformation" is too tame to contain what this new movement has in mind. The kind of transformation it has in mind is radical, from the inside out and from the bottom up, and the liberation it has in mind is economic—who has power, who has money, and who should have power and money. Liberation theology is now growing in corners of North American and European Christianity in unnoticed ways and with implications that are far-reaching, and it is revolutionizing as well what the word "kingdom" means.

For some, to use the expression "liberation theology" is to evoke one kind of liberation—namely, Latin American—and to evoke one theologian, Gustavo Gutiérrez. But I want the expression to span various forms of liberation theology by mapping the various contributions some major thinkers have made to how we today understand kingdom theology. I will begin with the architect of the social gospel, the German Baptist Walter Rauschenbusch; then look at the German theologian Jürgen Moltmann; and then Gustavo Gutiérrez, the premier liberation theologian. But this

237

theology did not stop with Gutiérrez. It spawned, or expressed, other forms of liberation, like the feminist liberationist thought of Rosemary Radford Ruether and African American liberationist approaches like that of Brian Blount. Contemporary progressive Christian thinking in the United States, whether one finds it among Roman Catholics like Elizabeth Johnson at Fordham University or among the emergent voices like Brian McLaren, is, in its various forms, a riff on liberation theology where the central drives are justice and peace as manifestations of holistic salvation.

Here's a map: from Rauschenbusch our sense of salvation is translated into the social and systemic in the public sector; from Moltmann a new sense of hope spawns an ever broader sense of salvation as liberation from all oppressive forces; from Gutiérrez we find the first genuine Marxist contribution to what liberation and salvation and kingdom mean, where now salvation includes a social revolution from the bottom up directed at the powers of capitalism. Finally, I will sketch briefly how liberation theology as kingdom theology empowered women and African Americans to turn the gospel of Jesus toward their own needs for liberation from injustices. The impact of this varied story is that kingdom theology moves from the transformation of the various spheres of society as God's cosmic rule to a concrete focus on the social liberation and empowerment of the oppressed people of our day. Kingdom theology, shaped as it is now by these two major streams of thought—the transformation and liberation approaches—has become a combination of good people doing good things in the public sector and an activistic striving to undo injustices and establish justice against the oppressive systemic forces of, most especially, capitalism and colonialism.

Walter Rauschenbusch: Salvation as Social Salvation

So, first to Walter Rauschenbusch, who was a German Baptist nurtured theologically by his father and at Rochester Theological Seminary. While a student and imbibing some influence from theological study in Germany,[23] Rauschenbusch came to repentance but later realized that this conversion experience was the first stage of a journey recognizing not only personal sins but also systemic sins, and aiming toward not only personal salvation but also systemic salvation. It was his pastoral work—once again illustrating that pastoral work and theology often create the most dynamic expressions of both theology and discipleship—at Second German Baptist Church in Hell's Kitchen in New York City that reshaped Rauschenbusch from a traditional evangelical into the architect of the social gospel and that inspired him to apply his idealistic perception of socialism to his theology, which was itself formed out of an idealistic perception of socialism. This new Rauschenbusch rose meteorically in the American religious landscape. He formed the heart of the American mainline, with notable impacts on others (like the Niebuhr brothers), for much of the twentieth century. The liberation theology so characteristic today of the American mainline drew some of its energy from Rauschenbusch because in Rauschenbusch we gain a profoundly expanded sense of both sin and salvation. Sin is both individual and social, and salvation is both individual and social.

The heart of Rauschenbusch's vision was that the teachings of Jesus could become a reality in American society. At this point Rauschenbusch sounds like a transformationist. But Rauschenbusch's vision was focused on economics, politics, education—everything. For Rauschenbusch, this was striving for the kingdom of God. One can say, then, that for him the kingdom of God is a transformed earthly social reality through the implementation of the social and moral vision of Jesus. The major terms of the day were "social Christianity" and the "social gospel" as opposed to the reduction of Christianity to the personal salvation and personal influence that he found in the typical transformationist approach to the Christian's relationship to society. His orientation was far more structural in his focus on economic liberation for the poor, or, to use other terms, social salvation. His famous expression, which serves to introduce how he understood evangelism, is found in these words: the kingdom of God "is not a matter of getting individuals to heaven, but of transforming the life on earth into the harmony of heaven."[24] For Rauschenbusch, personal redemption was part of social redemption, but the latter was the driving force.

Although Rauschenbusch's work included the writing of many books, nothing is perhaps more expressive of his work's essence than his 1904 article in the *Independent* called "The New Evangelism."[25] In this article Rauschenbusch was quick to claim that true evangelism will be sensitive not only to the "primitive, uncorrupted and still unexhausted power" of

239

Jesus but also to the "life of our time." The times have changed, he argued, so there is the need for a more comprehensive understanding of the gospel. "It is a lack of Christian humility to assume that our gospel and *the Gospel* are identical." That gospel is at work, and here he taps on a note that is characteristic of the liberation approach to kingdom, outside the church: "It is not because the religious spirit has failed. It runs surprisingly strong, but it runs largely outside the churches." Why? Because the church is irrelevant: "About the most pressing questions arising there [in society] the church as a body is dumb."

This classic essay of his was unfolded in his two major books, *Christianity and the Social Crisis* (1907) and *A Theology for the Social Gospel* (1917), which is the fullest expression of Rauschenbusch's vision. In this book he emphasizes that "the salvation of the individual is, of course, an essential part of salvation." This is why Rauschenbusch was often called an "evangelical liberal." But the gospel is bigger and salvation is bigger. "If sin is selfishness, salvation must be a change which turns a man from self to God and humanity." More yet: "Complete salvation, therefore, would consist in an attitude of love in which he would freely co-ordinate his life with the life of his fellows in obedience to the loving impulses of the spirit of God, thus taking his part in a divine organism of mutual service." Perhaps his most potent line of all now: "Salvation is the voluntary socializing of the soul." There is a kind of eschatology at work in Rauschenbusch, a kind that shows up in powerful form some fifty years later in Jürgen Moltmann. Here are Rauschenbusch's words: "In primitive Christianity the forward look of expectancy was characteristic of religion," and thus "this [hope] is the aspect of faith which is emphasized by the social gospel. It is not so much the endorsement of ideals formulated in the past, as expectancy and confidence in the coming salvation of God . . . [that] this is a good world and that life is worth living. It is the faith to assert the feasibility of a fairly righteous and fraternal social order. . . . It is faith to see God at work in the world and to claim a share in his job." Finally, "Other things being equal, a solidaristic religious experience is more distinctively Christian than an individualistic religious experience." This sense of solidarity becomes central to Rauschenbusch, and I close with this line: "The saint of the future will need not only a theocentric mysticism which enables him to realize God, but an anthropocentric mysticism which enables him to realize his fellow-men in God."

In the context of this book, the fundamental importance of Rauschenbusch, though he was not the first,[26] is his connection of the expression "kingdom of God" with social activism in the public sector on behalf of others, especially the poor and marginalized. Liberation theology will enhance this tune as it makes salvation social. What is perhaps more notable is that an increasing number of America's evangelicals, whether they know of Rauschenbusch or the social gospel movement, are forming an early twenty-first-century version of the social gospel. A case has been made, and I think here of the recent study by Tim Suttle, that evangelicalism is compatible with the social gospel, given the early combination by Rauschenbusch of both a personal and social salvation.[27] To varying degrees Christian activists like John Alexander, Jim Wallis, Mark Hatfield, Sharon Gallagher, Samuel Escobar, and Ron Sider have both learned from and adapted insights derived from the social gospel.[28]

But social gospeling comes, almost inevitably but not necessarily, at a cost to the church. John Howard Yoder observed the impact of the social gospel movement in these words: "The emphasis has constantly been laid upon turning one's attention away from the church and what goes on within in order to discern instead what it is that God, independently of the church if need be, has been doing in the world, namely, in the structures of society and their evolution, so that, having discerned his working, the church can welcome it and join it."[29] Instead of calling the world to the church, which is the church's mission, the world solicits the church to aid the world's progress.

Jürgen Moltmann: Political Theology as Worldly Hope for Liberation

The great German theologian of the late twentieth century and the beginning of the twenty-first century is Jürgen Moltmann.[30] In a German prison camp in Scotland, Moltmann found both faith and the foundation for a new theology when he perceived the significance of Christ suffering for us and entering into our pain and guilt and shame. Moltmann took these insights and fashioned in his *A Theology of Hope* a powerful expression of a social vision. Building on the "atheist" European philosopher Ernst Bloch, Moltmann nurtured that philosophy into a theology of hope by cultivating three shoots: the concept of God's promise, the resurrection of the crucified Christ as God's promise for those suffering and for the world, and a belief in human history (the world) as the mission of God's kingdom. There is less overt socialism at the core of Moltmann than we will find in Gutiérrez, though Moltmann is socialist. A major difference must be noted before we even get to the Latin American theologian: Moltmann stands in the position of privileged power over against Gutiérrez's conscious stance with the poor and their preferential treatment in the plan of God in human history. With each of these theologians Moltmann can say, "Every eschatological theology must become a political theology, in the form of a theology that is socially critical." Swedish theologian Arne Rasmusson, one of the more astute scholars on contemporary political theologies, considers Moltmann's major contribution as "his attempt to show the relevance of Christian faith to the social and political movements (or at least to the Christians who sympathize with them) which have dominated radical political thought and action during the last three decades."[31] Perhaps more important, Rasmusson defines what "political theology" means for Moltmann's entire endeavor: "Political theology, according to Moltmann, is not a theology about the political, and it does not want to politicize theology."[32] So what is political theology's purpose? Rasmusson continues: "The purpose is instead to analyse and reconstruct theology *as a whole in the light of its political functions.*"

Moltmann in some ways became the European spokesperson for the centrality of liberation theology as political theology, and because of the wide influence of his voice, I want here to cite the famous lines of the Bangkok World Mission Assembly in which Moltmann was hard at work bringing his views into ecclesial significance. I will quote from the section called "Salvation and Social Justice in a Divided Humanity." It begins with a section on the mission of God, and it opens with God sending Christ into the world to liberate and to empower others to participate in the "Messianic work." Christ is the liberator: "He takes the inevitability out of history. In him the Kingdom of God and of free people is at hand." That is, Christ is the liberating savior, and he brings a "comprehensive wholeness in this divided life." Drawing on a constant theme found in the liberation stream, Moltmann says, "As evil works both in personal life and in exploitative social structures which humiliate mankind, so God's justice manifests itself both in the justification of the sinner and in social and political justice. As guilt is both individual and corporate, so God's liberating power changes both persons and structures." This mission of God now gets a fulsome statement for the ages: "Therefore we see the struggles for economic justice, political freedom and cultural renewal as elements in the total liberation of the world through the mission of God." Notice what we see here. As with the transformation approach's emphasis on the cosmic kingdom of God, so with liberation theology: a cosmic sense of kingdom means a cosmic sense of salvation as liberation. Moltmann, in my view, is still much closer to the transformation model when it comes to how the church impacts society, though he is far more focused on economics than we saw in Kuyper. Liberation theologians were already quickly moving well beyond Moltmann, and he would strive to keep pace with the surging ideas among the liberation theologians.

Now back to the Bangkok World Mission statement. Section 2 concerns "Salvation and Liberation of Churches and Christians," which speaks to the issues of the blindness of the wealthy and capitalistic societies to their own entrapment in oppression and injustices and which expresses a Marxist approach to liberation. "Without the salvation of the churches from their captivity in the interests of dominating classes, races and nations, there can be no saving church." Hence the church must develop solidarity with all, particularly the poor, and so at Bangkok there is this yearning: "We are seeking the true community of Christ which works and suffers for his Kingdom." The church, then, must become missional and "not merely the refuge of the saved but a community serving the world in the love of Christ."

Section 3 develops the four dimensions of salvation. Salvation works in the "struggle for economic justice against the exploitation of people by people." It works "for human dignity against political oppression of human beings by their fellow men" and "for solidarity against the alienation of person from person." Finally, it works "in the struggle of hope against despair in personal life." This may sound abstract, but this timely

Bangkok statement had concrete situations in the world in mind, so that "salvation is the peace of the people in Vietnam, independence in Angola, justice and reconciliation in Northern Ireland and release from captivity of power in the North Atlantic community, or personal conversion in the release of a submerged society into hope, or of new life styles amidst corporate self-interest and lovelessness." The proper means for this struggle to make its impact entails the use of "political power" and "cultural influence," but what about violence? Here are the final words of the statement: "But in the cases of institutionalized violence, structural injustice and legalized immorality, love also involves the right of resistance and the duty 'to repress a tyranny' (Scottish Confession) with responsible choice among the possibilities we have. One may then become guilty for love's sake, but can trust in the forgiveness of guilt. Realistic work for salvation proceeds through confrontation, but depends, everywhere and always, on reconciliation with God."

In little more than fifty years we have moved well beyond Kuyper and Rauschenbusch. With Moltmann we see that the mission of God is salvation, is liberation, is the kingdom of God (and here kingdom of God has become social liberation of the oppressed), is a prophetic critique of the ruling oppressing powers, and is vigorous pursuit of social justice and social peace. It is noteworthy at this intermediate point in our discussion where the church fits. Moltmann, in almost Anabaptist fashion, speaks of the church as "contrast society" or the "people of the coming kingdom," even if his emphasis is more on the struggle for especially economic justice in the world. This means world and church are not so neatly distinguished as in the Anabaptist visions.[33] It would be fair to say for Moltmann that the church is a friendship of those committed to following in the way of Jesus, a way that identifies with the poor and works in society to eliminate injustices. The mission of God is liberation of the entire world unto freedom, justice, and peace, and the church's task is to discern that activity of God in the world and cooperate.

This Moltmannian theology explains, then, the soteriology of the Bangkok statement, where salvation seems swallowed by the elimination of systemic injustice and the establishment of systemic justice. One catches a glimpse of this in Moltmann's budding universalism with respect to how he understands Jews and Judaism: "Israel [historic and modern day] and Church are two different forms of the kingdom of God in history, and they must recognize one another in their difference and respect one another in their common ground if they want to bring hope for the coming of God to the peoples of the earth." As he was to say in the 1980s, "Jews and Christians are the Lord's witnesses, each in their own way." But to what? They are "united in their hope for a messianic kingdom."

The transformationist model of even so conservative a scholar as Abraham Kuyper focused quite explicitly on a radical distinction of church and kingdom, and kingdom became God's cosmic rule over all the spheres of human life. But the church is still the heartbeat of God's work in this world. The liberation theologians capture that same cosmic kingdom and plan of God for this world but will, in effect, strip it of its ecclesial center and turn kingdom theology into public liberation. Perhaps the one who did this most forcibly is the Latin American theologian Gustavo Gutiérrez, who wields a much sharper Marxist razor than we find in Moltmann. In Gutiérrez the Christ-transforming model so dear to Niebuhr and the North American Christian traditions is deconstructed, and in its place we find a Marxist liberation hermeneutic.

Gustavo Gutiérrez: The Marxist Razor

Public sector kingdom activism took on a very special form in 1971 when Peruvian theologian-priest Gustavo Gutiérrez wrote his colossally influential *A Theology of Liberation*,[34] giving to kingdom theology a liberation theme that far transcended the economically paternalistic tones of Rauschenbusch and even the Eurocentric approach of Moltmann. Everything changes with Gutiérrez, for instead of a message of care *for* the poor on the part of the wealthy—indeed, white-establishment condescending benevolence—the message became a revolt of the poor against the wealthy (American capitalist system) by disestablishing the powers that be for a new society of justice and peace for all.

For Gutiérrez theology is "critical reflection" on praxis and not simply theologizing out of the text or on the basis of a history of theology. Theology is done in context and for that context.[35] The elements at work in Gutiérrez include love, spirituality, anthropology, and the life of the

245

church, as well as philosophy, Marxism, and a robust eschatology. Inherent to Gutiérrez's vision are his convictions about the rightness and possibilities in Marxist economic theory and history. This means that liberation itself is an economic form of liberation and a process for individuals and societies to become more responsible and less capitalist. Yet, for Gutiérrez, Christ is the origin of all liberation, and he liberates from sin (which is a break in friendship with God and others) and liberates unto a life of freedom (which is love for God and others). Here he sounds at the surface level as no different than Kuyper, Rauschenbusch, and Moltmann. But Gutiérrez's liberation is framed mostly in terms of the public sector. As he puts it, "Social praxis is gradually becoming more of the arena itself in which the Christians work out—along with others—both their destiny as humans and their life of faith in the Lord of history." This is not an option or secondary; as he puts it, we are dealing here with *"the very meaning of Christianity."* The download for this book is clear: liberation is kingdom work and liberation is salvation, and this means kingdom and social realities are the primary place of God's work in this world. "To work, to transform this world, is to become a man and to build the human community; it is also to save." The eschatology is clear here as well: "Human history, then, is the location of our encounter with God, in Christ." That is, liberation from injustice is where we encounter God and lean into the kingdom of God.

Liberation as salvation as kingdom as human history and progress then raises the important question pressed from the very start against Gutiérrez's vision of liberation: What about the church? The answer one gets from Gutiérrez, though he softens the blow at times, is a radical decentering of the church. The church is summoned into the world to participate in the struggle by and for the poor for justice, peace, and power. For him the church's role can be seen in these words: in Latin America "the Church should be politicized by evangelizing." Which is a way of saying genuine kingdom work is work done through the church's people in the public sector on behalf of the elevation of the poor into justice and power, and, to make that happen, there must be a decentralization of the capitalist powers. In other words, "Gutierrez delegates to the world the responsibility of shaping the church's mission and consequently part of its identity."[36]

Salvation is, then, either redefined or expanded, depending on one's theological context. Some of the sharper (perhaps "jaw-dropping" would be better) lines I've read are from Orlando Costas, who said:

> Every moment that dignifies human life,
> that promotes equitable economic relations,
> and that encourages solidarity among individuals and peoples . . .
> can be said to be, therefore, a manifestation of the saving power of
>   the gospel.[37]

Salvation and kingdom are social actions that liberate and redeem and reconcile.

The contextualized location of Latin American liberation theology provides a setting, and a setting is the location for all theology and all liberation. These aren't ideas; these are people in need of salvation as economic liberation and empowerment. Gutiérrez, both at the time of but especially after his magisterial work, became increasingly aware of both the particular form all Latin American liberation theology would become but also the commonalities between all forms of liberation, whether one thinks of the Africans of South Africa, African Americans, or the women of the world, each of whom illustrates yet another particular set of peoples in need of liberation. In fact, in 1977 there was a famous showdown between James Cone, one of America's most influential African American theologians, and liberation theologians in Mexico City, when Cone prophetically called attention to the plight of blacks in Latin American contexts. His probing question was, "Where are your black liberation theologians?" He was suggesting, then, that Latin American theologians sometimes were structurally analogous to white North American theologians! Cone was followed by Dora Ace Valentin, who pushed against everyone by saying that 50 percent of the population is women, and there were no women liberation theologians present. Her question that haunted both Moltmann and Gutiérrez was, "Where are the feminist liberation theologians?"[38]

So Gutiérrez's original work was not complete. This theologian went on to develop both spiritual and local dimensions of his proposals.[39] What matters in this context is that in each of these liberation proposals the word "kingdom" was increasingly connected to the word "liberation" or "salvation," and these are understood largely as occurring in the public sector and at the economic, social, cultural, and national levels. What is increasingly diminished in each of these is the place of the church as well as the need for personal redemption. Cosmic perceptions of the kingdom were increasingly consumed by economic and political theories.

Brian Blount: African American Realities

Uniting all its various manifestations, liberation theology begins with experience—not just any experience or even a religious experience, but with the condition of oppression and poverty. Liberation theology learns to read the Bible and do theology from that condition and for that condition. Hence, in our brief look at Gutiérrez's seminal work on liberation theology we observed that liberation theology includes as part of its "information gathering" the praxis of the poor and the pastor or theologian in the midst of the poor. This connection of praxis and theology needs another connection: the theology developed out of this oppressive condition is a kingdom theology in which the fundamental theme is liberation or freedom. Every "species" of liberation theology begins with a different set of impoverished conditions, but each begins there. One might also add that advocates of liberation from different originating conditions, like Moltmann who sat rather comfortably if also compassionately in his European professorship, learn to listen to the oppressed and do a theology on behalf of the oppressed and for the oppressed, and they often also learn then to get out of the way. Neither America nor the American churches would ever be the same without the social and liberation theology of Martin Luther King Jr., but I have chosen here to look at the second generation of African American liberation theology.

Brian Blount is an African American liberation theologian with a specialization in New Testament studies. He has been a Presbyterian pastor in Newport News, Virginia and a professor at Princeton Theological Seminary, and is now the president of Union Presbyterian Seminary in Richmond, Virginia. His important study on New Testament ethics through the lens of an African American liberation hermeneutic, *Then the Whisper Put on Flesh*,[40] opens with a familiar theme: "Our context shapes the kinds of questions we bring to the biblical material." His context is the African

American context; mine is a white privileged (largely invisible)[41] context. Because he is a minority, he is invisible; his hermeneutic makes the African American visible. Furthermore, his self-conscious posture of reading the Bible from his condition strikes the person in power as biased, while the person in power only rarely breaks through to see that he or she too reads from a condition—only the condition in this case is of power. In other words, the whisper of God's word takes on flesh in concrete situations, and we need to be alert to our own location.

Speaking of location, Blount in James Cone–like fashion looks directly at white privilege and utters these words: "That status of recognition [or power] belongs to the conglomeration of Euro-American scholars, ministers, and layfolk who have, over the centuries, used their economic, academic, religious, and political dominance to create the illusion that the Bible, read through their experience, is the Bible read correctly." In other words, and this is so important, the methods being used derive from the ones already reading the Bible. We may think the methods permit us to transcend our location, but the methods themselves emerge from our location and, furthermore, support and sustain that location. The method at work in biblical studies, by and large, is the method developed by white privilege. In Blount's words, then, "The whisper took on a white flesh." What happens, he is asking, when the whisper takes on "a flesh of color"? That is precisely what Blount does in his many books and lectures. Blount proposes beginning with the African American slave. That condition of the Africans led to the development of a liberation lens as they learned to cope with their new world and their oppression—hence, African American liberation theology. "Israel's myth became their myth" as they reworked the exodus experience some three thousand years later. The result is undeniable: "Jesus, all of a sudden, means freedom—social and political freedom."

What strikes many of us as going just too far, but is characteristic as much of Gutiérrez as of Blount, is that liberation becomes the canon within the canon: "Where it [the text] is not [in line with liberation], the text, because of the frailty of the humans who composed it, must be challenged and, if need be, resisted as much as the system of slavery it was purported to support." Or, as James Cone expresses the same,

I still regard the Bible as an important source of my theological reflections, but not the starting point. The black experience and the Bible together in dialectical tension serve as my point of departure today and yesterday. The order is significant. I am *black* first—and everything else comes after that. This means I read the Bible through the lens of a black tradition of struggle and not as the objective Word of God. The Bible is therefore one witness to God's empowering presence in human affairs, along with other important testimonies.[42]

But don't think we can simply dismiss Cone or Blount when they turn liberation against the Bible and its interpreters. The text itself turns against our oppressions enough that nothing need be denied to encounter the God who opposes injustice and oppressions. This kind of reading of the Bible creates a culture of resistance to those in power because, as Blount affirms, "this lens already existed in the biblical story itself."

This liberation theology is a kingdom theology for Blount. "New Testament ethics, then, at least the synoptic version, is apocalyptic, future, kingdom ethics." It begins with Jesus, and this leads him to the question of questions: "But is he also representative of a future kingdom that drives the present and all those who live in it toward the kind of historical transformation that prefigures and therefore inspires the liberation of those who are oppressed? My answer is yes." Kingdom is liberation, is salvation, is political and social liberation. In other words, and all these words are italicized by Blount, "*this lens of liberation . . . exists in the synoptic texts through the symbolic imagery and implications of the kingdom.*" He sketches that kingdom liberation ethic in Mark through the notion of boundary breaking, in Matthew through the liberating ethics of a "visible institution," and in Luke through the ethics of reversal. John, he argues, proposes active resistance.

Elisabeth Moltmann-Wendel: Feminist Liberation

There is not sufficient space here to cover the spectrum of feminist liberation theologies.[43] Instead I will point to one well-known feminist enlightenment story, that of Elisabeth Moltmann-Wendel.[44] Elisabeth's story is that of the East German scholar in a conservative German world who, after World War II in West Germany, found a voice in the emergence of liberation theology. As she says it, "Suddenly I was drawn into the great upheaval which was affecting Blacks, Latin American Christians, students, minorities and those without rights all over the world. And I did not need to speak *for* them. I could speak about *myself*." The permitted voice in the German church at the time was the male voice, and it was decidedly impersonal.

The church, as she saw it, was the problem, even though she had caught the possibilities of revolutionary thinking as a teenager in home Bible studies. "We live," she said, "in a state which has always wanted order more than justice; a church which never wanted the kingdom of God; and a society which could never become it." As she puts it, "My revolution had begun with Kate Millett and not with Mary Daly, and that meant for me the revolution had to begin with society." Even as a university student she confessed that those who withdrew from the public sector had no appeal for her: "My motivation was almost the reverse: theology had to extend into politics." But Moltmann-Wendel experienced the all-too-common tension of a family life. When her husband, Jürgen Moltmann, was growing in fame and ever more often gone from home, it led to marital tension, "since he put his missionary tasks above his care for the family." Elisabeth's theological vision was the vision of so many liberation and feminist theologians: "It was no longer the traditional German Pauline Christ, crucified and risen . . . but the Jesus of Luke 4 who proclaims freedom to the prisoners, promises the gospel to the poor, and heals the stricken."

Her story can't be told in full here, but the heart of Elisabeth Moltmann-Wendel's feminist theology combines learning to read the Bible as a woman and in fellowship with other women—from one writing and speaking project to another, where she could share a platform with other women and liberation voices—with the discovery of what "woman" means in the twentieth and twenty-first centuries. Kingdom theology for her is the vision of a society and fellowship liberated from the systemic oppressions of a male-dominated culture and a theology that legitimates that culture. This could take shape in a changed church: "The church as a hope for women; the church as a place for the process of women's discovery of themselves, through which the church would in turn change." Her liberation work began at home with Jürgen, and these are some of the most memorable lines of their experience: "The master in the man must die so that the brother who is ready for open friendship can be born. It will be important for men to learn to listen and sit at the feet of women, as Mary sat at Jesus' feet."

Feminist liberation theology is at times full-scale revolution, seen perhaps most visibly in Elisabeth's journal notes that reframe the doctrine of justification, which to remind us is the heart of all German Protestant theology.

> Perhaps the best thing is to have discovered a feminist doctrine of justification:
>> I am good—
>> I am whole—
>> I am beautiful.
>
> Jürgen has understood. At the Community Service conference they listened. In Brunswick and in Sindelfingen, where it began, some were open-mouthed. It remains to be seen whether I can clarify it further.

At work here is her discovery of the unconditional love of God for her as a woman, and being the kind of activist Christian woman—not a man's wallflower—who could bring home the message of kingdom liberation.

Where We Are Today

This liberation theology approach to the kingdom focuses on social justice and peace through the liberation of the oppressed, in a variety of contexts. This stream, I think, has overflowed its banks and is flooding the church of the United States with a highly politicized framework for understanding the Christian life. More and more people today perceive the Christian calling to be fundamentally about relief of the poor and release of the oppressed, and this is largely enacted in the public sector where the primary energy is spent on political power and social activism. An increasing number of white evangelicals are in the grip of this vision, and they tend to offer a Moltmannian version of liberation with hues of feminist and African American liberation concerns. I shall contend that this stream, if it stays within the banks, has much to offer the church and society. But if it runs loose, it floods the other streams, colonizes the kingdom into little more than political action devoid of the gospel of the kingdom itself, and thereby strips the church of its calling in this world.

But I need to sharpen this critical gaze. Liberation theology's kingdom theology has been embraced by the surging growth of progressive Christians, including blocs and blocs of (often young) evangelicals, and it is now the default definition of kingdom for the majority. InterVarsity Christian Fellowship staff member and Anglican deacon Tish Harrison Warren, at the blog *The Well*, expresses the kingdom vision of many today:

> I am from the Shane Claiborne generation, and my story is that of many young evangelicals. I grew up relatively wealthy in a relatively wealthy evangelical church. Jesus captured my heart and my imagination when I was a kid. I was the girl wearing WWJD bracelets and praying with her friends before theater rehearsal. It did not take long before I began asking questions about how the gospel impacted racial reconciliation and poverty. I began to yearn for something more than a comfortable Christianity focused on saving souls and being generally respectable Republican Texans.
>
> I entered college restless with questions and spent my twenties reading Marx and St. Francis, being discipled in the work of Rich Mullins, Ron Sider, and Tony Campolo, learning about New Monasticism (though it wasn't named that yet), and falling in love with Peter Maurin and Dorothy Day. My senior year of college, I invited everyone at our big student evangelical gathering to join me in protesting the School of the Americas.
>
> I spent a little while in two different intentional Christian communities, hanging out with homeless teenagers, and going to a church called "Scum of the Earth" (really). I gave away a bunch of clothes, went barefoot, and wanted to be among the "least of these." At a gathering of Christian communities, I slept in a cornfield and spent a week using composting toilets, learning to make my own cleaning supplies, and discussing Christian anarchy while listening to mewithoutyou. . . .
>
> Now, I'm a thirty-something with two kids living a more or less ordinary life. And what I'm slowly realizing is that, for me, being in the house all day with a baby and a two-year-old is a lot more scary and a lot harder than being in a war-torn African village.[45]

Her story is the typical story of many today: the story from a personal spiritual gospel to a social gospel and then on to . . . what will come next? That is why this book was written.

Contemporary kingdom theology tends mostly to be liberation theology articulated by white people on behalf of the oppressed and poor and marginalized, who (by the way) more often than not have themselves moved beyond anything whites have to offer. The transformation approach pointed to a biblical reality: the cosmic reign of God. Walter Rauschenbusch represents those who expanded salvation to the social. Liberation theology has made salvation almost entirely social. This is not a slippery slope, nor is it a "give 'em an inch and they'll take a mile." The social is profoundly important to the Bible's sense of kingdom, but the social dimension of salvation has become a totalizing force in much kingdom thinking today. Progressive kingdom theology has become too often an emasculated kingdom of those whose theology is framed to make reparations for past injustices. As such it functions as little more than the puppeting echoes of progressive Western liberalism and politics with a thin veneer of soteriology slathered on top of what is little more than a feeble attempt to salve a guilty conscience over a sinful history. Many evangelicals and progressives today are steamed up about their opportunity to change the world and to be significant and to do something important. For all the "good" this movement can do and is doing, I contend that, far more important, it is largely a shame-based movement masking a shallow gospel and an inept grasp of what kingdom means in the Bible. One wonders at times if kingdom theology for many is religious language used to baptize what to most other observers is merely good actions done by decent people for the common good. Is kingdom language, then, the attempt to make something wholly secular somehow sacred?

What has now happened in our Christian culture needs to be faced directly. The liberation approach overtly decentralizes the church as it strives to undo the injustices at work in the systems of this world. Ironically enough, many proponents in the transformation approach are leading one Christian after another out of the church to do kingdom work in the public sector because it perceives over and over the kingdom as larger than the church. Its framing story is that the kingdom is cosmic and speaks of the universal rule of God in this world. One can therefore do kingdom work and have nothing to do with the church. Kingdom work, in other words, has become good things Christians do in the public sector, and church work is what Christian people do within the confines of the church. *Kingdom Conspiracy* attempts to reconstruct a kingdom theology rooted in church, not the public sector.

A Test Question

In my years of talking about kingdom theology there is one question to which I go when I want to know where a person stands or when I want to get a student to think more articulately about where she or he stands on this kingdom issue. The question is this: Did Gandhi do kingdom work?

For the Christ-transforming-culture approach the answer is on a spectrum from the ambivalent "Not really but kind of" to "No." Since his work is parallel to what God's church is called to do, since his work is good and just . . . for these reasons and plenty of others, Gandhi, though clearly not a Christian, in some sense did kingdom work for many in the transformation approach. In the liberation theology approach the answer is, "Yes, Gandhi's peace work was kingdom work because Gandhi did God's will." Anyone establishing justice and peace is doing kingdom work regardless of their faith. I say, "No, only kingdom people do kingdom work, and since Gandhi is not a kingdom person he did not do kingdom work."

AFTER WORDS

My thanks to Northern Seminary, to our president Alistair Brown, to Deans Karen Walker-Freeburg and Blake Walter, to my colleagues David Fitch, Cherith Fee Nordling, Bob Price, Michael Quicke, Claude Mariottini, and Sam Hamstra. Thanks to the students in my kingdom class in the winter of 2013, who carefully explored each reference to kingdom in the New Testament to see if any referred to actions done in the public for the common good, and to my Jesus class at Northern for probing the implications of kingdom.

Mark Thiessen Nation made general comments on the earliest draft of this manuscript when the mission dimension was barely visible. Thanks to David McGregor and Tabor Adelaide for filling my ears with Barth's perspective on kingdom. To Chris Wright for providing some e-copies of articles. Josh Graves and Jonathan Storment pointed me to a few ideas that needed to be brushed up. My thanks to the youth ministers and to leaders in Churches of Christ for the feedback to my lectures; to the Sentralized conference in September 2012; for the kind invitation from Brian Zahnd to give lectures to the Faith and Culture conference in St. Joseph, Missouri; and especially to the Word Made Fresh Lecture in Chicago with Tom Wright responding. My thanks to Tom Oord and Don Thorsen. Also my thanks to Gary Schwammlein for the annual invitation to speak to international leaders at the Partnering to Prevail conference at Willow Creek Community Church, and to Jeff Greenman for honoring me with an invitation to speak on kingdom and politics at the 2013 Wheaton Theology

Conference. Thanks to Chris Backert and J. R. Rozko for inviting me to address these topics at the first Missio Alliance Conference in Arlington, Virginia, and for a similar invitation to the Ecclesia Network of church planters. My thanks to Regent College, not the least Ken and Joan Braun, along with the Lewises, Waltkes, Houstons, and Greenmans, and Jonathan Wilson for hospitality and conversation in the summer of 2013. To many at Abilene Christian University for the invitation to give Summit lectures, and to the students and faculty who interacted with me, including Randy Harris, Jim Martin, and Mike Cope. When this manuscript was all but done, I was given the opportunity by Mike Glenn to address leaders at Brentwood Baptist Church, and I'm grateful to them, and everyone else, for kingdom-church conversations. Thanks to Ingrid Faro, Kim Karpeles, Carol Marshall, and Michelle Van Loon for the invitation to speak at the Trinity Women's Theology Conference, where I heard stories of women whose local churches were suppressing their gifts; and so this book comes with the reminder that sometimes kingdom-as-church realities must hotly criticize local church realities.

Every author needs a good editor; at least I do. So, many thanks to Bob Hosack, Tim West, Bethany Murphy, Arika Theule-Van Dam, and Jess Reimer at Brazos for their admirable attention to details. My friend and agent Greg Daniel has been more supportive and helpful than words can express. I am grateful to Tara Beth Leach for compiling the indexes.

Finally, I express my deepest love to my wife, who makes kingdom more a reality in our home than I deserve.

Thanksgiving 2013

NOTES

Chapter 1 Skinny Jeans Kingdom

1. Tim Suttle, *An Evangelical Social Gospel? Finding God's Story in the Midst of Extremes* (Eugene, OR: Cascade, 2011), 7, 73.

2. See Ryan Gregg and Ryan Brymer, "Derek Webb Explains Himself (Finally)," *FaithVillage.com*, Sept. 10, 2013, http://www.faithvillage.com/article/c2f4c8cdb 3394cc4958446df7f3c63bf/derek_webb_explains_himself_finally.

3. See Matt Conner, "Derek Webb Grows Up," *ChristianityToday.com*, Sept. 4, 2013, http://www.christianitytoday.com/ct/2013/october/derek-webb-grows-up -i-was-wrong.html.

4. Jim Wallis, *On God's Side: What Religion Forgets and Politics Hasn't Learned about Serving the Common Good* (Grand Rapids: Brazos, 2013), 52–54. This book was reissued in paperback in 2014 with the title *The (Un)Common Good: How the Gospel Brings Hope to a World Divided*.

5. Charles Marsh, *The Beloved Community: How Faith Shapes Social Justice, from the Civil Rights Movement to Today* (New York: Basic Books, 2005), 207–16.

6. Walter Wink, *The Powers That Be: Theology for a New Millennium* (New York: Doubleday, 1998).

7. Tyler Wigg-Stevenson, *The World Is Not Ours to Save: Finding the Freedom to Do Good* (Downers Grove, IL: InterVarsity, 2013).

8. For an introduction to how kingdom theology today is one variant after another on Constantinianism, see appendix 1; for a more academic introduction to the development of kingdom theology as political theology in the twentieth and twenty-first centuries, see appendix 2.

9. Walter J. Houston, *Contending for Justice: Ideologies and Theologies of Social Justice in the Old Testament* (London: T&T Clark, 2006), 52–98.

10. Louise W. Knight, *Jane Addams: Spirit in Action* (New York: Norton, 2010), xiv, 61, 105–6, 161. For discussion of her faith, see pp. 21, 22, 28, 45–46, 54, 55, 57, 71, 75, 259. For a more extensive look at Addams's early years, see Louise W. Knight, *Citizen: Jane Addams and the Struggle for Democracy* (Chicago: University

of Chicago Press, 2005). Jane Addams wrote a splendid memoir, *Twenty Years at Hull-House, with Autobiographical Notes* (New York: Signet Classics, 1961). For a collection of Jane Addams's writings, see Jean Bethke Elshtain, ed., *The Jane Addams Reader* (New York: Basic Books, 2002). The most important collection of her theories is Jane Addams, *Democracy and Social Ethics* (New York: Macmillan, 1902).

11. Jean Bethke Elshtain, *Jane Addams and the Dream of American Democracy: A Life* (New York: Basic Books, 2002), 76.

12. For similar criticisms, see Stanley Hauerwas, *Against the Nations: War and Survival in a Liberal Society* (Minneapolis: Fortress, 1985), 107–21.

13. I think of the noble work to save trees by Wangari Muta Maathai, described in *Unbowed: A Memoir* (New York: Alfred A. Knopf, 2006). We can ask the same question of Maathai: Was her effort to save and grow trees in Kenya kingdom work?

Chapter 2 Pleated Pants Kingdom

1. The literature here is enormous. I recommend two texts that focus on the history of this scholarship, the first a sampling of scholars and the second a survey of major areas of study: Bruce D. Chilton, ed., *The Kingdom of God*, Issues in Religion and Theology 5 (Philadelphia: Fortress, 1984); Wendell Willis, ed., *The Kingdom of God in 20th-Century Interpretation* (Peabody, MA: Hendrickson, 1987). Two texts that examine "kingdom" in the Bible are George Eldon Ladd, *The Presence of the Future: The Eschatology of Biblical Realism* (Grand Rapids: Eerdmans, 1974); and George R. Beasley-Murray, *Jesus and the Kingdom of God* (Grand Rapids: Eerdmans, 1986). For a very good sketch of both biblical and theological studies, see Mark Saucy, *The Kingdom of God in the Teaching of Jesus in 20th Century Theology* (Dallas: Word, 1997).

2. Karl Barth, *The Christian Life*, in *Church Dogmatics* IV.4 (Lecture Fragments) (Grand Rapids: Eerdmans, 1981), 246.

3. The Hebrew word is *malkuth*, and the Greek term is *basileia*.

4. Why? We can't be certain, but I suspect three factors were at work. First, "rule" shapes Protestant scholarship while "realm and rule" have more presence in both Roman Catholicism and Eastern Orthodoxy. Protestant polemics may have suggested that seeing "realm" was too Catholic or Orthodox. But this raises a second important factor: "realm" tied "kingdom" to national politics, to the "realm" of one's government, and this too became worrisome to biblical scholars as modernity continued to fragment nations and continents. To be viable, religion had to transcend nation and government, which leads then to a third factor: perhaps "realm" tied Jesus' kingdom vision too closely to Judaism and less to a universal religion so that the rise of anti-Semitism, however subtle, had some effect on this discussion. These three factors were at work; whether there are more would require more than I know about nineteenth-century language. Perhaps the most influential study reshaping the conversation is by Gustaf Dalman, *The Words of Jesus*, trans. D. M. Kay (Edinburgh: T&T Clark, 1902), 91–147. Gerhard Lohfink, in a very recent study that sees the same mistake, points once again to German scholarship

that emphasized (1) the purely religious view of kingdom, (2) the otherworldliness of the kingdom, and (3) the fear that it might be equated with the church. See Gerhard Lohfink, *Jesus of Nazareth: What He Wanted, Who He Was*, trans. Linda M. Maloney (Collegeville, MN: Liturgical Press, 2012), 53–56. He points his finger at Johannes Weiss while I have pointed at Dalman.

5. Ladd, *Presence of the Future*, 218.

6. I have focused on Ladd because of his influence, but many scholars across the spectrum use similar ideas. For instance, Douglas Oakman translates "kingdom" with the word "power" in *The Political Aims of Jesus* (Minneapolis: Fortress, 2012), 45–78. Bruce Chilton thinks more in terms of "God acting in strength" in *Pure Kingdom: Jesus' Vision of God* (Grand Rapids: Eerdmans, 1996). Oakman revives the older theories of Reimarus that Jesus was a this-worldly political activist who was misunderstood by his followers, and Chilton roots his understanding of Jesus and the kingdom in the *Targum to Isaiah*. By far the most extensive study of kingdom as a redemptive dynamic can be found in the evangelical scholar George Beasley-Murray, *Jesus and the Kingdom of God*. Beasley-Murray sees kingdom as "saving sovereignty." My final example is Karl Barth's well-known understanding of kingdom of God as the presence and redemptive acts of God in *The Christian Life*.

7. Rudolf Schnackenburg, *God's Rule and Kingdom*, trans. John Murray (New York: Herder & Herder, 1963), 95. Emphasis added.

8. John G. Stackhouse Jr., *Making the Best of It: Following Christ in the Real World* (New York: Oxford University Press, 2008), 21. I see some tension in this sentence with his earlier description of kingdom at pp. 19–20.

9. Ibid., 259.

10. N. T. Wright, *Simply Jesus: A New Vision of Who He Was, What He Did, and Why He Matters* (New York: HarperOne, 2011), 207–31.

11. George Ladd, for instance, devotes exactly two pages to "Jesus and Social Ethics," and says there "is little explicit teaching on social ethics in the Gospels." This illustrates the fundamental weakness of the "redemptive dynamic" approach. See Ladd, *Presence of the Future*, 302–4, quote from 303.

12. A good example is how the word "kingdom" is used in the informative and useful book by Jordan Seng, *Miracle Work: A Down-to-Earth Guide to Supernatural Ministries* (Downers Grove, IL: InterVarsity, 2013), 30.

13. Marilynne Robinson, *When I Was a Child I Read Books* (New York: Farrar, Straus & Giroux, 2012), 158.

14. Others can be found in appendix 1 and appendix 2.

15. Carl F. H. Henry, *Confessions of a Theologian: An Autobiography* (Waco: Word, 1986), 145, 270–71 (five tenets guiding *Christianity Today*); Andy Crouch, *Culture Making: Recovering Our Creative Calling* (Downers Grove, IL: InterVarsity, 2008); James K. A. Smith, *Desiring the Kingdom: Worship, Worldview, and Cultural Formation*, Cultural Liturgies 1 (Grand Rapids: Baker Academic, 2009); James K. A. Smith, *Imagining the Kingdom: How Worship Works*, Cultural Liturgies 2 (Grand Rapids: Baker Academic, 2013); Miroslav Volf, *A Public Faith: How Followers of Christ Should Serve the Common Good* (Grand Rapids: Brazos, 2011); Os Guinness, *The Global Public Square: Religious Freedom and the Making of a*

Safe World for Diversity (Downers Grove, IL: InterVarsity, 2013); James Davison Hunter, *To Change the World: The Irony, Tragedy, and Possibility of Christianity in the Late Modern World* (New York: Oxford University Press, 2010). An important Kuyperian/Reformed study of political theory is David T. Koyzis, *Political Visions and Illusions: A Survey and Christian Critique of Contemporary Ideologies* (Downers Grove, IL: InterVarsity, 2003). It is not without significance that Koyzis's index to his book contains no entry on the church.

16. Timothy Keller, *Center Church: Doing Balanced, Gospel-Centered Ministry in Your City* (Grand Rapids: Zondervan, 2012), 181–245.

17. Stackhouse, *Making the Best of It.*

18. See also the suggestive proposal of "living lightly" in John C. Nugent, *The Politics of Yahweh: John Howard Yoder, the Old Testament, and the People of God*, Theopolitical Visions 12 (Eugene, OR: Cascade, 2011), 196. And see pp. 191–210 for his more comprehensive approach to Christian living: Christians are to be cities of exile, cities of refuge, cities of sacrifice, and cities on a hill.

19. An excellent discussion, from the angle of creation theology and holding on to the need for a theology of the world within a redemption of creation, can be seen in Jonathan R. Wilson, *God's Good World: Reclaiming the Doctrine of Creation* (Grand Rapids: Baker Academic, 2013), 199–206.

20. Paul has similar teachings. See 1 Cor. 7:31 ("For this world in its present form is passing away"); cf. 1 Cor. 2:12; 3:19. This world, then, is in need of reconciliation (2 Cor. 5:19).

21. Stanley Hauerwas and William H. Willimon, *Resident Aliens: Life in the Christian Colony* (Nashville: Abingdon, 1989), 96.

22. A balanced study is Christopher J. H. Wright, "The World in the Bible," *Evangelical Review of Theology* 34, no. 3 (2010): 207–19, quote from 207. One of the few who study culture who also examines the Bible's use of "world" is Smith, *Desiring the Kingdom*, 187–90. Smith sees two themes at work: the world as "structure" (created by God and good) and the world as "direction" (sinful, idolatrous). Many have similar ideas; see Stackhouse, *Making the Best of It*, 14–18.

23. It is not without pain that I refer here and elsewhere to the work of John Howard Yoder, a man whose writings have influenced many, including me, but whose legacy, it must be noted, will always be a trail of sexual abuse. See Mark Oppenheimer, "A Theologian's Influence, and Stained Past, Live On," *NYTimes .com*, Oct. 11, 2013, http://www.nytimes.com/2013/10/12/us/john-howard-yoders -dark-past-and-influence-lives-on-for-mennonites.html?_r=0.

24. John Howard Yoder, *The Royal Priesthood: Essays Ecclesiological and Ecumenical* (Scottdale, PA: Herald Press, 1998), 56, 62.

25. Stanley Hauerwas, *The Peaceable Kingdom: A Primer in Christian Ethics* (Notre Dame, IN: University of Notre Dame Press, 1983), 100. On this topic, see 59–63, 99–102.

26. Hauerwas and Willimon, *Resident Aliens*, 94.

27. Robinson, *When I Was a Child*, 49.

28. Christian Wiman, *My Bright Abyss: Meditation of a Modern Believer* (New York: Farrar, Straus & Giroux, 2013), 52.

29. Maria Edgeworth, "An Essay on the Noble Science of Self-Justification," in *The Art of the Personal Essay: An Anthology from the Classical Era to the Present*, ed. Phillip Lopate (New York: Anchor Doubleday, 1994), 150; Marilyn Chandler McEntyre, *Caring for Words in a Culture of Lies* (Grand Rapids: Eerdmans, 2009), 44.

Chapter 3 Tell Me the Kingdom Story

1. Elizabeth Achtemeier, *Not Til I Have Done: A Personal Testimony* (Louisville: Westminster John Knox, 1999), 12, 16–17, 18, 19, 20.

2. Brandon K. McKoy, *Youth Ministry from the Outside In: How Relationships and Stories Shape Identity* (Downers Grove, IL: InterVarsity, 2013), 164–66.

3. I tell the C-F-R-C story as the story of oneness in my book *The Blue Parakeet: Rethinking How You Read the Bible* (Grand Rapids: Zondervan, 2008). I tell the A-B-A' story from a different angle in *The King Jesus Gospel: The Original Good News Revisited* (Grand Rapids: Zondervan, 2011), 136–42, 148–53.

4. James Thurber, *The Thurber Carnival* (New York: HarperPerennial, 1995), 13.

5. Barth, *Christian Life*, 233.

6. A good example of ignoring church in the larger narrative of the Bible can be seen in D. A. Carson, *Christ and Culture Revisited* (Grand Rapids: Eerdmans, 2008), 44–59. When he summarizes his biblical theology on p. 81, there is once again a noticeable absence of "church." I'm not seeking here for a word but for a pattern of thinking that the church is the locus of God's work today. What pains Carson's discussion is his claim that he is giving the "nonnegotiables" in biblical theology.

7. N. T. Wright, *Jesus and the Victory of God*, Christian Origins and the Question of God 2 (Minneapolis: Fortress, 1996), 226.

8. N. T. Wright, *The New Testament and the People of God*, Christian Origins and the Question of God 1 (Minneapolis: Fortress, 1992), 215–43, with quotes from 217, 232.

9. Carey C. Newman, ed., *Jesus and the Restoration of Israel: A Critical Assessment of N. T. Wright's* Jesus and the Victory of God (Downers Grove, IL: InterVarsity, 1999).

10. Wright, *New Testament and the People of God*, 243.

11. See John H. Walton, *The Lost World of Genesis One: Ancient Cosmology and the Origins Debate* (Downers Grove, IL: IVP Academic, 2009); Walton, *Genesis 1 as Ancient Cosmology* (Winona Lake, IN: Eisenbrauns, 2011).

12. But see John Bright, *The Kingdom of God: The Biblical Concept and Its Meaning for the Church* (Nashville: Abingdon, 1981), 17–44. A more extensive study of the political theology that emerges from Genesis through 2 Kings, one that touches on the theme I am discussing in "Plan B," can be found in J. Gordon McConville, *God and Earthly Power: An Old Testament Political Theology (Genesis–Kings)* (New York: T&T Clark, 2008), esp. 133–47.

13. Another translation would be, "The matter was evil in Samuel's eyes." The word "king" is the problem here; Samuel, the last of the judges and the first of the prophets, is not, however, a king and so his sons are not kings. That the elders

want to replace his sons does not seem the issue to Samuel; his concern is their desire for a "king."

14. 1 Sam. 8:5 (cited in the text) has an interesting parallel in Deut. 17:14–15 where, without disregarding the revelation of YHWH to Samuel, the author looks beyond this primal act of rebellion to the days of kings in the land and what the requirements will be for that king. Even within 1 Sam. 8–13, there is some tension between favor and disfavor toward a monarchy.

15. I am indebted to my friend Joel Willitts in this section.

16. Prophets arise to speak against the king. Notice Hosea 13:11.

17. The so-called King Yahweh psalms (e.g., 89, 93, 96–99) are seen by many as the assertion of YHWH as king over against a human king; as such, they correspond to the Plan B element of our approach. See on this J. Gordon McConville, "Law and Monarchy in the Old Testament," in *A Royal Priesthood? The Use of the Bible Ethically and Politically; A Dialogue with Oliver O'Donovan*, Scripture and Hermeneutics 3 (Grand Rapids: Zondervan, 2002), 69–88.

18. See Wright, *New Testament and the People of God*, and *Jesus and the Victory of God*.

19. John Bright: "The Servant? He is Israel; he is the true and loyal Israel; he is the great Servant who will be leader of the servant people—all in one!" See his *Kingdom of God*, 151.

20. This theme is developed in N. T. Wright, *How God Became King: The Forgotten Story of the Gospels* (New York: HarperOne, 2012). I disagree with Tom's posing of a kingdom theology over against creedal orthodoxy.

21. Jonathan T. Pennington, *Heaven and Earth in the Gospel of Matthew* (Grand Rapids: Baker Academic, 2009), 253–330.

22. Barth, *Christian Life*, 248–49.

23. Dietrich Bonhoeffer, *Life Together and Prayerbook of the Bible*, ed. Eberhard Bethge, trans. G. L. Müller, Dietrich Bonhoeffer Works 5 (Minneapolis: Fortress, 1996), 36, 37.

24. George Eldon Ladd, *A Theology of the New Testament*, rev. ed., ed. Donald A. Hagner (Grand Rapids: Eerdmans, 1993). Originally published in 1974.

25. Predictably, the Wesleyans listed H. Orton Wiley and John Wesley at the top; Ladd was not on their list.

26. John A. D'Elia, *A Place at the Table: George Eldon Ladd and the Rehabilitation of Evangelical Scholarship in America* (New York: Oxford University Press, 2008).

27. Carl F. H. Henry, *The Uneasy Conscience of Modern Fundamentalism* (Grand Rapids: Eerdmans, 2003). First published 1947.

28. On Yoder, see Stanley Hauerwas, *Hannah's Child: A Theologian's Memoir* (Grand Rapids: Eerdmans, 2010), 243–47.

29. Suzanne Selinger, *Charlotte von Kirschbaum and Karl Barth: A Study in Biography and the History of Theology* (University Park: Pennsylvania State University Press, 1998).

Chapter 4 Kingdom Mission Is All about Context

1. James D. G. Dunn, *Jesus Remembered*, Christianity in the Making 1 (Grand Rapids: Eerdmans, 2003), 390, 391–92, 393–96, 398.

2. A listing of good books could begin today and not end until a month from now, so I mention only two: Shaye J. D. Cohen, *From the Maccabees to the Mishnah*, Library of Early Christianity 7 (Philadelphia: Westminster, 1987), 124–73; E. P. Sanders, *Judaism: Practice and Belief, 63 BCE–66 CE* (Philadelphia: Trinity Press International, 1992), 315–494.

3. This ties into our Plan B feature of the A-B-A' story.

4. Quotations from the *Psalms of Solomon* are from the translation of R. B. Wright in *The Old Testament Pseudepigrapha*, ed. James H. Charlesworth (New York: Doubleday, 1985), 2:665–69.

5. Mark 3:18 has "Simon the Cananaean," but the NIV 2011 takes the entirely legitimate liberty of rendering "Cananaean," which comes from the Hebrew word for zeal or jealousy, as "Zealot" in accordance with the parallel in Mark 3:17.

6. N. T. Wright, *Scripture and the Authority of God: How to Read the Bible Today* (New York: HarperOne, 2011), 115–42. I explore this in McKnight, *Blue Parakeet*.

7. Kevin J. Vanhoozer, *The Drama of Doctrine: A Canonical-Linguistic Approach to Christian Theology* (Louisville: Westminster John Knox, 2005), 32–33.

8. Wayne Gordon, *Real Hope in Chicago: The Incredible Story of How the Gospel Is Transforming a Chicago Neighborhood* (Grand Rapids: Zondervan, 1995), 169–70.

9. His story is told in Tim Dickau, *Plunging into the Kingdom Way: Practicing the Short Strokes of Community, Hospitality, Justice, and Confession* (Eugene, OR: Cascade, 2011). My account is based on pp. 4–26. Emphasis added.

10. I sketch the ideas of looking, listening, linking, and loving in Scot McKnight, *Embracing Grace: Discovering the Gospel That Restores Us to God, Creation, and Ourselves* (Brewster, MA: Paraclete, 2012), 72–87.

11. Hunter, *To Change the World*. I use the word "seemingly" because it is not entirely clear to me just how "faithful witness" and "power" are connected by Hunter.

12. See John Howard Yoder, *The Priestly Kingdom: Social Ethics as Gospel* (Notre Dame, IN: University of Notre Dame Press, 1984), 49–54, for an excellent sketch of early Christian responses to cosmic politics.

13. Steven Wilkens and Mark L. Sanford, *Hidden Worldviews: Eight Cultural Stories That Shape Our Lives* (Downers Grove, IL: InterVarsity, 2009).

14. Dickau, *Plunging into the Kingdom Way*, 105–18.

15. See Scot McKnight and Joseph B. Modica, eds., *Jesus Is Lord, Caesar Is Not: Evaluating Empire in New Testament Studies* (Downers Grove, IL: IVP Academic, 2013).

16. So the conclusion of Morten Hørning Jensen, *Herod Antipas in Galilee: The Literary and Archaeological Sources on the Reign of Herod Antipas and Its Socio-Economic Impact on Galilee*, 2nd ed., Wissenschaftliche Untersuchungen

zum Neuen Testament 2.215 (Tübingen: Mohr Siebeck, 2010). See also Alan Storkey, *Jesus and Politics: Confronting the Powers* (Grand Rapids: Baker Academic, 2005), 75–94.

17. On this I benefited from chap. 10 in John Howard Yoder, *Revolutionary Christian Citizenship*, ed. John C. Nugent, Branson L. Parler, and Andy Alexis-Baker (Harrisonburg, VA: Herald Press, 2014), 132–37.

18. Hauerwas and Willimon, *Resident Aliens*, 30.

Chapter 5 Kingdom Is People

1. Betsy Halperin Amaru, "Land, Concept of," in *The Eerdmans Dictionary of Early Judaism*, ed. John J. Collins and Daniel C. Harlow (Grand Rapids: Eerdmans, 2010), 866.

2. David Frankel, *The Land of Canaan and the Destiny of Israel: Theologies of Territory in the Hebrew Bible*, Siphrut: Literature and Theology of the Hebrew Scriptures 4 (Winona Lake, IN: Eisenbrauns, 2011), 382. Emphasis added.

3. The name means "My father, the king."

4. See D. A. Carson, "Kingdom, Ethics, and Individual Salvation," *Themelios* 38, no. 2 (August 2013), http://thegospelcoalition.org/themelios/article/kingdom_ethics _and_individual_salvation.

5. Lohfink, *Jesus of Nazareth*, 25. The thrust of Lohfink's sketch of kingdom is to show that it must be connected to the people of God (pp. 39–71). I was unaware of the happy similarities of our approaches to kingdom until after I had written this entire manuscript.

6. The king's rule leads to a law, and the extent of the king's rule leads to a land. That the king rules implies also that the king saves or redeems the people. These are the elements of kingdom: king, rule, redemption, people, land, and law.

7. Paul S. Minear, *Images of the Church in the New Testament* (Philadelphia: Westminster, 1960).

8. See Walter Rauschenbusch, *A Theology for the Social Gospel* (Louisville: Westminster John Knox, 1997), 133–45.

9. Alfred Loisy, *The Gospel and the Church* (Buffalo: Prometheus Books, 1988), 145.

10. Jim Botts, "The Church vs. the Kingdom," *ChurchLeaders.com*, http:// www.churchleaders.com/outreach-missions/outreach-missions-articles/148827 -the-church-vs-the-kingdom.html. Emphasis in the original.

Chapter 6 No Kingdom outside the Church

1. Ladd, *Theology of the New Testament*, 109.

2. Bright, *Kingdom of God*, 236.

3. H. Richard Niebuhr, *The Purpose of the Church and Its Ministry: Reflections on the Aims of Theological Education* (New York: Harper & Brothers, 1956), 19–20.

4. Ibid (emphasis added).

5. Ibid (emphasis added).

6. Dallas Willard, *The Divine Conspiracy: Rediscovering Our Hidden Life in God* (San Francisco: HarperSanFrancisco, 1998), 25, 26, 27.

7. Gustavo Gutiérrez, *A Theology of Liberation: History, Politics, and Salvation,* rev. ed. (Maryknoll, NY: Orbis, 1988), 32.

8. Ibid., 91.

9. Ibid., 143–44.

10. See Leonardo Boff, *Ecclesiogenesis: The Base Communities Reinvent the Church*, trans. Robert R. Barr (Maryknoll, NY: Orbis, 1986); Veli-Matti Kärkkäinen, *An Introduction to Ecclesiology: Ecumenical, Historical and Global Perspectives* (Downers Grove, IL: IVP Academic, 2002), 175–83.

11. This pun could be translated punningly today as, "You are Rocky, and on this rock I will build my church."

12. E. B. White, "The Ring of Time," in Lopate, *Art of the Personal Essay,* 541.

13. Wright, "The World in the Bible," 216.

14. Undoubtedly tension arose, and the book of Acts and especially Paul's letters reveal the tensions. What occurs in the move from Israel to Israel Expanded entails a shift from an ethnic identity to a fictive, family identity. On this, see Joseph H. Hellerman, *The Ancient Church as Family* (Minneapolis: Fortress, 2001), 59–126.

15. For an exceptional study of church, see Paul Trebilco, *Self-Designations and Group Identity in the New Testament* (Cambridge: Cambridge University Press, 2012), 164–207.

16. Hellerman, *Ancient Church as Family*; see esp. p. 6 for the comparative chart.

17. C. K. Barrett, *Church, Ministry, and Sacraments in the New Testament* (Grand Rapids: Eerdmans, 1985), 13, 25.

18. Dietrich Bonhoeffer, *The Young Bonhoeffer, 1918–1927,* ed. Hans Pfeifer et al., Dietrich Bonhoeffer Works 9 (Minneapolis: Fortress, 2003), 316.

19. Rudolf Schnackenburg, *The Church in the New Testament,* trans. W. J. O'Hara (New York: Herder & Herder, 1965), 188. Schnackenburg fears that if we make the church too close to the kingdom, we will turn the church into a "church of glory" and fail to see its imperfect realities today; I contend right back that he has made the kingdom only a "kingdom of glory" and so fails to see the current realization of kingdom as messy. Thus we see the common failure in comparison: kingdom is perfect; church is imperfect.

20. Truth be told, Wayne is a colleague of mine at Northern Seminary. This story can be found in Gordon, *Real Hope in Chicago.*

21. Ibid., 108 (emphasis added).

Chapter 7 Kingdom Mission as Church Mission

1. Melissa Steffan, "1,500 Pastors Who Deliberately Broke Politics Law Gain Unexpected Ally," *Christianity Today*, August 14, 2013, http://www.christianity today.com/gleanings/2013/august/grassley-ecfa-commission-endorsements-pulpit -freedom-sunday.html.

2. Yoder, *Priestly Kingdom,* 93.

3. Someone who is working out his theory of justice on the basis of biblical texts is Nicholas Wolterstorff, *Justice: Rights and Wrongs* (Princeton, NJ: Princeton University Press, 2008), and *Justice in Love* (Grand Rapids: Eerdmans, 2011).

4. I explain both justice and peace in Scot McKnight, *One.Life: Jesus Calls, We Follow* (Grand Rapids: Zondervan, 2010), 57–84.

5. John Howard Yoder, *Body Politics: Five Practices of the Christian Community before the Watching World* (Scottdale, PA: Herald Press, 2001).

6. A really good example can be found in David E. Fitch and Geoff Holsclaw, *Prodigal Christianity: Ten Signposts into the Missional Frontier* (San Francisco: Jossey-Bass, 2013), 66–82.

7. For a full discussion of this theme, see Joseph H. Hellerman, *When the Church Was a Family: Recapturing Jesus' Vision for Authentic Christian Community* (Nashville: B&H Academic, 2009).

8. Ibid., 144–62.

9. The word "order" is better than "submit" since the latter implies inferiority, the very thing the kingdom reality in the church deconstructs. The Greek word for "submit" is *hypostasso*, meaning to "order under," but in this case there is not over-under order but a radical new fellowship of equals.

10. See the discussion in Arne Rasmusson, *The Church as* Polis: *From Political Theology to Theological Politics as Exemplified by Jürgen Moltmann and Stanley Hauerwas* (Notre Dame, IN: University of Notre Dame Press, 2009), 231–47.

11. I take this from Volf's quotations of Michel de Certeau; see Volf, *Public Faith*, 91.

12. Yoder has often been accused of being "sectarian," which when properly defined would be both accurate and affirmed but at the same time not leading to disengagement with world or culture. For a defense of Yoder's cultural theology, see Branson L. Parler, *Things Hold Together: John Howard Yoder's Trinitarian Theology of Culture* (Harrisonburg, VA: Herald Press, 2012).

13. The most extensive discussion of this is that of John H. Elliott, *1 Peter: A New Translation with Introduction and Commentary*, Anchor Bible 37B (New York: Doubleday, 2000), 84–103.

14. Bruce W. Winter, *Seek the Welfare of the City: Christians as Benefactors and Citizens*, First Century Christians in the Graeco-Roman World (Grand Rapids: Eerdmans, 1994), 37. I reformatted his prose.

15. Miroslav Volf, "Soft Difference: Theological Reflections on the Relation between Church and Culture in 1 Peter," *Ex Auditu* 10 (1994): 16–19.

16. A succinct summary of what Wayne Gordon and John Perkins advocate can be found in John M. Perkins and Wayne Gordon, *Leadership Revolution: Developing the Vision and Practice of Freedom and Justice*, ed. Randall Frame (Ventura, CA: Regal, 2012), 142–51. Their more recent sketch of local community development is found in Wayne Gordon and John M. Perkins, *Making Neighborhoods Whole: A Handbook for Christian Community Development* (Downers Grove, IL: InterVarsity, 2013).

17. Jay Pathak and Dave Runyon, *The Art of Neighboring: Building Genuine Relationships Right Outside Your Door* (Grand Rapids: Baker Books, 2012).

18. Fitch and Holsclaw, *Prodigal Christianity*; Lance Ford and Brad Brisco, *The Missional Quest: Becoming a Church of the Long Run* (Downers Grove, IL: InterVarsity, 2013).

19. Stackhouse, *Making the Best of It*, 222. I do not, however, agree with all the directions John takes this observation in the pages that follow (223–59), where he concludes with his statements about the kingdom being everywhere (cited above).

20. Crouch, *Culture Making*, 23, 24, 67, 189.

21. J. R. R. Tolkien, *Tree and Leaf* (Boston: Houghton Mifflin, 1989), 75–95.

22. An important new book along this line is by Steven Garber, *Visions of Vocation: Common Grace for the Common Good* (Downers Grove, IL: InterVarsity, 2014). Like Crouch, Garber's book does not make the church central enough to the "culture" God is making through Christ.

23. Marsh, *Beloved Community*.

24. There's too much to read here. In addition to Marsh's *Beloved Community*, I recommend Curtiss Paul DeYoung, Michael O. Emerson, George Yancey, and Karen Chai Kim, *United by Faith: The Multiracial Congregation as an Answer to the Problem of Race* (New York: Oxford University Press, 2003); Korie L. Edwards, *The Elusive Dream: The Power of Race in Interracial Churches* (New York: Oxford University Press, 2008); Efrem Smith, *The Post-Black and Post-White Church: Becoming the Beloved Community in a Multi-Ethnic World* (San Francisco: Jossey-Bass, 2012).

25. Stanley Hauerwas, *The Hauerwas Reader*, ed. John Berkman and Michael Cartwright (Durham, NC: Duke University Press, 2001), 462. Emphasis added.

26. For example, Jürgen Moltmann, *The Church in the Power of the Spirit: A Contribution to Messianic Ecclesiology*, trans. Margaret Kohl (Minneapolis: Fortress, 1993), 126–30. For the common exposition of the view that "the least of these" refers to followers of Jesus and not to the poor in general, see R. T. France, *The Gospel of Matthew*, New International Commentary on the New Testament (Grand Rapids: Eerdmans, 2007), 957–60.

27. Here are the references that matter: Matt. 5:22–23 (fellow Jews); 5:47 (fellow Jews); 7:3–5 (fellow Jews); 10:21 (fellow Jews); 18:15, 21, 35 (fellow believers); 28:10 (fellow believers).

Chapter 8 The King of the Kingdom

1. Wright, *Jesus and the Victory of God*; Wright, *How God Became King*.

2. Barth, *Christian Life*, 233–60. Quotes below from 237.

3. Other important psalms about the king are Psalms 2, 18, 20, 21, 45, 89, 101, 110, 132, and 144.

4. On titles, even if now dated, no book has yet exceeded Oscar Cullmann, *The Christology of the New Testament*, rev. ed., trans. Shirley C. Guthrie and Charles A. M. Hall (Philadelphia: Westminster, 1963).

5. Already in the second century: Ignatius, *To the Ephesians* 20.2; *Epistle of Barnabas* 12.10; Irenaeus, *Against Heresies* 3.16.7; 3.17.1.

6. Daniel Boyarin, *The Jewish Gospels: The Story of the Jewish Christ* (New York: New Press, 2012), 25–70, quote from 38.

7. A splendid sketch of "Son of God" in the Jewish world can be found in Adela Yarbro Collins and John J. Collins, *King and Messiah as Son of God: Divine, Human, and Angelic Messianic Figures in Biblical and Related Literature* (Grand Rapids: Eerdmans, 2008).

8. A friend and I coedited a book on seven accusations against Jesus by his opponents: he was a law-breaker, demon-possessed, a glutton and drunkard, a blasphemer, a false prophet, king of the Jews, and an illegitimate son. See Scot McKnight and Joseph B. Modica, eds., *Who Do My Opponents Say I Am? An Investigation of the Accusations against Jesus*, Library of Historical Jesus Studies 327 (London: T&T Clark, 2008).

9. A most important recent study in this regard is Michael Peppard, *The Son of God in the Roman World: Divine Sonship in Its Social and Political Context* (New York: Oxford University Press, 2011). For a fresh reworking of the evidence, see N. T. Wright, *Paul and the Faithfulness of God*, 2 vols., Christian Origins and the Question of God 4 (Minneapolis: Fortress, 2013).

10. These are the references to "Messiah" in the Gospels on the lips of Jesus: Mark 9:41; 12:35; 13:21; Matt. 22:42; 23:10; 24:5, 23; Luke 20:41; 24:46; John 17:3.

11. An exceptional sketch can be found in Craig A. Evans, "Messianism," in *Dictionary of New Testament Background*, ed. Craig A. Evans and Stanley E. Porter (Downers Grove, IL: InterVarsity, 2000), 698–707. Evans has an extensive bibliography. See also Kenneth E. Pomykala, "Messianism," in *The Eerdmans Dictionary of Early Judaism*, ed. John J. Collins and Daniel Harlow (Grand Rapids: Eerdmans, 2010), 938–42.

12. Evans shows how some texts played an important role in developing messianism (Gen. 49:10; Num. 24:17; Isa. 11:1–6).

13. Barth, *Christian Life*, 252–53. I have reformatted Barth's words.

14. Leonardo Boff, *Jesus Christ Liberator: A Critical Christology for Our Times* (Maryknoll, NY: Orbis, 1978).

15. Elisabeth Moltmann-Wendel, *Autobiography*, trans. John Bowden (London: SCM, 1997), 48, 108. For more on Moltmann-Wendel, see appendix 2.

16. *Incarnation of the Word* 54.3, in *Nicene and Post-Nicene Fathers*, Second Series, ed. Philip Schaff and Henry Wace (Grand Rapids: Eerdmans, 1953), 4:65.

17. Dickau, *Plunging into the Kingdom Way*, 2.

18. Gordon, *Real Hope in Chicago*.

19. David Rufful, "Kirsten Powers: How a Liberal Democrat and Former Atheist Came to Know Jesus Christ as Her Savior," *Young Conservative*, July 14, 2013, http://youngcons.com/kirsten-powers-how-a-liberal-democrat-and-former-atheist-came-to-know-jesus-christ-as-her-savior/.

20. Henry, *Confessions*, 45–47.

Chapter 9 Kingdom Redemption Unleashed

1. John's Gospel focuses on "eternal life" or just "life" instead of "kingdom." There is much speculation about why the change occurs, but as long as we keep our eye open for the people-nuances of "life" in John (sharing life with the Son and the Father as the vine and the branches, etc.), we will not suddenly think John has hopped the rails. Though there are nuances and differences between "eternal life" and "kingdom," there are more overlaps and similarities. For a study of this, see Paul Woodbridge, "Theological Implications of 'Eternal Life' in the Fourth Gospel," in *God's Power to Save: One Gospel for a Complex World?*, ed. Chris Green (Leicester: Inter-Varsity/Apollos, 2006), 55–78.

2. Richard Bauckham, *The Bible in Politics: How to Read the Bible Politically*, 2nd ed. (Louisville: Westminster John Knox, 2011), 143.

3. Exorcisms and healings, as well as miracles in general, have received intense research; see Graham Twelftree, *Jesus the Miracle Worker: A Historical and Theological Study* (Downers Grove, IL: InterVarsity, 1999); Craig S. Keener, *Miracles: The Credibility of the New Testament Accounts*, 2 vols. (Grand Rapids: Baker Academic, 2011).

4. Matt. 4:12–16; 8:17; 11:2–6; 12:15–21.

5. The "finger of God" echoes the work of God at the exodus; cf. Exod. 8:19. Some note, too, a connection to God writing the Ten Commandments with his "finger"; see Exod. 31:18; Deut. 9:10. See also the work of creation that God does with his "fingers," Ps. 8:3.

6. For a valuable sketch of prisons in the Roman Empire, see B. M. Rapske, "Prison, Prisoner," in *Dictionary of New Testament Background*, ed. Craig A. Evans and Stanley E. Porter (Downers Grove, IL: InterVarsity, 2000), 827–30.

7. At Qumran a text has been found connecting these very expectations with the Messiah (4Q521).

8. A typical early Christian example of this power at work is found at James 5:13–16.

9. C. S. Lewis, *The Screwtape Letters* (New York: HarperCollins, 2002), ix.

10. Graham Twelftree, "Demon, Devil, Satan," in *Dictionary of Jesus and the Gospels*, ed. Joel B. Green, Scot McKnight, and I. Howard Marshall (Downers Grove, IL: InterVarsity, 1992), 163–72, quote from 168.

11. Christopher J. H. Wright, *The Mission of God's People: A Biblical Theology of the Church's Mission*, Biblical Theology for Life (Grand Rapids: Zondervan, 2010), 273–78.

12. See "Evangelism and Social Responsibility: An Evangelical Commitment," Lausanne Occasional Paper 21, http://www.lausanne.org/en/documents/lops/79 -lop-21.html. Emphasis added.

13. See also the landmark Pontifical Council for Justice and Peace, *Compendium of the Social Doctrine of the Church* (Vatican City: Vatican Press, 2004).

14. John Goldingay, "Your Iniquities Have Made a Separation between You and Your God," in *Atonement Today*, ed. John Goldingay (London: SPCK, 1995), 39–53.

15. For a good discussion of the tensions, see James K. Beilby and Paul Rhodes Eddy, eds., *Understanding Spiritual Warfare: Four Views* (Grand Rapids: Baker Academic, 2012).

16. See D. G. Reid, "Satan, Devil," in *Dictionary of Paul and His Letters*, ed. Gerald F. Hawthorne, Ralph P. Martin, and Daniel G. Reid (Downers Grove, IL: InterVarsity, 1993), 862–67.

17. Scot McKnight, *A Community Called Atonement* (Nashville: Abingdon, 2007).

18. See D. G. Reid, "Principalities and Powers," in *Dictionary of Paul and His Letters*, ed. Gerald F. Hawthorne, Ralph P. Martin, and Daniel G. Reid (Downers Grove, IL: InterVarsity, 1993), 746–52. For further reading, see John Howard Yoder, *The Politics of Jesus: Vicit Agnus Noster*, 2nd ed. (Grand Rapids: Eerdmans, 1994), 134–61; Wink, *The Powers That Be*; Hendrik Berkhof, *Christ and the Powers*, trans. John Howard Yoder (Scottdale, PA: Herald Press, 1977).

19. This is seen well in Wright, *Simply Jesus*, 120–27.

20. G. B. Caird, *New Testament Theology*, ed. L. D. Hurst (Oxford: Clarendon, 1994), 118–35.

Chapter 10 Kingdom Is a Moral Fellowship

1. For the community nature of Jesus' ethics, see Hauerwas and Willimon, *Resident Aliens*, 69–92.

2. Scot McKnight, *Turning to Jesus: The Sociology of Conversion in the Gospels* (Louisville: Westminster John Knox, 2002), 1–25, 66–74; Scot McKnight and Hauna Ondrey, *Finding Faith, Losing Faith: Stories of Conversion and Apostasy* (Waco: Baylor University Press, 2008).

3. For further discussion, see Scot McKnight, *A New Vision for Israel: The Teachings of Jesus in National Context* (Grand Rapids: Eerdmans, 1999), 110–15.

4. The term "righteousness" means moral behavior that conforms to the will of God as taught by Jesus.

5. Martin Hengel, *Crucifixion: In the Ancient World and the Folly of the Message of the Cross*, trans. John Bowden (Philadelphia: Fortress, 1977); David W. Chapman, *Ancient Jewish and Christian Perceptions of Crucifixion*, Wissenschaftliche Untersuchungen zum Neuen Testament 2.244 (Tübingen: Mohr Siebeck, 2008). For a brief, reliable sketch, see J. B. Green, "Death of Jesus," in *Dictionary of Jesus and the Gospels*, ed. Joel B. Green, Scot McKnight, and I. Howard Marshall (Downers Grove, IL: InterVarsity, 1992), 147–48.

6. Dietrich Bonhoeffer, *Discipleship*, Dietrich Bonhoeffer Works 4 (Minneapolis: Fortress, 2001), 86–87. The most quoted line of Bonhoeffer's, far more poetic than Bonhoeffer's original line, was "When Jesus bids a man come, he bids him come and die." In the quotation above we find a more exact and far less poetic translation when it says, "Whenever Christ calls us, his call leads us to death."

7. On what follows, see my commentary *The Sermon on the Mount*, Story of God Bible Commentary (Grand Rapids: Zondervan, 2013).

8. Dunn, *Jesus Remembered*, 265–92; Tom Holmén, *Jesus and Jewish Covenant Thinking*, Biblical Interpretation Series 55 (Boston: Brill, 2001).

9. Leon Lamb Morris, *Testaments of Love: A Study of Love in the Bible* (Grand Rapids: Eerdmans, 1981); Thomas Jay Oord, *Defining Love: A Philosophical, Scientific, and Theological Engagement* (Grand Rapids: Brazos, 2010).

10. Oord, *Defining Love*, 15.

11. Niebuhr, *Purpose of the Church*, 35.

12. Rolf Rendtorff, *The Covenant Formula: An Exegetical and Theological Investigation*, trans. M. Kohl (Edinburgh: T&T Clark, 1998).

13. A very good sketch of how that kind of effort can be put into play can be found in Glen H. Stassen, *Just Peacemaking: Ten Practices for Abolishing War* (Cleveland, OH: Pilgrim, 1998).

14. For the most complete study, see Willard M. Swartley, *Covenant of Peace: The Missing Peace in New Testament Theology and Ethics* (Grand Rapids: Eerdmans, 2006).

15. McKnight, *Sermon on the Mount*, 130–38.

16. Shailer Mathews, *Jesus on Social Institutions* (New York: Macmillan, 1928), 103–4. Emphasis added.

17. McKnight, *New Vision for Israel*, 187–94.

18. Flannery O'Connor, *Flannery O'Connor: Collected Words*, Library of America 39 (New York: Library of America, 1988), 936.

19. See RJS, "It Is a Conundrum, Pt. 2," *Jesus Creed*, Nov. 21, 2013, http://www.patheos.com/blogs/jesuscreed/2013/11/21/it-is-a-conundrum-pt-2-rjs/.

20. Albert C. Outler and Richard P. Heitzenrater, eds., *John Wesley's Sermons: An Anthology* (Nashville: Abingdon, 1991), 347–57.

Chapter 11 Kingdom Is Hope

1. Wiman, *My Bright Abyss*, 56, 58.

2. A very good book on this topic is N. T. Wright, *Surprised by Hope: Rethinking Heaven, the Resurrection, and the Mission of the Church* (New York: HarperOne, 2008).

3. It is difficult to know what to make of the man who came with inappropriate attire but who (it is assumed) knew what to wear. It is likely this choice is an affront to the king's status and to the sanctity of the wedding banquet. This man illustrates the rejection of the invitation by those who were originally invited. On this parable, see Klyne Snodgrass, *Stories with Intent: A Comprehensive Guide to the Parables of Jesus* (Grand Rapids: Eerdmans, 2008), 299–324.

4. See McKnight, *New Vision for Israel*, 141n52, where I provide a lengthy set of parallels.

5. Marius Reiser, *Jesus and Judgment: The Eschatological Proclamation in Its Jewish Context*, trans. Linda M. Maloney (Minneapolis: Fortress, 1997), 304.

6. Gregory Claeys, ed., *The Cambridge Companion to Utopian Literature* (Cambridge: Cambridge University Press, 2010); Mary Ann Beavis, *Jesus and Utopia:*

Looking for the Kingdom of God in the Roman World (Minneapolis: Fortress, 2006).

7. Beavis, *Jesus and Utopia*, 9–52.

8. Beavis herself gets it wrong when she dismisses Israel from Jesus' kingdom vision, and she can only do so by spending pages proving sayings as inauthentic. See ibid., 85–102.

9. Wright, "The World in the Bible," 218.

10. This section draws on McKnight, *Sermon on the Mount*, 32–36.

11. On the history of happiness, see D. McMahon, *Happiness: A History* (New York: Atlantic Monthly Press, 2006); and my own essay on happiness studies, "Happiness: Given, Lost, Regained," *Books & Culture*, November/December 2008, 44–46, http://www.booksandculture.com/articles/2008/novdec/14.44.html.

12. D. C. Allison, *The Sermon on the Mount: Inspiring the Moral Imagination*, Companions to the New Testament (New York: Crossroad/Herder & Herder, 1999).

13. C. F. D. Moule, *The Meaning of Hope: A Biblical Exposition with Concordance*, Facet Books 5 (Philadelphia: Fortress, 1963), 54–55. Emphasis and formatting mine.

14. I distinguish between subjective (forgiveness) and objective (reconciliation) dimensions in the forgiveness process in Scot McKnight, *The Jesus Creed: Loving God, Loving Others* (Brewster, MA: Paraclete, 2004), 224–26.

15. Stewart Goetz, *The Purpose of Life: A Theistic Perspective* (New York: Continuum, 2012). All citations from Augustine and Lewis in this paragraph are from Goetz's discussion of the history of happiness; pp. 1, 10, 11–12, 16.

Appendix 1 The Constantinian Temptation

1. The word "Constantinianism" refers to far more than the emperor and his own ideas and influences. The term refers to the powerful legacy of combining church and state in all its forms, including what goes on in the name of Christ to this day. On Constantinianism, see the various writings of John Howard Yoder, in particular, *Priestly Kingdom*, 82–85, and *Royal Priesthood*, 192–203.

2. Yoder, *Priestly Kingdom*, 137.

3. Francis J. Bremer, *John Winthrop: America's Forgotten Founding Father* (New York: Oxford University Press, 2003); John M. Barry, *Roger Williams and the Creation of the American Soul: Church, State, and the Birth of Liberty* (New York: Viking, 2012).

4. Hauerwas, *Hauerwas Reader*, 459–80, quotes from 473. Emphasis added.

5. One of the more trenchant tellings of evangelicalism's involvement in politics is by Randall Balmer, *God in the White House: A History; How Faith Shaped the Presidency from John F. Kennedy to George W. Bush* (New York: HarperOne, 2008). Even more critical is his *Thy Kingdom Come: How the Religious Right Distorts Faith and Threatens America* (New York: Basic Books, 2007).

6. Koyzis, *Political Visions and Illusions*.

7. John Howard Yoder, "Reformed versus Anabaptist Social Strategies: An Inadequate Typology," *Theological Students Fellowship Bulletin* 8 (May/June 1985):

2–10, quote from 3. Yoder also contends that the Anabaptists took *sola fide* into the realm of epistemology, trusting Scripture alone, while the Reformed relied more on reason (p. 3). On how John Howard Yoder's "politics of Jesus" have become a politics of reading Yoder inaccurately, see the exceptional study of Mark Thiessen Nation, "The Politics of Yoder Regarding the Politics of Jesus: Recovering the Implicit in Yoder's Holistic Theology for Pacifism," in *Radical Ecumenicity: Pursuing Unity and Continuity after John Howard Yoder*, ed. John C. Nugent (Abilene, TX: Abilene Christian University Press, 2010), 37–56.

8. For the best history, I recommend William R. Estep, *The Anabaptist Story: An Introduction to Sixteenth-Century Anabaptism*, 3rd ed. (Grand Rapids: Eerdmans, 1996).

9. Yes, there's a bit of an irony in using the state to disestablish state interference in one's faith, but the creation of the wall of separation changed the history of this country and eventually much of the world. Muslim Constantinianism is still found throughout the world.

10. Jean Bethke Elshtain, *Sovereignty: God, State, and Self*, The Gifford Lectures (New York: Basic Books, 2008), 127–30.

11. Henry, *Confessions*, 394.

12. Hunter, *To Change the World*. Others make the same observations about the lack of influence. In February 2008, at a Trinity Law School conference, a team of scholars from across the spectrum of disciplines gathered to discuss the question, "How is it that evangelicals have been so ineffective at changing the political and social landscape of the United States in a positive way?" The papers were published: see Roger N. Overton, ed., *God and Governing: Reflections on Ethics, Virtue, and Statesmanship* (Eugene, OR: Pickwick, 2009). In a manner similar to Hunter's call for "faithful witness," Dallas Willard at the conference called for a gospel directly connected to and focused on character development (see pp. 74–91).

13. Balmer, *God in the White House*, 167.

14. Adolf Harnack, *What Is Christianity?*, trans. Thomas Bailey Saunders (Gloucester, MA: Peter Smith, 1978), 56.

15. James D. Bratt, *Abraham Kuyper: Modern Calvinist, Christian Democrat* (Grand Rapids: Eerdmans, 2013). See also appendix 2 of this book.

16. Michael Kazin, *A Godly Hero: The Life of William Jennings Bryan* (New York: Alfred A. Knopf, 2006).

17. David R. Swartz, *Moral Minority: The Evangelical Left in an Age of Conservatism* (Philadelphia: University of Pennsylvania Press, 2012), 267–69.

18. George M. Marsden, *Fundamentalism and American Culture: The Shaping of Twentieth-Century Evangelicalism, 1870–1925* (New York: Oxford University Press, 1980).

19. Christopher H. Evans, *The Kingdom Is Always but Coming: A Life of Walter Rauschenbusch* (Grand Rapids: Eerdmans, 2004).

20. Henry, *Uneasy Conscience*; Henry, *Confessions*.

21. Yoder, *Priestly Kingdom*, 172–95.

22. Allan R. Bevere, *The Politics of Witness: The Character of the Church in the World*, Areopagus Critical Christian Issues 111 (Gonzalez, FL: Energion, 2011), 40.

23. Swartz, *Moral Minority*.

24. William Jennings Bryan, *The Cross of Gold*, ed. Robert W. Cherny (Lincoln: University of Nebraska Press, 1996), 18, 24, 28.

25. Kazin, *A Godly Hero*, 61.

26. Gutiérrez, *Theology of Liberation*; Gutiérrez, *We Drink from Our Own Wells: The Spiritual Journey of a People* (Maryknoll, NY: Orbis, 2010).

27. Jürgen Moltmann, *A Broad Place: An Autobiography*, trans. Margaret Kohl (Minneapolis: Fortress, 2008).

28. See Jonathan Merritt, "The Rise of the Christian Left in America," *The Atlantic*, July 25, 2013, http://www.theatlantic.com/politics/archive/2013/07/will-the-religious-left-become-the-new-moral-majority/278086/.

Appendix 2 Kingdom Today

1. Gerhard Kittel and Gerhard Friedrich, eds., *Theological Dictionary of the New Testament*, trans. Geoffrey W. Bromiley, 9 vols. (Grand Rapids: Eerdmans, 1964).

2. Robert P. Ericksen, *Theologians under Hitler: Gerhard Kittel, Paul Althaus, and Emanuel Hirsch* (New Haven: Yale University Press, 1985), 70–76.

3. Susannah Heschel, *The Aryan Jesus: Christian Theologians and the Bible in Nazi Germany* (Princeton: Princeton University Press, 2008).

4. Mark Thiessen Nation, Anthony G. Siegrist, and Daniel P. Umbel, *Bonhoeffer the Assassin? Challenging the Myth, Recovering His Call to Peacemaking* (Grand Rapids: Baker Academic, 2013).

5. Eberhard Bethge, *Dietrich Bonhoeffer: A Biography*, rev. ed. (Minneapolis: Fortress, 2000).

6. Eberhard Busch, *Karl Barth: His Life from Letters and Autobiographical Texts*, trans. John Bowden (London: SCM, 1976), 207, 223, 255, 257, 259.

7. Thus, discussions of "creation mandates" or "creation orders" or "natural order" will meet firm rebukes from Barth.

8. Luther's approach needs to be seen in terms of transformation and influence—that is, of the kingdom of heaven influencing the kingdom of this world. An example of this approach to Luther is Martin Hengel, *Christ and Power*, trans. Everett R. Kalin (Philadelphia: Fortress, 1977), 69–82.

9. The most complete study of Christian engagement in society is by the Pontifical Council for Justice and Peace, *Compendium of the Social Doctrine of the Church*, http://www.vatican.va/roman_curia/pontifical_councils/justpeace/documents/rc_pc_justpeace_doc_20060526_compendio-dott-soc_en.html.

10. Francis J. Bremer, *First Founders: American Puritans and Puritanism in an Atlantic World* (Durham: University of New Hampshire Press, 2012).

11. H. Richard Niebuhr, *Christ and Culture* (San Francisco: HarperSanFrancisco, 2001). The best critique of Niebuhr can be found in the essay by John Howard Yoder, "How H. Richard Niebuhr Reasoned: A Critique of *Christ and Culture*," in *Authentic Transformation: A New Vision of Christ and Culture*, ed. Glen H. Stassen, D. M. Yeager, and John Howard Yoder (Nashville: Abingdon,

1996), 31–89. For an approach from the Reformed and C-F-R-C side, see Carson, *Christ and Culture Revisited*.

12. In another book, Niebuhr mapped American church history in its basic understandings of kingdom of God. For the Puritans it was the kingdom of God, or the sovereignty of God; for the nineteenth century and the rise of evangelicalism it was the kingdom of Christ; and for the twentieth century, among social gospel advocates, it became the kingdom on earth or the coming kingdom. See H. Richard Niebuhr, *The Kingdom of God in America*, reprinted with introduction by Martin E. Marty (Middletown, CT: Wesleyan University Press, 1988). Niebuhr's historical scheme proves yet again that he who writes the story controls the glory.

13. Richard J. Mouw, *Abraham Kuyper: A Short and Personal Introduction* (Grand Rapids: Eerdmans, 2011), 4, 22, 23–24, 41, 42, 57, 58, 96. For a recent sketch, see John Bolt, "Abraham Kuyper and the Search for an Evangelical Public Theology," in J. Budziszewski, *Evangelicals and the Public Square: Four Formative Voices on Political Thought and Action* (Grand Rapids: Baker Academic, 2006), 141–61 (see also pp. 55–72). The most complete study of his life is Bratt, *Abraham Kuyper*. Bratt also has collected important writings of Kuyper in James D. Bratt, ed., *Abraham Kuyper: A Centennial Reader* (Grand Rapids: Eerdmans, 1998).

14. A bald restatement of this is found in John Stackhouse, quoted above in chap. 2.

15. Mouw leaves out "church" in his maps on p. 42 of *Abraham Kuyper*.

16. See James K. A. Smith, "Naturalizing 'Shalom': Confessions of a Kuyperian Secularist," *Cardus*, June 28, 2013, http://www.cardus.ca/comment/article/3993/naturalizing-shalom-confessions-of-a-kuyperian-secularist/. Emphasis in the original.

17. Mark A. Noll, *One Nation under God? Christian Faith and Political Action in America* (San Francisco: Harper & Row, 1988), 146.

18. Niebuhr, *Christ and Culture*, 190–229, quotes from xii, 194, 196, 225, 228, 233, 238, 255, 256. Most agree that Niebuhr slated his five types so that the winner would be the transformation model, and I agree. Yet his "A 'Concluding Unscientific Postscript'" on 230–56 seems to be ignored by most. Here Niebuhr pushes in a more existential direction for determining how that transformation is to occur.

19. See the monumental effort of Gary Dorrien, *The Making of American Liberal Theology*, 3 vols. (Louisville: Westminster John Knox, 2001–6). The three volumes include vol. 1, *Imagining Progressive Religion (1805–1900)*; vol. 2, *Idealism, Realism, and Modernity (1900–1950)*; and vol. 3, *Crisis, Irony, and Postmodernity (1950–2005)*.

20. It has been observed by many that American mainline Christianity has so shaped American culture—at least the parts that it can shape—that the distinction is no longer visible. On this, see N. Jay Demerath, "Cultural Victory and Organizational Defeat in the Paradoxical Decline of Liberal Protestantism," *Journal for the Scientific Study of Religion* 34, no. 4 (1995): 458–69.

21. Here Niebuhr is riffing off the German philosopher of religion and historian Ernst Troeltsch, as well as the Danish philosopher Søren Kierkegaard.

22. Lonnie D. Kliever, *H. Richard Niebuhr*, ed. Bob E. Patterson, Makers of the Modern Theological Mind (Waco: Word, 1977), 63–72, 85–109. For his "theological relativism," see 70–72.

23. For the broader context of the social gospel, see David W. Bebbington, *Baptists through the Centuries: A History of a Global People* (Waco: Baylor University Press, 2010), 121–38.

24. Evans, *Kingdom Is Always but Coming*, xxvii.

25. I have used the anthology by Winthrop S. Hudson, ed., *Walter Rauschenbusch: Selected Writings* (New York: Paulist Press, 1984), 137, 139, 141, 143, 197, 199, 201, 202, 205, 206.

26. Ibid., 3–41.

27. Suttle, *An Evangelical Social Gospel?*.

28. A marvelous study of the "evangelical left" can be found in Swartz, *Moral Minority*.

29. Yoder, *Royal Priesthood*, 93.

30. Moltmann, *A Broad Place*, 108, 172–75, 267, 275.

31. Rasmusson, *The Church as* Polis, 45. The subtitle to this book reveals his hand: *From Political Theology to Theological Politics as Exemplified by Jürgen Moltmann and Stanley Hauerwas*. Moltmann does "political theology," a theology focused on the political realm, while Hauerwas does "theological politics," a theology where the church is a politic. Moltmann sees the kingdom work in the public sector while Hauerwas sees it in the church. My friend and colleague David Fitch observed in a private conversation that "political theology" is "theological claims put to the service of political questions," while "theological politics" is "political questions put to the service of theological claims." A. C. Thiselton gives political theology the label of "socio-pragmatic exegesis." See Anthony C. Thiselton, *New Horizons in Hermeneutics* (Grand Rapids: Zondervan, 1992), 379–470.

32. Rasmusson, *The Church as* Polis, 47.

33. Jürgen Moltmann, *The Way of Jesus Christ: Christology in Messianic Dimensions* (Minneapolis: Fortress, 1990), 116–36. Rasmusson concludes the same emphasis in Moltmann; see Rasmusson, *The Church as* Polis, 84.

34. Gutiérrez, *Theology of Liberation*, 32, 91, 106, 154.

35. For a good sketch, see João B. Chaves, *Evangelicals and Liberation Revisited: An Inquiry into the Possibility of an Evangelical-Liberationist Theology* (Eugene, OR: Wipf & Stock, 2013), 40–43.

36. See ibid., 78–85, quote from 83.

37. Quote from ibid., 117. I reformatted the lines.

38. Details can be found in Moltmann, *A Broad Place*, 227–32.

39. Gutiérrez, *We Drink from Our Own Wells*. For a sketch of developments, see Chaves, *Evangelicals and Liberation Revisited*.

40. Brian K. Blount, *Then the Whisper Put on Flesh: New Testament Ethics in an African American Context* (Nashville: Abingdon, 2001), quotes from 10, 15, 32, 34, 43, 48, 49, 50.

41. Power and privilege are largely invisible to those who are in power and who have privilege. On this, see Edwards, *Elusive Dream*.

42. James H. Cone, *God of the Oppressed*, rev. ed. (Maryknoll, NY: Orbis, 1997), xi. Emphasis in the original.

43. An older but valuable sketch is Thiselton, *New Horizons in Hermeneutics*, 439–52.

44. Moltmann-Wendel, *Autobiography*, quotes from x, xiii, xvii, 11–14, 19, 41, 48, 86, 104, 108. Emphasis and reformatting mine.

45. Tish Harrison Warren, "Courage in the Ordinary," *The Well Blog*, InterVarsity, April 3, 2013, http://thewell.intervarsity.org/blog/courage-ordinary.

SUBJECT INDEX

Subject Index

Scripture Index

287

288